D0071610

INSTITUTE

University
Associates

The Emerging Practice of
Organization Development

The Emerging Practice
of Organization Development

Edited by
Walter Sikes, Ph.D.
Allan Drexler, Ph.D.
Jack Gant, Ph.D.

Copublished by
NTL Institute for Applied Behavioral Science
and
University Associates, Inc.

Don:
My very best
to you —
Allan December 1989
Annapolis

© 1989 NTL Institute for Applied Behavioral Science

Printed in the United States of America
ISBN: 0-9610392-6-4

Library of Congress Cataloging-in-Publication Data

   1. Organizational change.   I. Sikes, Walter W. II. Drexler,
Allan. III. Gant, Jack, 1927- . IV. NTL Institute for Applied
Behavioral Science.
HD58.8.E46   1989
658.4'06—dc20   89-12622
                                                           CIP

**This book is copublished by NTL Institute for Applied Behavioral
Science, 1240 N. Pitt Street, Suite 100, Alexandria, Virginia 22314
and by University Associates, Inc., 8517 Production Avenue, San
Diego, California 92121.**

Some material in this book has been reprinted with permission from
other sources. The first page of each article cites the holder of the
copyright for that particular work, and any figures reprinted from
other sources provide source citations. To request permission to
reprint material for which NTL Institute holds the copyright, write
to the Publications Permissions Department of NTL Institute at the
address provided above.

Publications Manager, NTL Institute: Catherine A. Messina
Production Manager, University Associates: Deborah O. Stockton
Cover Design: Paul Bond

Table of Contents

I. The Background of OD

II. OD and Nonprofit Organizations

III. Ethics and Values in OD

IV. Pluralism and OD

V. Thoughts on the Practice of OD

VI. A Look Ahead

Biographical Sketches of the Contributors

Preface

This book was prepared in celebration of the 40th anniversary of NTL Institute for Applied Behavioral Science. NTL is generally recognized as the "inventor" of many of the processes associated with the field of organization development (OD), and all of the contributors to this book have been profoundly influenced by their involvement with NTL. Most of these authors are NTL members, and they represent a wide range of experience, age, viewpoint, educational background, gender, race, and ethnicity. Such diversity is appropriate for a book commissioned by NTL, as this organization has a strong commitment to pluralism.

We editors sought to produce a book containing the latest ideas of a varied, highly qualified group of OD practitioners and scholars. In beginning this project, we' hoped that the book's authors would write about the things they find most exciting in their current OD work. Their fulfillment of this hope delights us.

To our sorrow, two of the contributors died while the book was still in production. Robert Chasnoff had already finished his share of the work on a chapter, which his co-author, Peter Muniz, completed. Those of us who had the pleasure of knowing and working with Bob miss him greatly. We are privileged to publish material indicating the legacy of his rich and useful life. Ronald Lippitt, one of the founders of NTL Institute, co-wrote a chapter with Mikki Ritvo, which we are delighted to include in this book. Many consider Ron one of the more important teachers in this field, and all in the behavioral sciences are in his debt for his unique contributions. His death leaves us much poorer.

Finally, we thank Catherine A. Messina, the NTL publications manager, and other central office staff members of NTL Institute for assisting us in so many ways. Their work is appreciated.

Walter Sikes, Ph.D.
Allan Drexler, Ph.D.
Jack Gant, Ph.D.

Introduction to
The Emerging Practice
of Organization Development

Walter Sikes

For more than 40 years, NTL Institute for Applied Behavioral Science has generated much of the theoretical and practical work that has come to provide the basis for an emerging profession known as organization development (OD). I thus consider it highly appropriate that the celebration of NTL's 40th anniversary fostered the collection of new works about OD, written by persons greatly influenced by NTL. The chapters they have prepared cover a broad range of topics, all stemming from the authors' current interests.

The book opens with a section on the background of OD. It then moves to a section on the experiences and ideas of persons who have been devoting their energy to improving nonprofit organizations. The third section addresses the issue of morals, ethics, and values in OD. Following this, a section presents four chapters on the relationship of OD to race, gender, and cultural differences. The book's largest section presents an intriguing variety of insights into the practice of OD, drawing on the extensive experience of a dozen professionals in the field. Finally, a future-oriented section presents some profound challenges for those who wish to see OD fulfill its potential for improving organizations.

In the first chapter of the section on the **background of OD**, Thomas Patten, Jr., clearly and concisely reviews the roots of OD. He discusses the impact of the training group in thousands of organizational and laboratory settings, then examines how the field has been influenced by concepts from sociotechnical systems, psychology, social psychology, and anthropology. This chapter summarizes and integrates the theories of many major OD scholars.

Philip Hanson and Bernard Lubin have accumulated in the course of their practice about 100 questions that managers and others have asked about OD. After providing a useful definition of OD, they then answer 11 of the most frequently raised questions. The authors enrich our understanding of OD by examining it from the perspective of potential clients. Their discussion should be helpful to consultants as they deal with their clients, and to anyone seeking to understand OD.

The section on **OD and nonprofit organizations** begins with a chapter on organization development in social change organizations. L. David Brown and Jane Covey explore the dynamics of systems seeking to improve society, and describe the characteristics unique to these organizations. They present two cases illustrating how such organizations function and what consultants must address when they try to help them become more effective. Many of the authors' observations can also be applied to OD work with businesses, government agencies, health care systems, and educational institutions.

Jack Gant and Oron South present some ideas useful for OD work with schools. They draw on their long, rich experience with school systems, and offer clear, practical approaches solidly based on the principles of OD. The authors cite the characteristics of public education systems requiring modifications in the assumptions usually underlying OD efforts.

In discussing the application of OD concepts to higher education administration, Russell Rogers presents a useful analysis of such systems' idiosyncracies and how OD can be altered to serve them. He concludes that significant differences exist between the goals, values, and basic premises typical of OD and those of higher education administration. Nevertheless, he believes that OD can contribute to the efforts of colleges and universities to meet the demands of their changing environments, and describes how he thinks this can be achieved.

The section on **ethics and values in OD** begins with a chapter on values, human relations, and OD. Henry Malcolm and Claire Sokoloff make a case for creatively applying the principles of cooperation and mutual self-interest. They examine the link between organizational values and outcomes, emphasizing the need for management to develop effective strategies for influencing the actual behavior of persons doing the work of the organization. The authors suggest several specific ways to help produce that type of impact.

Some of the more difficult questions facing any organization involve developing appropriate responses to dilemmas of power and authority. Heywood and Catharine Martin explore these issues with respect to the consultant's involvement. They describe potential sources of organizational power and the consequences of consultants' relying on these, and recommend power bases for consultants.

Gene Boccialetti raises provocative questions about the appropriateness and utility of defining OD's values so as to make it one of the "forces of light." Given the complexity of organizations and their values, he recommends that the OD profession accept "fuzzier" values that will make practitioners more open to learning. He then makes a case for practitioners' raising issues related to values and ethics as subjects of inquiry, rather than seeking only to define fixed principles.

In the final chapter of this section, Lee Butler presents his views on the causes and consequences of collusion with organizational expectations. In discussing the psychological sources of collusion and the paradoxes involved, he describes the effects of socialization and norm building and how these contribute to collusion, particularly as this affects minority group members and women in organizations.

Many of the basic discoveries about group process and strategies for action and change came from work in race and community relations. OD's success in building more truly pluralistic organizations, however, has been limited. Although some clear gains have at in least part resulted from OD processes, some have accused OD of increasing the power of the powerful. OD's methods, however, have tremendous potential for facilitating the full inclusion of minority group members and women in organizational life. The four chapters in the section **on pluralism and OD** shed new light on some old concerns about the processes of inclusion—and exclusion.

Carl Jennings and Leroy Wells provide a new approach to analyzing the roots and effects of the racism systemic to many organizations in the U.S. They present a model addressing the economic and career disparity between blacks and whites, barriers to blacks' fulfilling their career goals, and whites' resistance to blacks' career advancement. The authors indicate that although their analysis focuses on relations between blacks and whites within organizations, their construct can also help one better understand the behavior of white men and how women and other minority groups members are treated.

In her chapter, Katherine C. Esty examines the development of women in organizations during the past 20 years. She states that during this period dramatic shifts have occurred in the ways OD practitioners perceive the needs of women managers and in the types of OD programs designed to address their problems. Despite the progress in meeting some of the needs of women, the author finds that most organizations still act as if all employees were men married to full-time homemakers. She predicts that for women to reach their full potential, a new set of women's needs must be addressed.

Before his death, Robert Chasnoff devoted much of his career to working in cross-cultural settings. Peter Muniz joined him in writing a chapter for this book. Together they present a model for better understanding situations in which members of more than one culture must deal with one another, with such situations including those of persons working in foreign lands, the existence of subcultures within organizations, regional groups within the U.S., and mergers and acquisitions of previously distinct organizations. The authors call their model "the cultural awareness hierarchy" and demonstrate how one may use it to increase the skills of those confronting cross-cultural situations.

Jimmy Jones and Jean Thomas Griffin discuss the use of group relations workshops in the black community. The methodology they present was developed by the Tavistock Institute and focuses on issues of power and authority. The authors consider these particularly relevant for minority group members, and suggest ways of making the programs more accessible and useful to black persons.

The section devoted to **thoughts on the practice of OD** contains the current ideas of practitioners and scholars. They address a wide range of topics and points of view. Daryl Funches discusses three gifts she considers central to OD practitioners' providing genuine help to their clients. Marvin R. Weisbord presents a method for helping a group devise its preferred future to support planning and community development. In my own chapter, I discuss seven principles I believe should be the basis of any effort to achieve personal or organizational change. Abraham Shani and Ord Elliott explore the similarities and differences among the design elements used by several leaders in the field of sociotechnical systems. Bernard Mohr distinguishes the open sociotechnical systems approach from the more traditional one, and examines the process dynamics necessary for successfully implementing the former. Robert Luke describes how to apply the principles of adult learning to management development. From another perspective on OD practice, Mikki Ritvo and the late Ronald Lippitt have contributed a chapter explaining their approach to shadow consulting (we are honored to publish this work on which Ron collaborated shortly before his death). Tom Armor discuses his ideas and experience in using computers as tools supporting OD efforts. The final chapter in this section allows us to benefit from Allan Drexler and Weld Coxe's insights into the marketing of OD services, and presents both principles and helpful hints.

The final section of this book takes **a look ahead** at the challenges OD faces for the future. Joseph Potts points to the need to integrate human systems with new technology, particularly computers. He helps us learn how organizations and consultants can make good use of computers in OD efforts.

At the close of the book, Peter Vaill issues a plea that we continue to recognize that OD is a process for improving processes. He urges us to maintain and extend our skills in helping clients design, implement, evaluate, and improve the substantive processes they require to pursue their missions, and discusses seven frontiers for OD to fill the need for new facilitative processes.

Vaill's challenge to OD practitioners seems an appropriate ending for a book celebrating NTL's first 40 years. Much has been accomplished, but more remains to be done. The hearts and minds of OD professionals must address the ongoing struggle to humanize organizations, resolve conflicts, use resources effectively, establish equity for all people, and encourage everyone to reach her or his full potential. We hope that the ideas of this fine group of OD experts will help us move toward achieving these goals before—much before—the next 40 years have passed.

Section I.
The Background of OD

Historical Perspectives on Organization Development

Thomas H. Patten, Jr.

When young people learning about applied behavioral science hear the term "OD," they frequently associate it with overdosing on drugs. Indeed, the term has never been universally clear, and OD experts themselves have often bickered over whether a notable difference exists between organization development versus organizational development.

After having spent about one-fourth of a century as an OD practitioner, I have come to consider OD to be the equivalent of improved management. That is, OD signifies all the concepts and methods used to improve the ways in which organizations are managed. It implies that management should be improved to change an organization's culture so that certain interpersonal and collective values become a way of life. One begins with trust, then moves to include—at a minimum—openness, authenticity, participation, democratic problem solving, innovation, and organizational justice. Thus, one may find it impossible to conceive of OD as existing in a Nazi concentration camp. Perhaps the concept may need alterations to fit today's "Third World" organizations. OD probably has a "Western" cultural bias, which would make it best understood historically as the product of behavioral scientists in the U.S. and England.

One can view the history of OD as either (1) a recapitulation of the contributions of specific behavioral scientists and institutions whose work has led to what today is known as OD, or (2) a record of the origins of and relationships among the main concepts of the behavioral sciences that form the roots of OD. Both streams of thought shed useful light on OD, and thus should prove valuable to OD practitioners, those training to become practitioners, managers, and students of OD. Knowledge and insights into the application of knowledge do not develop out of thin air. We thus need to understand the past and its effects on the present if we are to understand fully what we doing.

Individual and institutional contributions to OD

Wendell French (1982) has provided one of the more important formal histories of OD, for which all of us in this field are indebted. French explains that one source of OD is laboratory training, which consists basically of unstructured, small-group experiences in which participants learn from their own interactions and the group's dynamics. In 1946, Kurt Lewin, a German immigrant who did teaching and research at MIT, conducted a workshop for the Connecticut Interracial Commission that experimented with using discussion groups to achieve changes in "back-home" work situations. Lewin's field theory of social science and his concept of group dynamics, the change process, and action research greatly influenced the workshop staff members—Kenneth Benne, Leland Bradford, and Ronald Lippitt—who subsequently became leaders in designing workshops, conferences, and OD efforts.

The workshop staff learned that providing feedback at the end of each day to participants about their individual and group behavior (now known as "process") stimulated high levels of interest and apparently resulted in greater insight and learning than did more traditional lectures and materials on interracial matters (now known as "content"). Following this experience, Benne, Bradford, and Lippitt created the National Training Laboratory in Group Development in Bethel, Maine, in 1947. Their summer programs led to the T Group and sensitivity training (also called encounter group training, human relations or human interaction training, interpersonal skills training, or experiential training). Their organization evolved into NTL Institute for Applied Behavioral Science, which now offers many workshops, publications and degree programs throughout the year in various settings.

Other influences on Benne, Bradford, and Lippitt's work and the eventual emergence of OD include role playing and J. L. Moreno's work on sociodrama and psychodrama, which are therapeutic techniques also considered to be useful for healthy persons seeking to solve problems related to openness, authenticity, and other blocks to human energy. In addition, Bradford and Benne were influenced by John Dewey's philosophy of education, including his concepts of learning, change, and the transactional nature of humans and their environment. Benne was further inspired by the management theorist Mary Parker Follett, particularly by her ideas about cooperation, situational thinking, and integrated solutions to organizations' problems.

During the 1950s, as human relations trainers began to work with social systems more permanent and complex than T Groups, they felt considerably frustrated when seeking to use what was learned in laboratory education to solve the problems of organizations, including industrial firms. The personal skills learned in T Groups, particularly in groups of strangers in rural settings or resorts, proved difficult to transfer to intricate organizations. Occasionally, the emotional "high" a participant got from a T Group experience caused that person to act inappropriately upon returning to work, or be "out of sync" with the corporate culture. To function effectively, such persons had to make adjustments at work, which often required them to suppress what they had learned to regress to their former behaviors—which was, to say the least, counter-productive.

Such results led to the training of teams from the same organization. Upon returning to their organization, such teams could act as support groups for one another and forestall the regression and drop-off effects on learning obtained in T Groups comprising strangers. This newly identified focus on the total organization became an important connecting point in the theory and design of OD, as indicated in the work of Douglas McGregor, Herbert A. Shepard, Robert R. Blake and Jane S. Mouton, Richard Beckhard, Chris Argyris, Jack R. Gibb, Warren Bennis, Gordon Lippitt, Paul Buchanan, Edgar H. Schein, and other giants of OD. All of these persons had had experience as T Group trainers early in their careers.

Providing details about the professional careers of these individuals is beyond the scope of this chapter. French (1982) presents some of their major contributions, but one must consult many published materials on these pioneers to obtain an accurate, total picture. I consider it sufficient to say that through their work the term "organization development" was coined, perhaps simultaneously through the concepts of Blake and Mouton, Shepard, McGregor, and Beckhard. All of them had at least begun using the term "development group" in the 1950s, and OD does seem an appropriate label for characterizing the system-wide use of T Groups and related experiential learning efforts they administered in the organizations they sought to change. Moreover, OD connotes something quite different from the management or development typical of that era, terms essentially synonymous with the traditional training of managers.

OD also served as shorthand for "organizational planning and management development," a circumlocution that many found could be reduced to the first and last words. This abbreviation helped foster the recognition that organizational change often requires planning the organization's structure, changing its form, and supporting human resources management systems— along with training the affected managerial personnel to function in a new environment with new system—so as to facilitate "true" rather than "cosmetic" change (Patten, 1981).

This view of OD suggests that changes in an organization's patterns of interpersonal relations should be reinforced by consonant changes in the organizational chart, reward structures, methods of recruiting and selection, plans for promotion and succession, and the like. I call this a holistic view of OD, as it includes the behavior and technical systems of traditional personnel administration.

From Lewin to Likert

Lewin died in 1947, and much of the work he started at MIT continued at the University of Michigan, some under Ronald Lippitt, some under Alvin Zander (in group dynamics research), and some under Rensis Likert. French (1982) and others have pointed out that many of Lewin's colleagues at MIT formed the core group of Likert's Survey Research Center and Institute for Social Research at the University of Michigan, some of whom remained there until they either retired or died.

Likert's main contribution to OD was the development of survey research and feedback methods, a specialized form of action-oriented research that many now consider a sine qua non of OD. Likert's refinement of survey methodology was intended to demonstrate how a company or agency could best use the data gathered from employee attitude surveys to improve overall management and performance. To this extent, Likert greatly helped clarify OD as applied behavioral science geared toward management improvement, a way of defining OD that makes great sense, as indicated above.

The fundamental notion of giving feedback from attitudinal surveys to the managers and employees who generated the initial data has been widely endorsed, and now commonly occurs as an integral part of OD efforts. When the anonymity of individual respondents is ensured, the feedback greatly improves the practical value of these surveys. Survey results need interpretation, and their meaning becomes unclear without feedback. The efforts of Likert and those in Michigan to refine survey methodology, design questionnaires, and make valid, reliable use of the resulting data provided the bedrock for the further, substantive growth of OD.

A type of synergy of inestimable value has occurred at the Institute for Social Research. Although Likert has been dead for more than a decade, both the old guard and younger vanguard there have made methodological and theoretical advances in behavioral science that may be unequalled in the Western world.

Because of the work at the University of Michigan on OD, participant action research underlies most OD interventions conducted since the 1950s. Applications of OD thus have involved three "entities" in the design of a typical action research project: someone external to the organization who acts as a consultant in designing the change effort (called an "external change agent"), the client or client group—such as top management—seeking to alter the organization's status quo, and an internal group to whom management has delegated responsibility for producing change (called an "internal change agent"). The hallmarks of the action research model are collaboration among these entities through a preliminary diagnosis of the problems, data gathering from the client group (often using surveys or other instruments), data feedback to the client group and those who generated responses on questionnaires and interviews, data analysis and action planning by the client group, and taking action. Lewin, Likert, and those at the University of Michigan refined the action research model and many of its accompanying tools for OD.

Toward the end of his career, Likert's research and writing attracted the attention of high-level executives in the automotive industry, particularly those with General Motors and Ford. Under his intellectual leadership, various quality of work life and employee involvement programs were developed. We often tend to view such efforts as somehow being distinct from the armamentarium of OD interventions—that is, as not being OD in the strict sense. Yet no reason exists for denying that they are part of OD, and one could actually argue that they represent the zenith of OD efforts.

Sociotechnical systems

Thus far OD has been traced as if it had a distinctly American heritage. Such an ethnocentric view is incorrect. Instead, we should look across the Atlantic Ocean to the Tavistock Institute of Human Relations in London, which was founded in 1920 as an outpatient clinic providing therapy based on psychoanalytic theory and insights from the treatment of shell-shocked veterans of World War I. Tavistock's concepts of therapy had a group focus built into them, and concentrated on the individual only insofar as one manifested something on behalf of the whole group (Banet & Hayden, 1977).

The Tavistock approach known as "group relations" had its roots in the work of Wilfrid R. Bion—who was schooled in the psychoanalytic tradition of Melanie Klein—and A. K. Rice. In the 1940s and afterward, Bion conducted a series of studies of small groups that led him to conclude that individuals cannot be understood, nor their behavior changed, outside of the groups in which they live and survive. An aggregate cluster of persons becomes a group when interaction among members occurs, when members develop an awareness of the common relationships, and when a common group task emerges. When an aggregate becomes a group, the group behaves as a system with a primary goal of survival. Group members view the group as more than the sum of its parts, a shift in perception that makes a realistic understanding of change possible. Assumptions about group functioning and authority are learned (such as those Bion terms "dependency and counterdependency," "flight and fight," and "pairing and oneness"), and individuals learn from how groups function and change by examining these assumptions.

Eric Trist applied these and other Tavistock concepts to actual organizations, translating them into what is now known as the sociotechnical approach to restructuring work. Trist's evaluations of the human and technical consequences of the longwall method of coal production led to much behavioral science research in work redesign and the use of semiautomatic work teams. His work deserves to be called OD, for it consists of planned quality of work life interventions and emphasizes the importance of understanding social and technical matters and how they interact to efforts to plan and implement change.

English and American social scientists have interacted a great deal. For example, Tavistock leaders such as Trist and Bion had frequent contact with Lewin and Likert. Some prominent American OD experts—including Black and Bennis—have studied at Tavistock, and Tavistock founders such as Harold Bridger still come to the U.S. periodically to promulgate ideas and concepts. Moreover, we should not forget that the well-respected journal *Human Relations* was initiated by the joint efforts of Tavistock and American participants (French, 1982).

Fundamental behavioral science theory

Thus far this chapter has addressed individuals and institutions important to the evolution of OD. We also need a "map" of behavioral science theory to identify how OD was developed or fits in. Because many of the founders of OD had backgrounds in psychology, sociology, and social psychology, one should not be surprised that nearly all of them were interested in social interaction and networks of social relations.

During the past five years, the importance of culture in OD has been increasingly emphasized, and thus must be placed in a meaningful conceptual configuration. For many years, changing organizational culture has been a key concept for some OD practitioners.

The common meeting ground of the behavioral sciences is social interaction (see Figure 1). Social interaction is behavior resulting from the mutual awareness of human beings. The concepts and phenomena associated with arrows in Figure 1 are derived from the study of social interaction, and their identification and systematic articulation is the primary concern of the behavioral sciences. For example, sociology focuses on interaction in general rather than on the specific aspects of interaction in which other social sciences specialize (Patten, 1979).

Social psychology. Tools such as the Johari Window (Luft, 1970) and FIRO-B (Schutz, 1966), which have been widely used in OD efforts, have a manifestly social psychological nature. Moreover, the T Group—as used in OD efforts—is a socialization experience focused on the social self and the development of an open, authentic, and confrontational type of social personality. Mead's (1934) concepts of "I," "me," and the "generalized other" are implied in various quadrants of the Johari Window. Books about self-disclosure (e.g., Jourard, 1971), transactional analysis (e.g., Berne, 1964; Harris, 1973;

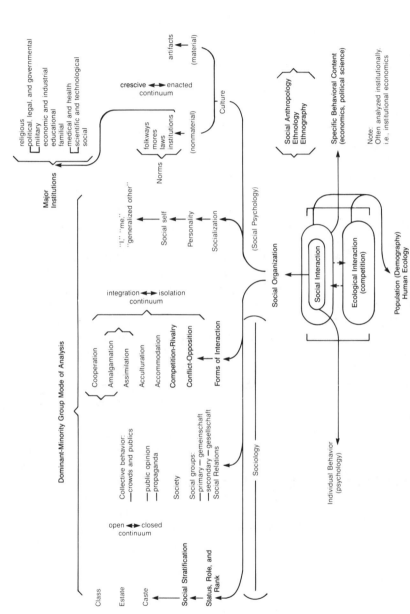

Figure 1. The interrelationships of behavioral science concepts and fundamental discipline
(Reprinted with permission from Patten [1979], copyright University Associates, Inc.)

Jongeward & Contributors, 1973) and self actualization (e.g., Shostrom, 1967) further suggest the relevance of social psychology to OD (Patten, 1979).

Social anthropology. In social anthropology, the key concept of culture is subdivided into the categories of material and nonmaterial cultures. Many group facilitators would argue that OD efforts seek to change clients' nonmaterial work cultures into other configurations, with such transformations often involving action research interventions to change norms.

In reality, one may define culture as constituting learned ways of doing things and thinking about things. This concept stems from observations of people's behavior that have the uncovered patterns of people's actions. The most useful studies examine the concrete behavior patterns of living persons, rather than artifacts and records of defunct cultures.

We know that the material culture affects the nonmaterial culture, and vice versa: Artifacts and technological systems affect social systems, and interventions should be recognized as sociotechnical by nature.

One may differentiate along a continuum the extent to which norms grow naturally or are enacted (see Figure 1). **Folkways** are norms that develop slowly and have the fewest moral implications; they are crescive, growing quickly. **Mores** have moral imperatives and a basis in reasoning (Barnes, 1948). **Laws** are formally enacted, and—when a sufficient number exist in a sphere or domain—become institutions (see the upper right corner of Figure 1). Many large institutions lead to work cultures of a pathologically bureaucratic nature, which have been the primary targets of OD efforts for the past 20 years.

OD efforts commonly try to intervene in large-scale institutions through their constituent sections (e.g., in industry, an effort might work through a particular company or department within a company) and focus on the changing aspects of interpersonal relationships so as to change work cultures and institutions.

Many have charged that OD practitioners ignore distributions of power and naively assume that changes in interpersonal relationships will produce institutional change, based on the belief that institutions are nothing more than interpersonal relationships "writ large"—which, of course, they are not. Sometimes, the changes an OD effort actually produces in a formal organizational structure prove to be more cosmetic than substantive, usually because the norms were not modified, the persons involved were merely shifted around or given new titles, or the final result was "business as usual" (Patten, 1975).

In sum, social organization is a concept basic not only to OD, but also to sociology, social psychology, and social anthropology.

Ecological and social interactions

The items below the heading "social organization" in Figure 1 are of prime interest to OD practitioners. Although space limitations prevent me from discussing at length the important connections between ecological and social interactions, I present some brief comments.

Figure 1 indicates that ecological interaction both influences and is influenced by social interaction. Ecological interaction has traditionally been viewed in terms of Darwin's concept of competition, but many types of ecological interactions actually involve cooperation. For example, to interact competitively—or even in conflict—opponents must reach some consensus on at least a few ground rules governing the situation. Therefore, one should perceive ecological interaction as involving opposition and cooperation, rather than competition.

Those who specialize in the study of ecology have formed the fields of demography and human ecology from that of ecological interaction. Few OD facilitators pay much attention to these specialties, however, although those working with groups have become keenly aware of the connections between ecological and social interaction, particularly when they have conducted interventions such as conflict management, team building between main office/subsidiary groups, and the like (Patten, 1979).

The integration/isolation continuum

The continua of integration/isolation and of open/closed social relations (see Figure 1) deserve greater attention than they have thus far received from those involved with OD. These continua help one interpret much of the behavior observed in organizations when conducting change efforts, and provide benchmarks for classifying various forms of social interaction.

In brief, the integration/isolation continuum distinguishes among forms of interaction ranging from the conflict and opposition found in groups isolated from one another to the state of cooperation, integration, cultural assimilation, and biological amalgamation. In between these extremes occur points along which one may accurately locate the interdepartmental or intergroup relations of those involved in an OD effort.

In the past decade, American industry has undergone an intense period of corporate mergers, acquisitions, and takeover attempts. Although the goal of these activities has been financial gain, descriptions of them refer to such colorful social images as "white knights," "poison pills," and "green mail." OD practitioners have seldom been asked to help ease the human suffering caused by such restructuring and to assist with the processes of assimilation and cooperation, but they have much to offer. The knowledge useful for OD interventions can be applied to helping client groups move toward integration and diagnosing where organizations are along the continuum.

The open/closed social relations continuum

At the extreme left in Figure 1, arrows indicate types of social relations and status, role, and rank. I refer above to social groups and to such phenomena as power, authority, and prestige as they relate to the political, economic, and social differentiation of individuals (Bendix, 1960). OD facilitators seldom, if ever, deal directly with systems of social stratification having cross-societal implications, although they do address the hierarchical structures of organizations and design OD efforts that consider status, role, and rank. Societal systems can be placed along a continuum of relatively open and closed social relations, according to social mobility (Davis, 1949). Caste systems are the most closed, class systems are the most open, and estate systems lie somewhere in between the two extremes.

According to Cooley (see Dewey, 1948) and Tonnies (see Heberle, 1948), social groups can be categorized as either primary (*gemeinschaft*) or secondary (*gesellschaft*) in nature. Primary groups are small ones whose members interact face to face, intensively, and deeply. Secondary groups are aggregates ranging from large groups to bureaucratic organizations of all sizes. Society is a group consisting of groups. The common denominator of primary and secondary groups and society is their structure by culture. In contrast, the collective behavior of crowds and the public, indicated by phenomena such as public opinion and propaganda, is relatively unstructured. The degree of relative structure in social relations has important implications for OD practitioners.

The dominant group/minority group mode of analysis

The top of Figure 1 presents a bracket indicating the range for the dominant group/minority group mode of analysis. All the concepts of social interaction presented beneath this bracket are potentially applicable to the analysis of power and interpersonal relations among members of dominant and minority groups in any society.

Many OD practitioners have helped organizations address problems of institutional racism, equal employment opportunity, affirmative action, and upward mobility for women and minority group members. These experiences generally prompt facilitators to work on problems related to the integration/isolation, open/closed social relations, and crescive/enacted continua, as well as problems of organizational solidarity, consensus, and work culture. Although some observers might remark wryly that in doing so OD practitioners are focusing on matters beyond their professional purview, Figure 1 suggests that, to the contrary, they are actually on familiar intellectual turf (Patten, 1979).

Conclusion

In tying together the themes of this chapter and coming to a conclusion, I want to discuss briefly the current interest of American management in organizational culture and corporate excellence. As the frequent references to this in the chapter should make clear, for years culture has been a prime concern of OD practitioners. Almost 20 years ago, in describing some of his early OD work for TRW Systems, Sheldon A. Davis (1967) stated explicitly that he sought to improve TRW's culture. Nearly as long ago, Robert R. Blake and Jane S. Mouton (1968) described clearly and elaborately how OD could be calibrated to yield corporate excellence.

The recent growth of interest in corporate cultures—and in changing them—stems from the work of Deal and Kennedy (1982). To bring the history of OD up to date, I must acknowledge the type of corporate culture case study (Davis, 1984) and intellectual symposia (Frost, Wakeley, & Ruh, 1974) on the leading edge of OD today.

Whether the spate of books on changing corporate culture will continue can only be guessed. OD has often been subject to fads. History is not bunk, however, and although the world does not run backwards in response to history, the past very much conditions the present. Consequently, a historical perspective on OD should be helpful, insightful, and fruitful for anyone who appreciates an understanding of context and roots.

REFERENCES

Banet, A. G., Jr., & Hayden, C. (1977). A Tavistock primer. In J. E. Jones & J. W. Pfeiffer (Eds.), *The 1977 annual handbook for group facilitators*. San Diego, CA: University Associates.

Barnes, H. E. (1948). William Graham Summer: Spencerianism in American dress. In H. E. Barnes (Ed.), *An introduction to the history of sociology*. Chicago: University of Chicago Press.

Bendix, R. (1960). *Max Weber: An intellectual portrait*. New York: Doubleday.

Berne, E. (1964). *Games people play: The psychology of human relationships*. New York: Grove Press.

Blake, R. R., & Mouton, J. S. (1968). *Corporate excellence through grid organization development*. Houston: Gulf.

Davis, K. (1949). *Human society*. New York: Macmillan.

Davis, S. A. (1967). An organic problem-solving method of organizational change. *Journal of Applied Behavioral Science, 3*(1), 3-21.

Davis, S. M. (1984). *Managing corporate culture.* Cambridge, MA: Ballinger.

Deal, T. E., & Kennedy, A. A. (1982). *Corporate cultures: The rites and rituals of corporate life.* Reading, MA: Addison-Wesley.

Dewey, R. (1948). Charles Horton Cooley: Pioneer in psychosociology. In H. E. Barnes (Ed.), *An introduction to the history of sociology.* Chicago: University of Chicago Press.

French, W. L. (1982). The emergence and early history of organizational development: With reference to influences on and interaction among some key actors. *Group and Organizational Studies, 7*(3), 261-277.

Frost, C. F., Wakeley, J. H., & Ruh, R. A. (1974). *The Scanlon Plan for organization development: Identity, participation, and equity.* East Lansing: Michigan State University Press.

Harris, T. (1973). *I'm ok—you're ok: A practical guide to transactional analysis.* New York: Bantam.

Heberle, R. (1948). The sociological system of Ferdinand Tonnies: "Community" and "society." In H. E. Barnes (Ed.), *An introduction to the history of sociology.* Chicago: University of Chicago Press.

Jongeward, D., & Contributors (1973). *Everybody wins: Transactional analysis applied to organizations.* Reading, MA: Addison-Wesley.

Jourard, S. M. (1971). *Self-disclosure: An experimental analysis of the transparent self.* New York: Wiley.

Luft, J. (1970). *Group processes: An introduction to group dynamics* (2nd ed.). Palo Alto, CA: Mayfield.

Mead, G. H. (1934). *Mind, self, and society.* Chicago: University of Chicago Press.

Patten, T. H., Jr. (1975). The white paper: A tool for OD. In J. E. Jones & J. W. Pfeiffer (Eds.), *The 1975 annual handbook for group facilitators.* San Diego, CA: University Associates.

Patten, T. H., Jr. (1979). The behavioral science roots of organization development: An integrated perspective. In J. E. Jones & J. W. Pfeiffer (Eds.), *The 1979 annual handbook for group facilitators.* San Diego, CA: University Associates.

Patten, T. H., Jr. (1981). *Organizational development through teambuilding.* New York: Wiley.

Schutz, W. C. (1966). *The interpersonal underworld.* Palo Alto, CA: Consulting Psychologists Press.

Shostrum, E. (1967). *Man, the manipulator.* New York: Bantam.

Answers to Questions Frequently Asked about Organization Development

Philip G. Hanson
Bernard Lubin

Intense systematic planned change efforts in various organizations have taken place for more than three decades. Recently, factors such as changing world markets, increased competition in many industries, the computerization of many industrial functions, employee discontent with working conditions in some industries, and the like have increased the pressure on organizations to engage in self-examination with the dual goals of increasing profits and making work environments more satisfying.

Such programs for change are known as organization development, organization renewal, organization improvement, or by the current term of organization transformation. As this relatively recent field of applied behavioral science has expanded, new concepts have emerged and old concepts have been reviewed. Thus, a new language has appeared that tends to obscure or alter the meanings of familiar terms while increasing our vocabulary. Although more books, courses, seminars, and workshops have become available, considerable misinformation and confusion exists.

For some time, we have been assembling questions consultants report that managers frequently ask about OD. We have also collected information from our colleagues and relied on our experience to devise relatively brief answers to these questions (recognizing, of course, that these answers themselves will be subject to change). This chapter presents some of these frequently asked questions and our answers to them.

© 1986 *Organization Development Journal*, "Organization Development: Answers to Questions Frequently Asked by Managers," *4* (4), pp. 40-46. Slightly modified by the authors. Reprinted with permission.

OD in general

What is OD? Organization development consists of planned efforts to help persons work and live together more effectively, over time, in their organizations. These goals are achieved by applying behavioral science principles, methods, and theories adapted from the fields of psychology, sociology, education, and management.

OD involves several steps. Although the process may vary, these are the typical procedures undergone in an OD intervention.

1. The consultant and client establish contact and determine what assistance the client needs and how they will work together.

2. The consultant gathers data about the culture of the client organization—that is, about how persons work together and the norms governing their behavior—through interviews, observations, instruments with rating scales, and the like.

3. A diagnosis is made of the state of the organization and the changes it should undergo to help it move toward its objectives.

4. The data collected are organized according to the goals the organization members feel must be achieved to improve the company; this constitutes the first phase of action planning.

5. Concrete interventions are planned and implemented to achieve the goals.

6. The interventions are evaluated to measure the extent of goal achievement.

7. Follow-up evaluations are administered periodically to track progress and provide ongoing diagnoses upon which to base further interventions.

The extent to which a manager and that person's staff become directly involved in these procedures depends upon the decisions made during the first step. The entire process, or parts of it, may be repeated in a cyclical pattern, with objectives changing in response to changes in the organization's needs.

Using the term "organization development" itself can sometimes interfere with a full understanding of what OD is, as clients occasionally perceive OD as somehow distinct from on-the-job issues and problems. That is, they may think, "When the consultant comes, it is OD time, and when the consultant leaves, it is time to get back to 'normal' work." Such a situation represents a failure to see the continuity of the OD process and the need for fully integrating the OD effort with issues related to ongoing work. In the broadest sense, OD represents any attempt to improve an organization by identifying problems, planning a way to deal with these problems, implementing these plans, and evaluating what has happened.

Because we live in a state of continuous change, goals established today may become obsolete tomorrow. Therefore, OD should not be considered a one-shot intervention by an external consultant, but rather an ongoing, long-term process in which managers and others become trained to diagnose their own organizations or work units, re-evaluate their goals, plan for ways to produce change, and review the results.

The following statements indicate some typical OD goals.

OD attempts to integrate individuals' needs for growth with organizational goals. The assumption here is that an organization can achieve its goals more effectively if it takes into consideration and supports individuals' needs. These include the need to assume more responsibility for decisions that affect one's work life, to receive recognition for competency rather than on the basis of status, to have open communication among co-workers, and to be creative and contribute to problem solving.

OD attempts to build into an organization some procedures that will be of long-term use in identifying internal problems and will lead to a better quality of solutions for these problems. OD attempts to change systems toward being more open. That is, it tries to legitimize self-examination, which has been denied in the past, and to open up areas to change that have not previously been open or have been considered ''untouchable.''

How does OD differ from good general management practices?

Good management practices are similar to OD if they provide the following:

- a commitment to using **all** resources available, particularly all human resources,
- clear and explicit assumptions by management,
- programs that are planned and anticipate some predictability and change,
- a readiness to address and integrate the emotional side of organizational life,
- a perspective from which the organization is viewed as a total system, with relationships among various components constituting the whole, that is influenced by its environment (e.g., adjacent systems), and
- reflections of a set of values or a philosophy, and not merely techniques somehow sanctioned as ''good.''

How is OD related to or distinct from training?

Training in general, apart from sensitivity training, may be considered a part of OD when the goals of the OD effort include helping persons develop skills and expertise for moving toward desired goals or change. Training in general may include workshops and seminars on managerial leadership, conflict management, problem solving, strategic planning, and the like. For example, an OD effort may seek to change the way managers function both independently and in work groups, which may require training to improve managers' skills related to the changes. OD focuses more on the organization than the individual, however, and involves more consultation than training.

What are some of the basic values of OD? Organizations essentially consist of networks of human relationships, and do not exist apart from the persons constituting them. **How** these persons work together affects the quantity and quality of the organization's products. Most OD consultants share some basic values related to helping persons and organizations function more effectively, including the following.

- People are basically healthy, self-motivated organisms who need to work in systems that respect them and their humanity.

- People will support what they help create. Individuals have a greater investment in and more commitment to their organizations if they participate in making decisions and solving problems affecting their work lives.

- One must examine one's own values and the extent to which these are reflected in one's behavior.

- One must accept that others have values different from one's own, and deal with these differences openly.

- Interpersonal relations constitute just as legitimate a matter of organizational concern as does task performance.

- To develop greater interpersonal effectiveness, one must address one's own leadership style and how it affects others.

- OD is an ongoing process requiring continuous diagnosis and concern for long-term effectiveness.

- The process by which work gets done is as important as the content of the work.

- One should learn about organizational dynamics and put that learning to use (e.g., one should determine how an organization is affected by both the subgroups within it and the environment outside it).

What is team building? Calling a group or work unit a "team" implies that it employs a particular process of working together, one in which team members identify and fully use one another's resources and mutual interdependence to facilitate more effective problem solving and task accomplishment. Thus, when team building is part of an OD effort, it usually involves having a team study its own processes (i.e., determine **how** members work together) and act to create a climate in which team members' energies are directed toward problem solving and making the best use of their resources. Perpetuating a climate in which individuals' resources are withheld and available energy is drained by maintaining protective or defensive facades is counter-productive to effective team functioning.

To help a team study how it works, a manager may ask an OD consultant to facilitate this process. When managers themselves have the skill to do this, they may help their own teams study their functioning. Consultants or managers may use several strategies for doing this, including helping teams develop process orientations, improving skills in self-observation, data gathering, and feedback, and assessing team members' leadership styles and their impacts on the teams. One important task of team building is helping a team develop a ''model of excellence'' against which to measure its performance. After identi-fying a team's norms and procedures, the team building effort should establish criteria for effectiveness, using behavioral and procedural targets. For team building to succeed, all team members must consider the self-study relevant for improving the team's functioning, and be committed to evaluating their own behavior.

The need for team building is indicated when managers and their teams recognize that the team exhibits symptoms of poor functioning. These include low productivity, unresolved conflicts among members that block understand-ing and take much of the team's time, failure to use members' resources ap-propriately, unclear or delayed decisions, confusion as to roles, responsibilities and deadlines, little or no participation at staff meetings, poor problem iden-tification, a combination of apathy, lack of creativity and defense of the status quo, and complaints from others that the team does not fulfill its responsibilities or respond to the needs of others outside the team.

Helping a team study its own processes and develop more effective ways of operating entails some risks. The activity may cause long-hidden conflicts and feelings to surface, thus increasing tension and anxiety. Members may fear that their future relationships with one another will suffer from the ''leveling'' and feedback. Despite these risks, however, team building may provide great rewards. These include revealing matters needing examination, developing more authentic ways for members to relate to one another, increasing members' ability to manage interpersonal conflicts, and creating an atmosphere in which members stop fighting among themselves and use their energy to solve prob-lems. Because of the risks and effort required, some conditions must be es-tablished if the team building is to succeed. These include the following.

- Those in a position of leadership must be committed to and involved in the effort. Team building cannot occur if the formal leader is absent, or if this leader demonstrates indifferences or cynicism toward the effort.
- The team leader must be willing to address her or his own role with respect to the team.

- All team members must be highly committed to and completely responsible for making the effort succeed. Anything less than complete responsibility creates the opportunity for members to develop a "wait-and-watch-the-other-guy" approach to the effort.
- All team members must be committed to studying their own processes and evaluating their own performance. These two activities never end, but persist throughout the team's existence.
- Team building cannot occur without team meetings. Having the manager meet individually with team members is no substitute for direct, face-to-face interactions among members, which they need to relate to one another as a group.
- Team building is not limited to special sessions, retreats, or visits from the consultant, but should occur on a day-to-basis at work. Team members must be committed to practicing what they have learned at special sessions and retreats.
- Team members must understand that team building is not a one-time-only event, but rather a continuous process of diagnosis, action planning, implementation, and evaluation.

OD and the manager/administrator

How can OD help a manager/administrator? OD can benefit managers and administrators in their daily work, including assisting them in the following tasks:

- raising one's level of consciousness of interpersonal and organizational effectiveness, and helping others increase their awareness of the "processes" of communication, interpersonal feedback, problem solving, leadership styles, decision making, and goal setting,
- clarifying goals and defining role functions,
- improving one's skills as an effective manager, communicator, and organization facilitator,
- creating a system in which the needs and desires of individual members can be realized in an organizational context, and
- helping individuals consider or understand some basic aspects of change and learning, such as developing an awareness of one's present state, examining how one's attitudes affect one's behavior, re-evaluating one's attitudes and experimenting with behaviors consistent with these, and learning new behaviors more appropriate to one's situation.

Managers perform various functions, such as administration, management, program implementation, service delivery, budgeting, supervision, planning, learning, teaching, and public relations. Their work demands the skills and expertise of a social change agent. The OD consultant can help a manager weld these complex functions into an effective organizational thrust.

How can an individual manager/administrator contribute to an OD program? Managers and administrators can contribute in several ways to the OD programs of their organization, all of which require a "pro-active" stance. These include the following:

- working with an OD consultant and other managers to learn more effective uses of the self in work relationships,
- obtaining more training through NTL Institute's programs or those similar to them,
- becoming more involved by joining a management team with the executive officers,
- reading pertinent material on OD,
- attending meetings and helping develop more effective ways of conducting and participating in them, and
- becoming an effective advocate for change whenever one sees the need for it.

OD consultation

What is an OD consultant? An OD consultant ideally is a person trained in the behavioral sciences—especially organizational behavior—who seeks to help an organization define and clarify its own issues, values, problems, and resources. The OD consultant collaborates with an organization in developing the best method of mobilizing its resources to address the issues it has identified, and ensuring that this is done in a way that is consistent with the organization's values. In more simple terms, the OD consultant is a professional person, usually from outside the organization, who seeks to help the organization function more effectively. In addition to "external" OD consultants, some organizations also have "internal" OD consultants among their employees.

What does an OD consultant do? Clients usually wait until they sense some discomfort before they bring in OD consultants. The stimulus may be a general feeling that the organization could improve, and needs help to do so. A consultant may then help the client clarify the organization's specific needs. Although the behavior of consultants may vary, they usually follow the pattern presented above in response to the question "What is OD?"

The consultant generally decides to become deeply familiar with the system and to formulate with the client some strategies for using what has been learned to benefit the organization. The consultant helps the client gather and analyze data about the organization and plan responses to these data. This may necessitate designing strategies and interventions. The consultant then works with the client to evaluate the progress made and impact of the interventions. The evaluations usually seek to determine whether or not the interventions fulfilled the objectives they were designed to meet.

How does OD consulting differ from other types of consulting? OD consulting differs from other types of consulting in that (1) it focuses on the process rather than the content of work (i.e., the OD consultant needs no technical expertise in performing the work itself) and (2) it is not prescriptive (i.e., the OD consultant does not give advice or solve problems for the client), because one of the consultant's goals is to help the client become better at diagnosing and solving problems.

What does one have to do to become an OD consultant for an organization? In many organizations, persons emerge who are interested in— and excited by—the work and role of the change agent. Often through their own initiative, such persons may begin to develop skills in training, consultation, and OD. This enables external consultants to gradually reduce the time they spend consulting to the organization, and allow the **internal consultant(s)** to assume more responsibility for the OD program. Prospective internal consultants may receive support from their organizations in obtaining training in OD from organizations such as NTL Institute.

With respect to personal criteria, an internal consultant benefits from having a high tolerance for frustration, being willing to settle for little short-term success in the hope of obtaining greater long-term payoffs, being open to influence and feedback from others, being willing to take risks and experiment with alternative strategies in the face of more traditional norms and procedures. With respect to goals for learning, an internal consultant benefits from learning as much as possible about the culture in which a client works, the client's values, the client's perceptions of her or his role, goals, and means of accomplishing them, and the organization's mission.

How can one evaluate an OD program? Although systematic evaluation is an important aspect of OD, often both the OD consultant and client avoid this. When evaluation does occur, it is usually informal, consisting of an oral response from managers to the question "How are we doing?" This stems in part from the perception of program evaluation as something requiring much sophistication in statistical design. Moreover, many confuse program evaluation with research and experimental design, something a typical manager lacks the skills to perform. Another problem is the difficulty of determining specific, measurable items reflecting the goals and objectives of an OD effort, or its byproducts. Finally, predicting exactly **when** the results of an OD program will emerge with sufficient visibility for measurement is difficult. Ongoing follow-up evaluation and feedback procedures are themselves the results of OD interventions.

Because of the importance of program evaluation, we feel we should shift the response from "how can" to "how to" and present some of the highlights of the evaluation process. Several strategies exist for evaluating the OD program in an organization, and these may or may not require help from an OD consultant with expertise in program evaluation. An evaluation effort, however, must be devised by the manager or supervisor involved in the project, along with that person's team. These persons must specify the goals of the program and determine the criteria (e.g., individual and team behavior, work performance, productivity, and the like) for measuring change. They should define these in a way permitting them to measure movement toward or away from these goals. Once they have defined the criteria, they must assess how the unit currently functions, how they wish it would function, and how they can tell when they have reached their goals.

Program evaluation need not be highly complicated. Measures can be as simple as recording the percentage of persons involved who answer a question with "yes" or "no." Once the manager and team have set criteria for success that appropriately reflect the department's goals—the most difficult part of program evaluation, and thus the part most frequently avoided—they can turn over the actual data collection to a clerk. The criteria for success provide a standard against which the department can measure its current functioning and how far it must go to reach its goals. We emphasize that periodic diagnostic evaluations must be provided to the team and used to critique the unit's performance, to continue setting goals, to plan and implement interventions relevant to the goals, and to evaluate the impact of the interventions. Thus, the cycle closes, only to be repeated when the need is apparent.

Conclusion

The questions presented above are some of the ones appearing in a larger list we have compiled (Hanson & Lubin, 1989). Some of the ones we chose not to include in this chapter apparently stem from growing concerns for fiscal restraints and diminished resources within organizations. Given the national trend toward "doing more with less," OD would seem a useful means of addressing shrinking resources, because it emphasizes tough-minded, efficient management within a context of human concerns and values.

REFERENCE

Hanson, P. G., & Lubin, B. (1989). *Organization development: Questions and concerns of managers.* Unpublished book manuscript.

Section II.
OD and Nonprofit
Organizations

Organization Development in Social Change Organizations: Some Implications for Practice

L. David Brown
Jane G. Covey

Introduction

Organization development (OD) in social change organizations (SCOs) resembles OD in government, hospitals, business, and industry in many respects. In our work with SCOs, however, we have found that these organizations face some special challenges. These challenges are not unique, but they are more pronounced in SCOs and are therefore more easily identified. In this chapter we identify the special characteristics and dynamics of SCOs and their implications for OD practice, and provide examples from our consulting experience. We do this to offer some generalizations useful to OD practitioners working with SCOs, and to suggest practical implications applicable to a variety of organizational settings.

What is an SCO? The term has been used to portray everything from an emerging political party to efforts to effect change for a transient local issue. We define SCOs as private voluntary organizations whose mission is to bring about social change. They are private rather than public agencies; they are voluntary in that those associated with them come together freely for a common purpose; they are organizations in that they are purposeful systems displaying some degree of formal structure.

SCOs are important to a pluralistic, democratic society because they act as mediators among individuals, the state, and corporate mega-institutions (Berger & Neuhaus, 1977). They provide a way for the voice of the minority to be expressed and heard. They are credited with the ability to address problems in innovative and economical ways, and so contribute to a dynamic society. SCOs challenge the status quo and tackle discrepancies between a society's values and behaviors.

Characteristics of SCOs

Social change missions. Social change missions emphasize the creation of better (more equitable, more innovative, more productive, more healthy) communities and societies. They articulate and work for visions of a better world. Social change missions commit SCOs to changing their environments. The mission of the Community Action and Peace Project,[1] for example, emphasizes creating peace and empowering the oppressed, especially those victimized by racism. It attempts to change the conditions that lead to war (e.g., by protesting U.S. military involvement in Central America) or social and economic oppression (e.g., by engaging families in solving problems of school desegregation), not just to ameliorate their effects (e.g., by sending humanitarian aid to victims of war). The Ghetto Community Development Corporation, for example, was formed at the initiative of the federal government after riots drew national attention to the lack of services, jobs, and opportunities for residents of black urban ghettoes (Brown, 1980, 1983). The corporation used federal funds and help from local business leaders to launch local ventures providing jobs and services to community residents, and implicitly seeks to counteract the effects of generations of white exploitation of blacks.

Emphasis on values and ideologies. Visions of change and development are central to SCOs. These visionary missions make values and ideologies central features of SCO life. Members of SCOs are motivated by shared social values, and they often justify the organization's activities in terms of such values. Ideologies underpin action by explaining linkages among what exists, what should be, and how changes can be accomplished (Beyer, 1981; Brown & Brown, 1983). The values of the Community Action and Peace Project, for instance, are rooted in a common religious base. The hours are long and the pay is poor, but volunteers and staff alike work extremely hard and often achieve extraordinary results. Individual members of the organization believe they are working for the highest ideals. The project also has a well-developed ideology that prescribes actions appropriate for its ideals, such as nonviolence and just and equitable human relations.

Diverse external constituencies. Given their links to both rich and poor populations, SCOs often have constituencies whose interests directly conflict with one another. Many SCOs bridge the gap between rich and poor, using resources from the former to enable the latter to act more effectively in their own interests. The Relief and Development Agency, for example, uses funds from private donors to launch small self-help projects in developing countries. The agency must deal with wealthy donors in the First World, impoverished peasants in the Third World, and governments in both. Similarly, the Ghetto Community Development Corporation works with three major constituencies—the federal government, elites in local business and government, and ghetto residents.

Loose organization. Finally, SCOs face complex tasks that require flexibility and local discretion. Their members are often ideologically antagonistic to formal and bureaucratic organization. Therefore, SCOs are often loosely organized. They often depend on informal expectations and leadership to guide behavior, and so are particularly vulnerable to challenges to the legitimacy of accepted norms and leaders. SCOs may be incapacitated by leadership transitions that would have little impact on more formal organizations. The Equality in Education Program, for example, which was founded and developed by a charismatic leader, almost foundered as she became less able to deal with new challenges. Loose organization allows innovation and local responsibility, but it also permits diffusion of energy, avoidance of critical issues, and/or escalation of internal conflict (Alderfer, 1979; Brown, 1980, 1983).

Resulting dynamics

These characteristics—social change missions, emphasis on values and ideologies, diverse external constituencies, and loose organization—contribute to organization dynamics that generate energy for achieving organizational missions, yet produce dysfunctional conflict and decision processes. For example, commitment to organizational values and ideology can motivate staff to prevail under difficult circumstances, but can also spark internal "holy wars" that preoccupy the organization and distract its workers from mission-related activities.

Constituency-based conflict. All complex organizations must manage conflict among diverse subunits. The more complex and unpredictable an organization's environment and tasks, the more resources it must expend to integrate subunits (Lawrence & Lorsch, 1967). SCOs must manage conflict driven by differences in constituencies and ideology, as well as differences in tasks. Diverse skills may be required to work with different constituencies. A Ghetto Community Development Corporation staff member who worked with both business people and ghetto residents complained, "I need to wear a dashiki over a three-piece suit and change back and forth in the car." Conflict among constituencies makes external demands greatly complicated. Fund raisers for the Relief and Development Agency feared that major donors would be alienated if the organization publicly supported left-wing positions advocated by the project staff.

When organizational subunits become aligned according to conflicting constituencies, conflict is common, and may be expressed in two ways. Subunits with stronger ties to their constituencies than to the rest of the organization may engage in conflict with other subunits inside the organization. Subunits that identify strongly with the organization and have weaker links to their constituencies, in contrast, are more likely to come into conflict with those constituents. The Community Action and Peace Project fits the first pattern: Major tensions in the organization since the 1960s have stemmed from the organization's capacity to respond to members who are not white, male, and middle class. Because the project includes constituents in active roles throughout the hierarchy of the organization, constituency-based conflict surfaces frequently inside the project. In contrast, the Relief and Development Agency requires most field staff to base their operations in the agency's headquarters rather than in the field. This policy strengthens the staff's ties to the home office and reduces potential conflict among project staff, management, and supervising committees.

Polarized values and ideologies. Members of SCOs tend to be strongly committed to organizational visions and rhetoric. Because they are highly sensitized to injustices and wrongs in the society, they are also quick to spot discrepancies between rhetoric and action in the organization. Lapses in affirmative action at the Relief and Development Agency, for example, evoked a scandalized reaction seldom seen in other organizations. Activists are generally strong subscribers to ideologies of change and will debate differences endlessly. Disagreements over task performance can become associated with ideological perspectives and thus transformed into moral battles. Fund raisers who wear three-piece suits and prefer a relatively hierarchical organizational structure may be considered ''bad'' by colleagues who are grassroots organizers, wear jeans, and prefer to make all decisions by consensus.

Decision making and learning problems. The special characteristics of SCOs affect their patterns of decision making. SCOs are particularly vulnerable to deadlock and paralysis, fiats and side deals, charismatic leaders, and ''disjointed incrementalism.'' Conflicts between powerful factions in such loosely organized systems can produce wars of attrition or systematic avoidance of controversial issues.

The Community Action and Peace Project, for example, became paralyzed by a deadlock over racial differences that crippled its customary methods of decision making. In other SCOs, side deals and political maneuvering allow for decision making by coalition without any explicit discussion of major issues. Staff members of the Relief and Development Agency believed that critical decisions were made through political bargaining with the director, despite the organization's professed commitment to participative decision making. In other organizations, the staff defers decisions to charismatic leaders, letting them resolve ambiguities or disagreements. The staff of the Equality in Education Program, for example, depended heavily on its director to handle complex decisions and felt helpless when she became less able to play that role. Finally, decisions may be made through a repeated trial-and-error process in response to new information and shifting sources of support, a method called "disjointed incrementalism" (Lindblom, 1959, 1979). For example, the Ghetto Community Development Corporation undertook new projects as federal funds, local business interest, and community support became available, but shifting concerns among its constituencies made it difficult to predict where resources might come from next.

For organizations that face outside complexities and turbulence of this kind, a capacity for organizational learning is central to effectiveness. Because the task of promoting social change is often inherently complex and difficult to predict, organizational subunits must be able to learn actively (Korten, 1980). This need for learning is increased by tensions among external constituencies. Incremental decision-making patterns represent one means of learning about complex problems and coping with conflicts among constituencies. Successful SCOs tend to grow in fits and starts; they succeed in one area, reap the benefits of that success, and then consolidate their gains. The International Relief and Development Agency, for example, grew tenfold in two years and then spent six years learning to operate as a larger organization. SCOs may have to engage in rapid organizational learning to deal with both internal and external change.

Paradoxes of success. For most organizations, success makes their niches in the social environment more secure and enables them to operate more efficiently. Because SCOs face unpredictable tasks and conflicting constituencies and seek to alter their environments, they may encounter paradoxes of success. Success may make the external position of an SCO more precarious or overload its internal capacity. The success of the Community Action and Peace Project in recruiting a multiracial staff, for example, led to organizational paralysis. The project's traditional style of making decisions by consensus was inappropriate in the face of emerging conflicts of interest among its members. The Relief and Development Agency's fund raising success overloaded its management capacity and indirectly led to a staff revolt against "autocratic" decision making. The Community Action and Peace Project empowered one constituency so well that the constituency required a significant redirection of project efforts.

Summary. Social change organizations display special characteristics that distinguish them from many other organizations: social change missions, emphasis on values and ideologies, multiple external constituencies, and relatively loose organizations. These characteristics cause special problems and dynamics, including subunit conflicts stemming from differences among constituencies and ideologies: conflict escalation arising from polarized values and ideologies, decision-making processes vulnerable to paralysis, fiat, charisma, or disjointed incrementalism, and paradoxes of success that reduce rather than

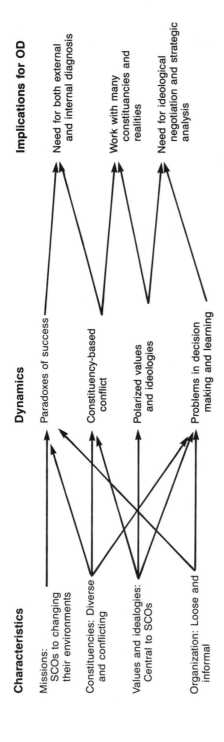

Figure 1. Characteristics and dynamics of social change organizations and their implications for OD

increase organizational security. Figure 1 depicts the relationship between these characteristics and organizational dynamics and their implications for OD practice.

Organization development in social change organizations

What are the implications of these characteristics and dynamics for OD in SCOs? In this section we describe some special problems of planned change in SCOs and speculate on the implications of those problems for OD.

External and internal diagnosis. SCOs' missions emphasize empowering disadvantaged groups or solving social problems. Unlike building automobiles or educating students, the tasks of SCOs require interaction with external agencies. Much of the internal behavior of SCOs flows from their relationships with external forces.

One cannot understand many events involving SCOs without considering their external context. For example, the Ghetto Community Development Corporation's difficulties in living up to the federal government's expectations is hard to comprehend without recognizing political changes in the larger context. The Johnson Administration's emphasis on providing jobs and services was replaced literally overnight by the Nixon Administration's emphasis on venture profitability. Consultants to SCOs must attend to external linkages like this to understand or foresee changes.

SCOs are often sensitive to external social issues that touch on core values and ideologies. The Ghetto Community Development Corporation's staff was sensitive to local and national histories of institutional and interpersonal racism, and that sensitivity affected relations among the staff members and among the staff, white business leaders, government officials, and black community members. The antagonism between the development corporation's staff and some business leaders, for example, can best be explained by the societal context in which it occurred. Consultants can easily become swept up in such large issues. The multiracial diagnostic team working with the corporation identified and addressed aspects of problems that a more homogeneous team might not have recognized (Alderfer, Alderfer, Tucker, & Tucker, 1980).

SCOs often fail to recognize the external sources of internal dynamics. For example, many staff members attributed the Ghetto Development Corporation's internal tensions to incompetence and interpreted their chief executive's indecision under pressure from incompatible constituencies as a "lack of leadership." Recognition of the external sources of the problem liberated the energy and creativity previously locked up in rationalization and self-protection. External diagnoses can focus attention on both internal dynamics and critical external boundaries.

Multiple constituencies, multiple realities. SCO subunits are differentiated by many forces, such as task specialization, external constituencies, occupational preferences, and real or perceived ideological differences. The variety of constituencies, the conflicts of interest among them, and their different—sometimes radically different—views of reality often pose special challenges to OD consultants. One cannot easily gain access to different stakeholders. When relations among SCO subunits are strained, the consultants' gaining access to one group may inhibit other groups' trust and thus undermine the consultants' access to them. Sometimes evidence that one group trusts the consultants will inhibit other groups' trust in them, and so subtly undermine the consultant's ability to recognize and explore different perspectives.

We were initially contacted by two representatives of the Relief and Development Agency—the executive director and the chairperson of the staff association—who represented the sides of the management and staff during a major organizational cleavage. We found, however, that significant tensions existed along racial, gender, and departmental lines as well. To develop our credibility, we had to have entry discussions and negotiations with many groups, and our "credentials" had to be checked repeatedly. Some staff members considered our initial diagnosis a management activity, until we refused to continue without the support of the staff association. Different groups tested us in different ways: Managers asked about our intellectual credentials and consulting backgrounds; staff members investigated our political ideologies and biases concerning participative management; people of color checked our sophistication and sensitivity with respect to race relations.

Building credibility is not easy when confronted with so many diverse subsystems. Our consulting team consisted of a black woman and a white man, which enabled us to connect with many relevant subgroups, but we could not empathize equally well with all of them. In our experience, organizational entry with diverse constituencies requires one to be willing to recognize and explicitly describe one's own values and biases, and to demonstrate understanding and respect for those with different viewpoints.

For SCOs, entry has other complexities. Different stakeholders often have different perceptions, interpretations, and evaluations of the same events. Consultants accuustomed to analyzing situations in which they find substantial agreement about major issues may consider SCO staffs bewilderingly inconsistent. For example, an unsuccessful Relief and Development Agency effort to achieve agency-wide participation in designing a new compensation plan was described by some staff members as "a management power grab," by other staff members as "a bureaucratic runaround," and by many managers as "staff unwillingness to face differences or make decisions." To learn about such multiple views of reality, consultants have to listen empathically to very different perspectives and interpretations.

The influence of multiple views of reality can become painfully obvious when consultants share their preliminary diagnoses with staff members. OD's success often depends on agreement over the definitions of and explanations for problems, as then provides the basis for effectively planning change. Consultants risk being "caught in the cross fire" when different constituencies push for the ratification of their own descriptions of the situation. Our first diagnostic report to the Relief and Development Agency evoked objections about pro-staff bias from management; the second draft drew a similar charge of a pro-management bias from staff activists; the third and final version was grudgingly accepted as "balanced," albeit somewhat offensive to all parties.

Planning by ideological negotiation and strategic analysis. OD seeks to help organizations identify future states and implement changes necessary to achieve them. Strategic or long-range planning is undertaken as environments change or when existing organizational arrangements are no longer effective. For SCOs, planning typically begins with a definition of the future state, expressed as value preferences. In the Community Action and Peace Project, for example, programs are initially defined in terms of values. The South African situation demands action because of the project's positions on racism and violence, not because it represents an opportunity to attract new donors or to gain public recognition. SCOs often make choices that may actually harm their organizational stability and success in conventional terms, but fit their values. For example, the American Civil Liberties Union sought to protect the civil liberties of neo-Nazi groups, even though this cost it support from people concerned about anti-Semitism.

Planning in SCOs relies on ideological agreements that link values to behavior with explanations of cause-and-effect relationships (Brown & Brown, 1983). Because different constituencies perceive different realities, however, they often have different theories as to what the SCO should do to achieve its mission. In the Community Action and Peace Project, serious ideological differences exist with regard to racism: Some hold an "integrationist" view that seeks to bring minority group members into the mainstream while leaving cultural and structural power arrangements essentially intact. Others believe that racism will persist until cultures and structures are modified to include the interests, beliefs, and preferences of people of color, a view one might describe as a "transformationist" ideology.

We have seen long-range planning efforts become bogged down and key decisions end in stalemate because of unresolved ideological differences. Deadlocked organizations cannot adapt to changing environments, and suffer from constant internal turbulence stemming from the underlying conflict. Those consulting to paralyzed SCOs may need to facilitate ideological negotiations before undertaking more commong planning steps. OD consultants may hesitate to encourage such negotiations because they demand an awareness and skills not typically associated with the collaborative processes leading to win-win solutions (Covey & Brown), 1983).

Ideological negotiations can be direct or indirect. In direct negotiation, a third party can help the organization reframe the ideological issue. For example, the planning committee of the Community Action and Peace Project reconceptualized the issue of institutional racism in terms of "becoming a multicultural organization." This redefinition allowed people to go beyond the paralyzing cycle of guilt, denial, and defensiveness invoked by the "racist" label. Our experience with SCOs suggests that efforts to reframe ideologies or articulate new values can be major forces for planned organizational change. The right concept expressed in locally comprehensible terms can liberate dammed-up resources of talent and energy, as it did for the Community Action and Peace Project. To develop ideas for expressing relevant values and ideologies, however, requires more than a superficial understanding of organizational cultures. Consultants may need to go beyond questionnaires and interviews to develop such understanding. In our work with the project, we invested considerable time in participant observation, then worked jointly with the client to frame statements of organizational realities.

Conclusion

We argue that OD efforts involving SCOs require consultants to pay attention to these organizations' particular characteristics and dynamics. We have found several innovations useful: Making external diagnoses, managing multiple conflicting clients, and assisting ideological negotiation for strategic planning. These adaptations have led us to examine the OD paradigm in more general terms. We believe that the OD paradigm needs modification and expansion to be relevant to SCOs and to exploit its potential for contributing to social change. In another work (Brown & Covey, 1987), we argue that the OD paradigm needs a broader basic metaphor, a more comprehensive analytic framework, a greater range of interventions, more attention to learning and inquiry, and an expanded view of potential impacts. We discuss some applications in this chapter, but much work is needed. SCOs may differ from government, business, and service agencies more in degree than in kind: Constituency-based conflict is common in many loosely organized systems, and commitment to values is a key factor in high-performing organizations in many contexts. The lessons from SCOs may have wide applicability for OD, both as it is currently practiced in organizations and as it might be practiced in the service of worldwide social change and development.

NOTE

1. All organization names are pseudonyms.

REFERENCES

Alderfer, C. P., Consulting to underbounded systems. In C. P. Alderfer & C. Cooper, *Advances in experimental social process* (Vol. 2). New York: Wiley.

Alderfer, C. P., Alderfer, C. J., Tucker, L., & Tucker, R. (1980). Diagnosing race relations in management. *Journal of Applied Behavioral Science, 16*(2), 135-166.

Berger, P. L., & Neuhaus, R. J (1977). *To empower people: The role of mediating structures in public policy.* Washington, D.C.: American Enterprise Institute for Public Policy Research.

Beyer, J. (1981). Ideologies, values and decision making in organizations. In P. Nystrom & W. Starbuck (Eds.), *Handbook of organizational design* (Vol. 2). New York: Oxford University Press.

Brown, L. D. (1983). *Managing conflict at organizational interfaces.* Reading, MA: Addison-Wesley.

Brown, L. D. (1980). Planned change in underorganized systems. In T. Cummings (Ed.), *Systems theory for organizational development.* London: Wiley.

Brown, L. D., & Brown, J. C. (1983). Organizational microcosms and ideological negotiation. In M. Bazerman & R. Lewicki (Eds.), *Bargaining inside organizations.* Beverly Hills, CA: Sage.

Brown, L.D., & Covey, J. G. (1987). Development organizations and organization development: Implications for the organizational development paradigm. In W. E. Pasmore & R. Woodman (Eds.), *Research in organizational development* (Vol. 1) (pp. 59-88). Greenwich, CT: JAI Press.

Covey, J. G., & Brown, L. D. (1985). *Beyond strategic planning: Strategic decisions in nonprofit organizations* (Working Paper No. 5). Boston: Institute for Development Research.

Korten, D. (1980). Community organizations and rural development: A learning process approach. *Public Administration Review, 40* (480-510).

Lawrence, P. R., & Lorsch, J. W. (1967). *Organization and environment.* Cambridge, MA: Harvard Business School.

Lindblom, C. E. (1959). The science of muddling through. *Public Administration Review, 19* (79-88).

Lindblom, C. E. (1979). Still muddling, not yet through. *Public Administration Review, 39* (17-526).

OD in Public Education: Areas for Development

Jack Gant
Oron South

Organization development originated in the private sector, and its basic concepts and practices have been tailored to reflect the organizational reality of industry. Public school systems represent a quite different organizational reality requiring a different approach to OD practice. This chapter aims to (1) outline the nature of the major differences between private-sector organizations and school systems and (2) describe the type of OD practice we have developed for school systems. Although this chapter concentrates on systems for kindergarten through the 12th grade, some of what we discuss can also be applied to the college level.

Public education: A "nonsystem" system

If General Motors, with all its divisions, is said to constitute a system, then the public education organizations of each state are what Schon (1971) calls a "nonsystem" system. Weick (1976) and March (1978) refer to educational organizations as loosely coupled systems. These observations indicate that a state's school districts are not organically related to its department of education, which is supposed to implement the policies and procedures of the governor and legislature. Although the system is hierarchical, no chain of command connects school districts with the department of education. The loose coupling label also applies to operations within school districts, as we discuss further below.

A certain degree of unity of purpose and perspective exists among the managers and executives of organizations such as General Motors. Such unity cannot be found among administrators in public education. Some are elected, some appointed; some have tenure, others do not; some have strong power bases, others weaker ones.

Public education systems tend to be highly centralized and to feature forms of management that rely on standardization and "doing things by the book."

At a time when many industries are decentralizing their organization and management and becoming more people oriented, legislators are seeking to increasingly centralize and standardize education through merit pay plans based on standardized evaluations, consistent course requirements, longer school days and school years, standardized curricula, and the like.

Schools are **administrative** units, not managerial ones; they administer programs, course grades, and requirements. Schools thus are essentially collections of programs and grade levels. Legislators enjoy having their names associated with particular programs and procedures, or with increased course loads and longer school days. Parents and special-interest groups also prefer to identify with programs or course grades rather than with schools. Until recently, this focus meant that almost no pressure was exerted to strengthen school organization and management. Except in rare cases, the role of general manager that is common to business does not exist in school systems.

Changes in state leadership, which occur as often as every two years, cause educational programs to lose their champions at the state level and new programs to be enacted. Even changes in leadership at the national level affect school programs. These frequent shifts in focus and emphasis create a highly unstable environment for administrators and teachers. Moreover, new programs often lack adequate funding and resources, causing difficulties in attempting innovation. Constant changes in policy mean teachers and administrators seldom have the time to help new ideas fulfill their potential.

Examining the principles used to organize educational systems illuminates the ways the programmatic focus is reflected in structure. A major function of state departments of education and school districts is school curricula/instruction. Each curriculum division consists of coordinators or supervisors in charge of language arts, social studies, mathematics, vocational education, science, kindergarten through third grade, third grade through sixth grade, and so forth. The program ''line'' extends from the department of education to the school district to the school. School district coordinators advise principals about program matters, including teacher selection, and may furnish them with data on performance evaluation. In some districts, the program coordinators' job descriptions actually specify that they are to supervise teachers. This supervision constitutes a structure somewhat **outside** the principal's jurisdiction, and contributes to the loose coupling by dividing responsibility for the teachers.

To understand the organizational reality, one must note that many school boards do not confine their activities to formulating policy, but are also actively involved in management. In 1985, secondary school principals and school district administrators attending a statewide conference were asked to estimate the distribution of power in their districts among school boards, superintendents, district staffs, principals, and teachers (power was defined as the ability to influence daily decisions and activities). For some districts, 65% of the power was perceived as being exercised by the board, 5% by the superintendent, 5% by the principals, and no more than 10% by the teachers (they were usually considered to exercise about 5% of the power). These results are consistent with those obtained from surveys conducted previously. The low level of power teachers are estimated to wield supports the argument of Darling-Hammond (1985) of the Rand Corporation that the most important need in American education is the professionalization of teaching. Such professionalization is expected to give teachers greater control over the content of their work.

We also wish to point out that school systems are budget driven rather than market driven (Niskanen, 1971). The governor and legislature are the "market" for a state's school system products and services. This means that school systems must constantly negotiate with the governor and legislators on matters of price, quality, and quantity. It also means that school systems provide only as much information as required, and that legislators withhold as much information as possible from schools on what they will pay them. Efforts to use market mechanisms to motivate teachers and administrators often do not work because of a failure to recognize the differences between market-driven and budget-driven systems.

As noted above, no organic chain of command exists between state departments of education and local school systems. To compensate for this, legislators seek to use the budget to motivate administrators and teachers to do what the legislature desires. Merit pay programs are examples of this. To "justify" raising teachers' pay, legislators tie raises to acceptance of a standardized evaluation system. Similarly, legislatures often offer districts additional funds for adopting favored programs or procedures. Such actions almost always increase the infrastructure, and hence increase the difficulty of making changes. In effect, as do school board members, legislators seek to manage from the center.

In light of the programmatic focus and budget practices, one should not be surprised that resources for organizational change are minimal. Money is hard to obtain, and time even more so. During the school year, getting even two hours of people's time a week for organizational skills training is difficult.

Organizational change is also hard to achieve because the "unit of change" generally is considered to be the principal and/or teachers. Many assume that school performance will change if teachers change. We have found that consultants often introduce or reinforce this orientation by focusing on teacher or administrator behavior.

Areas for development

Much of our work focuses on areas that must be developed if the change prescribed from outside is to be managed. For the past 20 years, legislatures and school districts have heavily focused on tasks. This has had the cumulative effect of producing tremendous organizational stress and strain at the school center, as not much has been done to help schools develop new management technology and practices for handling greater work loads. Our efforts thus are addressed at improving capacities through new technology, structures, and a greater sense of countervailing power. Most of our work has addressed the areas discussed below.

Coordination

The emphasis on programs, performance, and productivity has created a need for coordination across programs and across school boundaries so that the system's effects can be magnified. As schools develop data bases for different student groups, more coordination is needed for tracking information throughout the system. We have found that changes in students' values, lifestyles, and ways of learning are making changes in the system. To deal with their future, those working in secondary schools must examine students in elementary and middle schools.

In addition to pointing out the value of improving coordination, we have also sought to identify organizational structures for acquiring and using information and then making necessary plans. We also work on the faculty's team development and lines of communication so as to increase teachers' sense of power.

Action planning and action taking

Teachers and administrators rely on parliamentary procedures that are more useful for legislative debating than for planning and taking action. We do not consider this practice effective for management, for legislators do not have to implement what they enact. We thus emphasize the difference between debate and discussion, and stress building commitment and coordinating action. The team in charge of coordination and planning takes an integral part in making policy and in planning and taking action. This also increases teachers' sense of power.

Building data bases

We stress the need for more comprehensive data bases, and for systems that do not require as much time from principals and other administrators. Many of the school systems we have worked with depend on personal data bases and word of mouth for planning and making decisions. We recommend that planners and administrators not rely on such impressionistic information and instead use more systematic methods for collecting and analyzing data. Early in the process, we receive some of the sensitive data so that we may tabulate it and make suggestions for analysis. Coordinating and planning teams find that such data base management gives teachers more freedom to express their perceptions.

Building and maintaining communication structures

The emphasis on interpersonal communication has caused the structural aspects of communication to be largely overlooked. When we begin working with a school for the first time, we discuss how it is organized. Then we develop an organization chart indicating communication channels. In our experience, this is generally the first time a faculty has seen such a chart. In presenting the chart, we discuss how consciously adhering to the structure's communication channels can save time, increase the accessibility of key persons, and maintain contact more effectively. Moreover, we point out the harmful consequences of a teacher's feeling entitled to bypass the structure. In the case of a principal who habitually bypasses the structure, we recommend that the faculty create a quota of how many times the principal may do so. Finally, we get school personnel to agree to change the structure if it is not working. Many times we have found that no clear agreement exists as to the functions of various structural elements, such as grade groups, departments, faculty meetings, administrative councils, or planning and coordination councils.

Role development

As change becomes the status quo, principals and teachers must change also. As highly active legislators provide new tasks, principals must build relationships to counteract the strong task orientation of the school district and state officials. Principals must also become power brokers, finding ways to exercise more power than the systems make available. This can be done through communication, team building, and determining how to get more funding from superintendents. Teachers must assume organizational roles and become more attentive to lateral relationships. Once the purposes of and relationships among various subunits are recognized and agreed upon, roles and lateral relationships gain power.

Increasing a sense of power

As indicated above, we help increase a sense of power through more effective communications, aiming to get teachers to see that the structures and processes outlined help save them time and keep them connected to one another. We also use the following methods.

Once we worked with a planning team from a school with a history of having a divided faculty, and found that when the next school year began nearly one-fourth of the faculty would be new to the school. We indicated how this influx of new teachers could help change the balance of power, if the team quickly developed a process for orienting the new teachers. We later found that the process used proved effective, and that when school began the climate was considered much more positive than previously.

Whenever we have had the time, we have worked on diminishing the power of the rumor mill. Doing this calls for getting all the teachers to make public the opening lines they have heard with rumors, such as "Did you hear" and "Guess what?" It also includes developing ways of recognizing good work and extraordinary effort.

Another strategy for increasing a sense of power is to reduce the opportunities for making people feel powerless. For example, principals often feel vulnerable during faculty meetings, which provide forums for anyone seeking to get the attention of all the teachers. Based on this, we have taught ways of working with large groups and making each element of the structure function effectively. Some of these methods are as simple as writing brief, clear meeting minutes and distributing them promptly.

Planning

We generally become involved with both the structure and the process used in planning, and with the relationship issues that surface when new structures and processes are established. For example, in one high school whose principal wanted a new planning structure, we advised the faculty during the meeting in which the planning council would be selected. We insisted that the selection not be done by secret ballot, and that a negotiation process be used enabling those involved to have clear expectations. We stressed that the council members should represent the school as a whole, and after their selection helped the members develop ways of working and of keeping in touch with the faculty. When the council completed its initial work, we recommended that it give a report on this to the faculty and seek its assent.

Another case involved a school district that conducted planning by having the teachers in each school submit plans for the next year, which were then modified by the principal and sent to the school district administrators as a single school plan, which was in turn modified by the district, consolidated with plans for other schools, and sent to the state officials as a district plan. We advised the superintendent and district staff to make plans separate from the school plans, and recommended that the principals do their own planning. At first this proved quite difficult, as the old planning process had resembled curriculum planning—that is, those making plans tended to set down desired goals—rather than organizational analysis. Once they caught on to the new process, however, the superintendent and principals greatly altered their plans, for organizational analysis taught them that they could reach only a limited number of goals.

Work methods

The above discussion should indicate that we work from our own diagnoses of the state of the overall system, not just the client's presentation of the problem. In effect, we work simultaneously from a micro and macro perspective. Consistent with Deming's (1975) view, we have found that at least 80% of the problems we encounter are caused by the system itself.

Readers should also note that we spend more time improving capacities than solving problems. Principals and teachers have become overwhelmed with new tasks, without benefiting from a corresponding effort to increase their abilities to cope with the cumulative impact of the changes affecting them. One principal told us he identified strongly with a cartoon he had seen, which depicted a donkey hitched to a wagon overloaded with hay, on which someone was about to throw enough more hay to break the wagon. "I feel like that jackass," he said. "I agree with the individual bales put on my wagon; most of them do good things, and I have been for them. But now I'm overloaded, and my teachers are overloaded."

Because of the shortage of time available, we try to use half a day at the beginning or end of a school year to address the work to be done during the next school year. If possible, lunch is eaten during part of that time. We usually begin this session by asking those present to assess what they consider good about the previous school year and what they would like to do differently. We want the teachers to recognize what they have done **collectively** and to learn one another's agenda. In our experience, this usually represents the first time a faculty has performed such an analysis. Because criticism is more common than praise, many teachers are amazed at how many worthwhile things have been done during the previous school year. For the next hour or two, we use carefully planned agenda. During this meeting, we more actively make suggestions, aid in restructuring, and perform evaluations than we would when working for a client system that could give us more time.

We emphasize that communication and information are paths to power. We also point out that information in various forms is a product of social process. One must therefore make certain the process is credible.

To facilitate self- and group evaluation of the impact of the cognitive styles of individuals and the group, we use such instruments as the Learning Style Inventory or the Myers-Briggs Type Indicator. These help communicate the message that personal factors other than professional certification are important for work groups and teams. We have found that according to the Myers-Briggs Type Indicator, most principals have an "SJ" temperament, and thus should prefer stability and routine and resist high levels of change. Helping them understand and accept this information, and to use the strengths of the team members, has proven beneficial.

Such instruments are particularly useful when facilitators have little time in which to work, as they make quite an impact. Participants may not remember details about the resulting reports, but we have found that they get the message. Teachers tend to recognize that cognitive differences account for the range of behaviors they confront in the classroom every day. The instruments also help school boards more clearly understand the dynamics of board meetings and why decision making tends to take a particular form—and to change form when various board members are absent.

Finally, when working with school systems we stress the corporate nature of the undertaking. For example, before a faculty meeting we once suggested that a principal say something similar to the following statement.

> Look around you. The people in this room are responsible for the quality of high school education in this community. We are the ones who ultimately will decide what will be taught and how it will be taught. We are the ones who establish the nature of the faculty-student relationship. We have a lot of power.

This encourages teachers to accept change processes from the beginning, to recognize that they are responsible for what happens in schools, and to believe that they have decision-making power. They come to realize that, in essence, the system is theirs.

Summary

As do companies in the private sector, public school systems need organization development. OD has produced valuable results in the field of education. When used in schools, however, the approach must vary from that used in business. As we indicate above, public school systems differ from their industrial counterparts with respect to chain of command, unity of purpose, structure, transitions, and general organizational realities. OD consultants to school systems thus must focus first on understanding how these systems are unique. Second, they must understand that the ways teachers and principals view their organizations—and themselves as members of these organizations—differ from the views of members of private-sector organizations. Those in education thus are motivated by different types of forces.

Our experience suggests that because of these differences, the effectiveness of OD in public school systems requires using the following strategies.

- Help school systems increase their capacity for managing change through interprogram coordination and planning.
- Develop systemic skills and norms supporting action planning and action taking.
- Assess, adjust, and facilitate comprehensive communication channels.
- Help school system personnel identify and assume new roles.
- Provide training for school system personnel in building working relationships that will increase their sense of power.

As suggested above, OD consultants to public schools must remain aware of both the micro and macro systems at all times. Organizational elements of both systems can ultimately make principals and teachers operate schools less effectively. We have shown how working with the two systems can enable OD consultants to help make schools better places for students.

REFERENCES

Darling-Hammond, L. (1985). Valuing teachers: The making of a profession. *Teachers College Record,* *87*(2), 205-218.

Deming, W. E. (1975). On some statistical aids toward economic production. *Interfaces, 5*(4), 1-15.

March, J. G. (1978, February). American public school administration: A short analysis. *School Review, pp.* 217-250.

Niskanen, W. A., Jr. (1971). *Bureaucracy and representative government.* Chicago: Aldine-Atherton.

Schön, D. (1971). *Beyond the stable state.* New York: Random House.

Weick, K. E. (1976, March). Educational organizations as loosely coupled systems. *Administrative Science Quarterly, pp.* 1-19.

Applying Organization Development Concepts to Higher Education: Initial Considerations

Russell R. Rogers

Introduction and context

In their book *Higher Education in Transition,* Brubacher and Rudy (1976) document the history of higher education from 1636 through 1976. Specifically, they
trace the institution of higher education through an evolutionary process more
characterized by the effects of change than by the effects of permanence. Clearly,
this "transition" is not complete. Indeed, the pace seems to be accelerating.
Words such as "transition," "transformation," "trauma," "retrenchment,"
"curtailment," "re-examination," "alternative," and "adaptation" appear frequently in the titles of current publications created to capture the essence of
higher education's metamorphic process.

Higher education faces the threat and/or challenge (the danger and/or
opportunity) of substantive change. This change involves much more than
unstable external support systems and poor internal coordination. The period
in which students—that is, education's customers—filled classrooms to learn
from dedicated professionals seems to have passed. Oversized budgets will
probably not appear within the next decade, if ever again. Stable salaries and
relatively flat operating costs have given way to fluctuating inflation and
expensive salary indexing. At the same time, the customer base for higher education has changed from a group of people between 18 and 22 years of age to
a more diverse collection of adult learners, many of them seeking immediate
payoffs from their tuition investment. This situation has resulted from both
our society's increasingly pragmatic orientation as well as from changes in values
inherent to the process of adult development itself.

In *The State of the Nation and the Agenda for Higher Education,* Bowen asserts that the early 1980s is a time of uncertainty and pessimism among educators. They have already experienced or they fear demographic decline, reduced student aid funds, diminished appropriations, continuing inflation, and lukewarm popular and political support. Their goals range from sheer survival to maintenance of the status quo. (1982, p. 155)

In addition to confronting changes in contingencies and constituencies, the community of higher education has recently had to address three major reports criticizing the present condition of curricula and calling for educational reform (Association of American Colleges, 1984; Bennett, 1984; National Institute of Education, 1984).

The scenario facing higher education is serious, perhaps bleak. The field must undergo metamorphic adaptations or face eventual extinction reminiscent of the demise of the dinosaurs, who apparently ran into mortal trouble when conditions changed and they did not. For higher education, conditions today are changing with respect to constituencies, contingencies, and curricula. Educators must now determine how they will respond.

The problem

Obviously, society constantly changes. In retrospect such changes often appear significant, yet they generally occur through such small adjustments that they do not seem dramatic at the time and take forms that organization members can assimilate and adapt to "naturally." Roeber asserts that

organizations have been able to adapt themselves to slow changes in their environments by making small concessions to pressures, and through the import of new personnel and the diffusion of new ideas. Through these unstructured, untutored, and unconscious adaptive responses organizations have "tracked" changes in their environment[s], much as the rear wheels of a long trailer track the changes in direction at the front. But such natural processes are no longer appropriate when the environment changes rapidly. (1973, p. x)

Higher education now exists in such an environment. Today's educational organizations face changes occurring at rates exceeding the scope of natural assimilation processes, and lack sufficiently comprehensive methods for adjusting and adapting to the turbulence. To enhance its effectiveness, achieve excellence, and ensure its survival, higher education clearly needs its administrative leaders—in full collaboration with faculty members—to develop conscious, explicit processes for managing change. These processes must include strategies for "defining missions, setting objectives, allocating resources, and coordinating efforts for the institution" (Corson, 1975, p. 18) amid conditions of rapid change.

Faced with this mandate for change, and recognizing the multiple and complex variables associated with such change, many educational administrators have been directed to find or develop methods that both accomplish change and preserve—or even strengthen—the integrity of their institutions' purposes and effectiveness. They face a situation similar to that confronting business organizations in the 1960s and 1970s.

Prior to the 1960s, the major approaches to management education consisted of teaching general "principles of management." As long as business organizations remained internally simple and their environments uncomplicated and stable, such approaches seemed appropriate. When business organizations became larger, more complex, and situated in environments characterized by accelerated change, however, the principles of management and intuitive approaches proved insufficient. The need for alternatives—and for confidence in the likelihood that these could improve the circumstances facing businesses— became apparent. To answer this need, organization development (OD) emerged as an applied discipline within business organizations.

The similarity between the complex, unstable, and rapidly changing conditions that business organizations have encountered and those now confronting higher education raise some major questions: Because higher education administration (HEA) has virtually no historic precedent, collective experience, or policy directive to guide it in managing the envisioned transition and/or retrenchment ahead, can OD help the HEA leadership accomplish the crucial tasks it faces? If so, how?

Research purpose and methodology

In The Governance of Colleges and Universities, Corson argues for a "rational modification of organizational forms and processes" that institutions of higher education inherit "from other fields of endeavor" (1975, p. 89). In accordance with Corson's directive, and to both establish a foundation and build a model for "rationally modifying" OD for its possible role in HEA, I undertook the following steps:

1. explored the fundamental OD literature to derive and determine a consensus regarding the basic premises, values, and purposes of OD;

2. explored the fundamental HEA literature to derive and determine a consensus regarding the basic premises, values, and purposes of HEA;

3. conducted a comparative analysis of the relationship between the basic premises, values, and purposes of OD and of HEA;

4. developed a framework for model building based on model theory;

5. developed a descriptive model in accordance with both the comparative analysis and model theory.

6. submitted a model and guidelines to three separate expert panels for critique (one panel consisted of OD consultants, one of HEA theorists, and one of HEA practitioners); and

7. revised the model and guidelines in accordance with the responses and suggestions of the three panels.

Findings

Based on the assumption that the fields of OD and HEA had become sufficiently developed to be represented in their literatures, I conducted an analysis of each field, which yielded 11 basic premises, 8 core values, and 8 fundamental goals per field. I then compared these premises, values, and goals to ascertain the nature of their intersection. From this, I determined that the relationship between OD and HEA was congruent at best, and tenuous at worst. Figure 1 uses a Venn diagram format to illustrate the revised model and depict the intersection (congruence) and lack of intersection (tenuousness) between the "sets" of OD and HEA.

As a theoretical and/or conceptual model, Figure 1 clarifies the degree to which OD and HEA intersect. This suggests the following guidelines and/or caveats for any attempt to integrate OD within HEA.

1. One must understand both OD and HEA and recognize the dynamics involved in their interplay. The model suggests that a clear perspective on the congruities and incongruities between the two fields is a prerequisite for any attempt to integrate them.

2. The areas of congruence between OD and HEA offer the firmest foundation upon which to base—and initially empower—an OD intervention within HEA.

3. One must analyze the areas of incongruence between OD and HEA for each individual higher education setting to determine the areas in which OD may need to be adapted. Because higher education exists as the "host" organization and OD as the "guest" intervention, OD must be adapted to suit HEA, rather than have HEA change to accommodate OD. The foremost goal is improving HEA's effectiveness through a process **aided** by OD—not commandeered by OD. In this regard, I suggest the following considerations.

OD practitioners must proceed cautiously when addressing human irrationality and affect within higher education organizations. Indeed, they must ground themselves in the language and cultural currency of higher education, which consists of facts, information, logic, expertise, and rational argument. The existence of irrationality and affect in higher education must be attended to covertly.

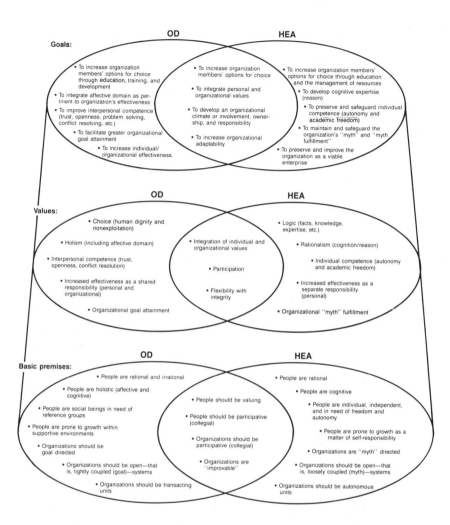

Figure 1. A theoretical model for integrating organization development within higher education administration

Although in business situations OD typically relies on the power that emanates from the organization's goals (legitimate power, expert power, skill power, and strategic resource power), OD consultants involved with HEA must adapt their source of influence from legitimate power per se to referent power, a contingency of myth-directed organizations. Weick asserts, ''Core beliefs are crucial underpinnings that hold loose events together. If these beliefs are questioned, action stops, uncertainty is substantial, and receptiveness to change is high" (1982, p. 392). The "referent" for HEA is a thorough knowledge of and ability to articulate the "myth" that connects the various loosely coupled aspects of the particular higher education institution.

Ultimately, the goal of both HEA and OD is an **effective** organization in which **effective** individuals and **effective** groups act and interact through **effective** processes to accomplish established objectives. To integrate OD within HEA, one must clearly understand the relative meaning of such "effectiveness." For example, Cameron (1980) presents a review of four major approaches for evaluating effectiveness, each emanating from a different understanding of the term. I outline each approach below, highlighting the idiosyncracies of higher education organizations that may thwart its applicability.

1. **Effectiveness as goal accomplishment.** The closer an organization's "output" comes to meeting its goals, the more effective it is. This approach is most appropriate when organizations have clear goals.

   HEA difficulties: Higher education organizations have vague goals, and employ ambiguous criteria for effectiveness in order to keep the organization adaptable, flexible, and capable of responding to diverse expectations and demands.

2. **Effectiveness as system resources.** The more an organization can obtain its needed resources, the more effective it is. This approach is most appropriate when a clear connection exists between the resources an organization receives and what it produces.

   HEA difficulties: No clear connection exists between the "input" or resources a higher education organization receives and its "output."

3. **Effectiveness as internal processes and operations.** The less internal strain and more benevolence and trust an organization demonstrates, the more effective it is. This approach is most appropriate when an organization's internal processes and procedures are closely associated with that which the organization produces.

   HEA difficulties: More than one type of higher education technology produces the same outcome, little information flow exists between the organization's work processes and results, and the connection between the organization's widely varying characteristics and products is ambiguous.

4. **Effectiveness as strategic constituencies.** The degree to which organizational stakeholders are satisfied indicates the organization's effectiveness. This approach is most appropriate when external constituencies exert a powerful influence on the organization's operations, or when the organization's behavior is largely reactive to the demands of a strategic constituency.

HEA difficulties: The loose coupling and semi-autonomous subunits characteristic of higher education organizations are the exact mechanisms used to limit the power that external groups exercise in relation to the organization.

An understanding of these idiosyncracies readily suggests that the meaning of "effectiveness"—and means of assessing it—must be clarified for each particular higher education organization and agreed upon by both the administrators and the OD consultants who are involved in a change effort.

Furthermore, those attempting to integrate OD and HEA must address two other aspects of increasing effectiveness: **accountability** and **responsibility.** The intention of increasing effectiveness presupposes a certain level of assessable accountability. Therefore, one must determine whether the rhetoric in support of "pursuing excellence and increasing quality" is more than just rhetoric. That is, is HEA willing and able to subject itself to the standards of accountability required for such pursuits? If not, interventions involving OD or any other strategy represent mere "window dressing" and probably should be aborted.

With respect to responsibility, OD claims at its very core to have an organizational perspective regarding effectiveness. OD contends that an organization has a stake and role in, and responsibility for, increasing its effectiveness. HEA, however, is based on an individualistic perspective in this regard. Within higher education, the locus and onus of responsibility for increasing effectiveness exist within the individually autonomous and academically "free" faculty member, not the organization per se. The mere consideration that OD has possible applicability to HEA assumes that higher education organizations could benefit from developing a more organizational perspective. In light of this divergence, the OD assumption must be clarified and negotiated with respect to each particular higher education setting.

4. OD efforts must proceed cautiously in promoting the values and goals of interpersonal competence in higher education organizations, insofar as these organizations are characterized more by autonomy and freedom than by transactions and shared responsibility. OD interventions must either be adapted to shape a new type of interpersonal competence for those facing minimal task-related interaction, or carefully seek to enhance and facilitate increased interaction without violating higher education's revered concepts of autonomy and academic freedom.

Recommendations

Based on the findings discussed above, I have devised six recommendations for those considering the intersection of organization development and higher education administration.

The sociocultural milieu in which the research took place, the components of OD, and the current state of higher education and its administration, suggest one recommendation. Numerous authors (Ferguson, 1980; Houston, 1980; Kanter, 1983; Lauderdale, 1982; Naisbitt, 1982; Peters & Waterman, 1982; Toffler, 1971, 1974, 1980; Yankelovich, 1982) find that society in general is changing, that a paradigm shift is causing society's basic premises, values, and goals to become more consonant with those of OD. Although the literature pertaining to this "emergent paradigm" (Lauderdale, 1982) may not necessarily refer directly to OD by name, futurist authors do seem to suggest that the sociocultural direction of society is, perhaps coincidentally, moving in the same direction as the premises, values, and goals purported by OD. The model presented in this chapter clearly depicts points of tension posed by merging OD and HEA, whether they are merged by name or world view, particularly if the convergence occurs without a careful integration of OD's premises, values, and goals and the distinctive characteristics of HEA. Toffler (1971) refers to such occurrences of change without integration as "future shock." A well-reasoned, planned OD effort that takes into account the distinctions and differences of the higher education enterprise may offer HEA the best means of negotiating the merger of OD and HEA, which will result in less organizational "shock" and more organizational "renewal" (Gardner, 1964). In this context, the model suggests that the result will be either a challenging agenda for integrating HEA with the paradigm of the future, or a formidable battle between HEA and that paradigm. By adapting OD in accordance with the distinctive and important qualities of higher education, practitioners in both OD and HEA may facilitate the integration and minimize the battle. In doing this, the practitioners might assume the role of a tutor preparing an organization for its role within the new paradigm.

My second recommendation stems from the substantial incongruence occurring between OD and HEA in the model. This incongruence suggests that for an OD effort to succeed within higher education, the effort must be confined to areas of congruence as it seeks to facilitate the organization's development. To address the basic premises, values, and goals not shared by OD and HEA, OD practitioners must adapt their strategies to reflect the important dynamics, idiosyncracies, and sensitivities that undergird HEA. The areas of congruence between HEA and OD offer a firm foundation upon which to base, earn credibility for, and—at least initially—empower OD efforts.

The following four recommendations stem from the third guideline listed previously in the findings.

- OD practitioners must exercise caution in dealing with human irrationality and affect, which are not considered integral to HEA.

- OD efforts must be grounded in different power bases for HEA than for business and industry (i.e., they must rely less on role power and more on referent—or core belief—power).
- For any particular setting, OD practitioners and HEA administrators must agree regarding the ultimate goal of organizational effectiveness (including defined accountability and locus of responsibility).
- OD practitioners must exercise caution in emphasizing values and goals related to interpersonal competence within HEA, given higher education's characteristics of autonomy, academic freedom, and low degree of task-related interaction.

Conclusion

The field of higher education is undergoing change, but with existing staff and few, if any, additional resources. Administrators are finding that change strategies honed during the 1960s and 1970s—a period of growth in higher education—have little value for this period of retrenchment. The new era demands a new strategy, one that recognizes individuals' needs and goals as well as those of the organization, that relies upon planned change, that encourages participation by all members of the organization, and that encompasses a sufficient variety of techniques that allow for addressing the contingencies of each situation. This strategy is within the purview of OD (French & Bell, 1978), and represents a ''new idea'' for higher education.

Most reasonable people will withhold their judgment long enough to entertain ''new ideas'' if they understand that they result from serious efforts to analyze a given situation and represent a straightforward rationale for addressing it. The model presented in this chapter is an example of this: The new idea for HEA is OD, and the situation is the current state of higher education and its administration.

Those seeking to apply this model—or some variation of it—must certainly reflect on it and come to a reasonable understanding of the assumptions, premises, philosophical postulates, intuitive insights, and logic it synthesizes before applying it in practice. Thus, the model and the guidelines it offers provide a conceptual ''blueprint'' for addressing the integration of OD and HEA and for outlining the contingencies involved in pursuing this integration. It does this **not** by advocating an immediate implementation of OD procedures, planning cycles, and intervention strategies (the literature abounds with examples of this), but rather by urging the prior consideration of basic premises, values, and goals for both OD and the nature of higher education. The failure to do this has compromised, or even precluded, the acceptance and long-term impact of many an idea.

Given the role and stature of higher education, the challenge of change it now faces, and the potential resourcefulness OD offers, the stakes are too high to toy with, ignore, or reject OD as a possible strategy for change. Rather, to consider OD a worthy ally and aid, practitioners in both OD and HEA will need to exercise perception, vision, and skill in areas in which OD can help and in which it must be adapted.

REFERENCES

Association of American Colleges. (1984). *Integrity in the college curriculum: A report to the academic community* (Report of the Association of American Colleges Project on Redefining the Meaning and Purpose of Baccalaureate Degrees). Washington, DC: Author.

Bennett, W. J. (1984). *To reclaim a legacy: A report on the humanities in higher education.* Washington, DC: National Endowment for the Humanities.

Bowen, H. R. (1982). *The state of the nation and the agenda for higher education.* San Francisco: Jossey-Bass.

Brubacher, J. S., & Rudy, W. (1976). *Higher education in transition: An American history, 1636-1976.* New York: Harper & Row.

Cameron, K. (1980, Autumn). Critical questions in assessing organizational effectiveness. *Organizational Dynamics,* pp. 66-80.

Corson, J. J. (1975). *The governance of colleges and universities.* New York: McGraw-Hill.

Ferguson, M. (1980). *The Aquarian conspiracy.* Los Angeles: J. P. Tarcher.

French, W. L., & Bell, C. H. (1978). *Organization development: Behavioral science interventions for organization development.* Englewood Cliffs, NJ: Prentice-Hall.

Gardner, J. W. (1964). *Self-renewal: The individual and the innovative society.* New York: Harper & Row.

Houston, J. (1980). *Life force.* New York: Dell.

Kanter, R. (1983). *The change masters.* New York: Simon & Schuster.

Lauderdale, M. (1982). *Burnout: Strategies for personal and organization life and speculations on evolving paradigms.* Austin, TX: Learning Concepts.

Naisbitt, J. (1982). *Megatrends.* New York: Warner Books.

National Institute of Education (1984). *Involvement in learning: Realizing the potential American higher education* (Report of the National Institute of Education Study Group on the Conditions of Excellence in American Higher Education). Washington, DC: Author.

Peters, T. J., & Waterman, R. H. (1982). *In search of excellence.* New York: Harper & Row.

Roeber, R. J. C. (1973). *The organization in a changing environment.* Reading, MA: Addison-Wesley.

Toffler, A. (1971). *Future shock.* New York: Bantam Books.

Toffler, A. (Ed.) (1974). *Learning for tomorrow.* New York: Vintage Books.

Toffler, A. (1980). *The third wave.* Toronto: Bantam Books.

Weick, K. E. (1982). Management of organizational change among loosely coupled elements. In P. S. Goodman (Ed.), *Change in organizations* (pp. 375-408). San Francisco: Jossey-Bass.

Yankelovich, D. (1982). *New rules: Searching for self-fulfillment in a world turned upside down.* Toronto: Bantam Books.

Section III.
Ethics and Values in OD

Values, Human Relations, and Organization Development

Henry Malcolm
Claire Sokoloff

Introduction

For the past 30 years, organization development (OD) authorities such as McGregor, Argyris, Beckhard, and Schein have demonstrated that human values have a clear and vital role in organizational life. Concepts such as trust, openness, honesty, fairness, mutuality, and integrity can be found on practically every page of the literature. In some organizational cultures these values are highly prized and taken seriously by management; examples include the "open door" policy at IBM, shared ownership at People Express, and 3M's practice of supporting innovative concepts by encouraging entrepreneurial behavior. Companies that appreciate human values demonstrate this through positive climates.

In other organizations, however, such values are merely espoused but not practiced. This is typical of the older, "sunset" corporations now faced with a need to revitalize themselves (including many in the steel, automobile, appliance, and manufacturing industries) and of long-established government agencies and public institutions such as hospitals, public school systems, and some voluntary institutions. When such organizations fall on hard times, they sometimes conclude that they must improve their "people management" and seek OD assistance.

In many other organizations, however, the role of values is seldom discussed. In fact, Theory X-style cultures almost seem antagonistic to the subject of human values in the work place. Mistrust is taken for granted, even labeled a sign of wisdom. Openness is treated as naive and dangerous. Honesty is used as a weapon or punishment. Fairness is violated every day by institutionalized norms of politics and power. Mutuality exists only as a negative value ("We will all go down together"), and integrity is practically unheard of. In short, in these firms decline and defeat have soured human values, and one has difficulty imagining that such companies would even seriously consider asking for help.

Faced with such disparity, OD practitioners are justified in wondering which types of organizations are honestly seeking OD assistance. Which will use the help if they contract for it, and which will benefit from it most?

Reaching the right people

Of course, the organization that has already discovered the importance of human values and their impact on performance probably already knows best how to use OD assistance. Even many troubled corporations facing buy-outs, Chapter 11, "downsizing," and the like are coming to recognize their need for OD. The subject of human values and organizational performance is beginning to be discussed much more freely.

The process of organizational value change, however, is complicated. Even such successful giants as Procter and Gamble, IBM, and GE, with all their highly trained managers, have not discovered the secret to how values are linked to actual performance. It simply is not obvious on the surface. Thus, although corporate commitment to values and people may be highly desirable, this does not guarantee success. That is why corporate-wide training programs seldom affect the behavior of first-line and mid-level managers. Learning what the corporation says it believes about people and people management is one thing; it is another to use this when one is back on the job and faced with deadline pressures, limited resources, daily conflicts among individuals and departments, and the frustration of having to settle for less than one has planned for.

The issue of concern for OD—and thus for managers—is determining not merely the "correct" values to teach managers, but the linkage between human values and human behavior. Douglas McGregor demonstrated years ago that a set of values exists that has a positive impact on the work behavior of most persons (Theory Y). Merely taking a public stand in favor of Theory Y values, however, does not always result in the desired behavior expected. Subordinates are far more conditioned to react to the actual behavior of their managers. Moreover, although they may actually believe that they have Theory-Y type managers, the subordinates' own performance is the true test of the managers' real values.

Therefore, this chapter seeks to describe the missing link between human values and organizational results. In so doing, we point out some of the assumptions and findings that have guided previous studies. We discuss the organizational context—that is, the work place—in which OD practitioners must learn to focus the value-performance issue for their clients. We also describe some remarkable research involving a well-known simulation exercise, The Prisoner's Dilemma, which demonstrates the crucial links between values and behavior. The chapter concludes with some recommended strategies for managers to consider for fostering more meaningful behavior change in their organizations.

Beyond values clarification

In the early 1980s, several behavioral scientists (such as Ouchi, Pascale and Athos, Gellerman, Peters and Waterman, and Schein) began to refocus on the subject of values. In particular, Schein alluded to earlier studies of "values clarification" and noted that a belief in the espousal of values resulted in an insufficient treatment of values—that is, not enough attention was paid to the linkage of behavior and values. Just because a person freely chose values from among alternatives, and then displayed these by publicly espousing them, did not mean that the individual had actually integrated these values into her or his behavior.

This is why the OD practitioner must approach the subject of values from the perspective of the impact of values on the work place. This is also why the subjects of motivation, ownership, decision making, leadership, team work, and the like are so important to the field. They represent the real world in which human values directly affect quality, productivity, and performance. OD consultants who try to influence their clients' organizations only through training and other behavior modification techniques may be **perceived** as helpful teachers. They are not, however, likely to witness their clients changing their own behaviors or those of their subordinates. That is where the need is felt most.

This is an important point, because managers are required to focus on outcomes. By definition, they manage systems and processes through which human beings work together to achieve specific results. For example, if a consultant discovers that workers in a particular organization believe that they cannot trust their managers—that their bosses are not open with them—then no matter what the managers claim to believe, their subordinates' attitudes, and especially their work performance, provide the real measure of which values actually govern the organization.

Values and the bottom line

The task requirements that bind manager and employee—and employee and work group—in the joint production of goods and services are unique. The products of work relationships are unlike the outcomes of almost any other relationship. In most human relations, the relationship itself is what matters.

Although other settings exist in which people work together to achieve common results, the pragmatic business environment provides a perfect setting for seeking behavior change under the aegis of mutual self-interest.

The work setting does not, however, justify the molding or conditioning of human behavior; the organization should not be an Orwellian "big brother." Attempts at that type of control usually take place only among closely bonded groups such as cults, religious orders, and zealous political sects. The work environment, however, has practical outcomes and goals, and achieving these is the natural preoccupation and focus of interest for the organization. When achieving those ends becomes important to the individual worker and work team, a type of mutuality is established. That mutuality is the situation OD strives to create between managers and workers.

Nothing is more important than this sense of mutuality to the effectiveness and quality of an organization's products and services. Management must strive to stimulate a strong sense of shared ownership in every employee, because otherwise an organization cannot do its best in the long run. Employees who identify their own personal self-interest with the quality of their organization's output understand mutuality and strive to maintain it in their jobs and work relations.

For several years, OD consultants and trainers have used a variety of techniques to help managers understand the importance of value-based behavior change. Many of these workshop techniques, based on OD research, emphasize the wisdom of establishing an environment of cooperation and trust rather than competition and suspicion. All too often, however, managers return to their jobs from these workshops claiming that although cooperation is a good value for other people, it cannot be achieved in their own organizations. Consequently, attempts to change behavior and values through training have been labeled "too soft" or "impractical."

Understandably, trainers and consultants have paid little attention to the esoteric literature on game theory and human behavior that has appeared in mathematics, philosophy, and psychology journals. This literature, however, when considered in light of OD principles, can be illuminating to managers trying to understand the concrete links between organizational values and behaviors.

One of the oldest and most commonplace methods of combining OD with simulation techniques is the training exercise game theorists call the Prisoner's Dilemma. This exercise has been used in hundreds of settings to teach managers and workers the greater merits of cooperation versus competition for meeting mutual needs. Based on the Prisoner's Dilemma, breakthrough research at the University of Michigan by Robert Axelrod (1980) generated a sophisticated computer model that both validates traditional OD principles and strengthens the link between these principles and a well-thought-out, effective strategy for bringing about behavior change.

In this game, two teams are pitted against each other. Players are told that the object of the exercise is to "maximize points" and that the way to maximize points is for each team to "vote" for one of two images or letters (usually "S" or "T"). Each team discusses the merits and pitfalls of each of the four possible outcomes (S/S, S/T, T/S, or T/T) and then selects a negotiator. The two negotiators discuss together how their teams should vote, and then return to their respective teams, which then decide how they should vote and submit their votes to a judge. Neither team knows how the other has voted until the judge reports the outcome. Following this, a second round begins. The game continues for at least 3 rounds and as many as 15. Figure 1 shows how points are allocated to the teams for each of the four paired choices.

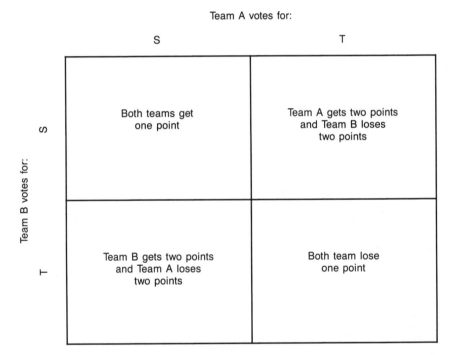

Team A votes for:

Figure 1. Scoring for the Prisoner's Dilemma

If both teams vote for S, each team receives one point. If both vote for T, each team loses one point. If Team A votes for S and Team B votes for T, Team A loses two points and Team B gains two points. Conversely, if Team

B votes for S and Team A votes for T, Team B loses two points and Team A gains two points. In sum, any team that votes for S loses two points if the other team votes for T.

Voting for S is therefore risky; a team that does this can lose two points while its opponent gains two if the opponent votes for T. If both teams vote for S simultaneously, however, they both gain. Voting for T is less risky; if both teams do so simultaneously, each loses only one point, and if only one votes for T, it gains two points while the other loses two, thus achieving a substantial advantage over its opponent.

Why would a team vote for S? The answer often is not apparent to the players. One reason is simple good faith: They are fulfilling an agreement made during negotiation. A second reason stems from the game's instructions, which state that the objective is to maximize points. Most managers who play the game assume that this refers to **their own team's** points, and that the best way to get the most points is to defeat the opponent. Because teams often find it impossible to see beyond self-interest, they equate maximizing points with getting two points per round. As a result, they tend to vote for T. When a team votes for T, however, particularly after its negotiator has promised the other team's negotiator it would vote for S, trust between the teams is severely impaired and both teams end up voting only for T. As a result, both teams continue to lose one point per round, their overall scores get smaller and smaller, and everyone loses. The lesson is that only a "win-win" strategy, in which both teams vote for S consistently, will produce a positive score. Unfortunately, however, the players seldom recognize that voting for S serves both teams' mutual self-interest.

TIT FOR TAT: The winning strategy

When he scrutinized the results of his computer tournaments, Axelrod realized he had uncovered a previously unrecognized key to effective relationship dynamics. Of all the strategies submitted to a worldwide competition for the Prisoner's Dilemma, only one consistently won out over the rest: TIT FOR TAT, by Anatol Rapoport of the University of Toronto. TIT FOR TAT is a two-line computer program comprising the following two statements: "Never be the first to defect in a relationship with an opponent," and "Whatever the opponent does, follow suit on the very next round." According to Rapoport, any strategies based on these two mandates eventually elicit a cooperative response and yield more points than any other approach. What could be more disarmingly simple? And exactly why does it work?

TIT FOR TAT is a relationship-building strategy based on a win-win strategy of mutual self-interest. Almost all the other tactics used in the tournament were designed to take advantage of the opponent sooner or later, thus representing relatively selfish attempts to gain points. To informed OD practitioners, the TIT FOR TAT strategy looks amazingly like an old team-building approach of establishing a sense of mutuality, wherein one team uses logic to influence the behavior of the other until both teams join forces in the win-win approach.

The four TIT FOR TAT principles. Axelrod discovered that TIT FOR TAT follows a deliberate set of steps designed to change the behavior patterns of as many opponents as possible. This is the same goal any behavioral scientist, trainer, or OD practitioner would promote. But unlike so many OD practitioners, who use the TIT FOR TAT philosophy as an idealistic strategy for appealing to the highest values in others, Rapaport's TIT FOR TAT operates on four critical principles that openly seek to affect behavior. That is, the goal of TIT FOR TAT is to win friends and influence opponents. The four TIT FOR TAT principles are the following.

1. **Never be the first to defect from the relationship or to take advantage of your opponent.** Do not send any signal to others that you intend to take advantage of them. Your goal for the relationship does not depend on your opponent's losing anything. You seek to gain something only if it can be gained together with your opponent. Never consider the opponent's loss to be your gain. Through TIT FOR TAT, one seeks to win while encouraging others to do the same.

2. **Make certain your opponent quickly realizes, however, that you can and will reciprocate if you are taken advantage of.** Your opponent may not necessarily want you to be a docile and accommodating victim, but your opponent certainly does not want to become entangled in a lose-lose situation. The very concept of competition requires a winner and a loser. TIT FOR TAT does not encourage a lose-lose outcome. If your opponent votes for a T, you do the same in the next round, following your opponent's lead. In doing so, you do not initiate any negative competitive behavior, you merely respond to the action of your opponent in kind. The reason for this is clear: The strategy of TIT FOR TAT is mutual gain and advantage. You respond to your opponent's attempt to gain an advantage over you by costing your opponent an endless series of losses. To return to a win-win stance, your opponent must select the high-risk S, knowing that you will vote T once more in response, to reverse the loss you received when your defecting opponent first tried to take advantage of you. Thus, TIT FOR TAT not only influences the behavior of the opponent by teaching the opponent an important lesson in self-interest, it also regains for you a certain advantage in point reversal.

3. **Forgive the other side for not having understood the superiority of mutual gain over selfish advantage.** The forgiveness of TIT FOR TAT is not forgiveness for the sake of goodness, nor is it a Biblical ''eye-for-an-eye'' response—it is forgiveness for the sake of self-interest. No good reason exists for making the opponent feel guilt or remorse. All you want is for the oppo-

nent to realize that TIT FOR TAT calls for you to reward cooperation and retaliate against competition. Remember, the objective is to change the opponent's behavior. Once an opponent realizes that its own self-interest is served by cooperating with TIT FOR TAT, the opponent becomes a partner and another step has been taken toward mutual gain.

4. **Make certain that every opponent (or person with whom you have a relationship) understands your needs and requirements.** Do not try to hide your intentions. A newly acquired partner will quickly revert to a competitive stance of self-interest if you try to conceal your real purposes. The lesson of TIT FOR TAT is that to create relationships that last and work, you must learn to become as open and honest with others as possible.

The working relationship

The applications of TIT FOR TAT for OD are clear. The work context is the most obvious setting for putting the TIT FOR TAT strategy to work. Axelrod's findings provide a way to focus more sharply on some traditional behavioral science concepts while demonstrating the superior logic of "reciprocal mutuality," the TIT FOR TAT objective. No longer must OD appear to be giving away the store or simply affirming the rightness of values over practicality. To demonstrate this, we reframe the four principles of TIT FOR TAT as four lessons for the manager-subordinate relationship.

Lesson 1. Do no defect from the relationship first, or seek to take advantage of others with whom you have an ongoing work relationship. Nearly every book on managerial or supervisory skills emphasizes the need to obtain the trust and confidence of one's subordinates. This need is at the heart of Lesson 1. The boss who takes advantage of a subordinate violates that subordinate's confidence and misuses her or his managerial authority and position. If this was done to achieve a personal objective, it represents a "defection," and the manager should expect the subordinate to act to protect himself or herself in the future.

In an average organization, people are taken advantage of countless numbers of times. Because of this, competent managers seek to rectify the situation by asking subordinates for feedback. To correct the problem, managers need to recognize that people want and need to have something to say about the what, how, where, and when of their jobs. Most have their own self-interest linked with achieveing positive outcomes for the organization. Thus, abusing a subordinate to obtain one's own ends is not only unfair, but has adverse consequences for the employee's initiative, self-management, and shared ownership of responsibility.

Lesson 2. Let subordinates know that you can and will respond to their defection from the relationship with strong and persistent acts of managerial

self-interest. Subordinates who share no sense of responsibility for the task, and either do a bare minimum amount of work or actively resist working collaboratively, are in effect defecting from the work relationship. Similar to teenagers caught in the contradictory emotions of adolescense, these employees usually feel that only the manager should have a sense of ownership for the job. That is, passive dependency and counterdependency are also forms of defection from the work relationship. Firing employees is a counterproductive response, though, and in many organizations is too difficult to accomplish.

Punishment has no place in the TIT FOR TAT strategy, because the entire purpose is mutual self-interest. Yet letting others know that a lack of commitment has its costs influences them to consider themselves partners in a venture. In such cases the manager should tell the uncommitted employee, ''If you do not want to be a partner in this effort, tell me what you do want,'' or ''I perceive that you are not interested in being a team player. If this continues, we will have to examine your role in this organization and find a more suitable position for you.'' The employee needs firm feedback that persistently and clearly communicates the message of reciprocity. The objective is to change the uncooperative behavior, not to elicit a defensive or self-protective response, or to encourage polarization or competition. As occurs with the TIT FOR TAT approach, this strategy may require several reciprocal actions by the manager before the subordinate realizes that failing to fully join in the organization's effort toward high performance, excellence, and mutual reward actually defeats the subordinate's own self-interest. If and when the subordinate does demonstrate a willingness to cooperate, the manager must quickly reciprocate in kind, this time positively and with appreciation and recognition.

Lesson 3. Forgive the subordinate (or the boss, if the situation is reversed) for not having previously appreciated the idea of mutual self-interest. Demonstrating one's commitment to outcomes and results is a powerful force on supervisors and managers. Sometimes a subordinate can use TIT FOR TAT to deal with a defecting and uncooperative boss. This situation is more dangerous for the employee, but the dynamics are the same. Every defection by a manager takes advantage of a subordinate and diminishes the worker's motivation and involvement. Subordinates can seek to change managers' behavior, even appearing to ''train'' them in collaboration, by demonstrating their willingness to see that the job gets done and that the boss's concerns are taken into serious consideration. By doing so, the employee is merely acting collaboratively, forgiving the boss out of true self-interest.

Lesson 4. Be open and honest about your needs, purposes, and intentions. Tricks, secretiveness, and game playing send signals that one is not really interested in collaboration. Some managers consider it a managerial prerogative to withhold information, which they only give to subordinates on a ''need-to-know'' basis. These persons do not seek to collaborate with subordinates, but to use information as a means of controlling them. That constitutes defection. Other managers, who are extreme introverts, unwittingly hide their intentions, wishes, and plans and are not accustomed to dealing publicly with others. These managers are defecting by default; they do not understand the importance of mutuality and maintaining a climate of openness.

Other applications of TIT FOR TAT

The key to TIT FOR TAT's effectiveness, therefore, is its strategy of using each of its four principles as a set of behaviors designed to affect the behavior of others. The desired outcome is helping others discover mutual self-interest and use this discovery to modify their own behavior. The game of the Prisoner's Dilemma uses a point system to represent self-interest; for managers and subordinates, the desired outcome is the effective accomplishment of work and all the rewards this brings.

The alert OD practitioner can see other ways to apply TIT FOR TAT, particularly to the relationship between the individual and the work group. How might a work team use TIT FOR TAT to achieve higher levels of cooperation among its members? Or how might work teams from different parts of an organization improve their interactions with TIT FOR TAT? The answers can be found by reviewing the four lessons:

1. Demonstrate the group's (or individual's) fundamental desire for cooperation, not competition.

2. Demand that others not take advantage of oneself or one's group, and make them realize that one can and will reciprocate if they do so.

3. Make others realize that they are not considered enemies or opponents, but are invited to become allies if they want a working relationship.

4. Demonstrate trust and openness by modeling the type of behavior one wishes others to enact.

Occasionally we meet managers who instinctively apply a TIT FOR TAT approach to their organizations. In them we immediately recognize such leadership traits as clarity of purpose, fairness with people, and firmness without sacrificing support. In these natural leaders we also see a combination of forgiveness and honesty mingled with determination to succeed and achieve great things.

We also have seen groups and small organizations whose work relationships proceeded according to TIT FOR TAT. We could not help noticing how everyone seemed to belong when the organization was characterized by the absence of defection and counterdependent behavior. We noticed, too, how readily any form of noncooperative behavior was noted and addressed. Those who had resorted to a moment of mistrust or suspicion of others were assured of eventual acceptance and forgiveness. We have even been a bit surprised at how openly people in these organizations dealt with problems—we found no hidden agenda, no political game playing, no hallway conferences in which "real" decisions were made.

TIT FOR TAT can even help people build strong and healthy interpersonal connections in many different types of relationships. Husbands and wives might benefit from firmer behavioral boundary lines. Parents might find children more responsive to a combination of firmness and forgiveness. And, as political scientist Robert Axelrod noted, one cannot avoid thinking of TIT FOR TAT's implications for international relations.

OD practitioners must continue to explore their own value choices even as they help clients recognize the clear behavioral requirements of assuming leadership and fulfilling the important values discussed above. As the OD challenge continues to expand, leading us toward to a world economy, we must be creative and conscientious about applying the principles of cooperation and mutual self-interest both at home and abroad.

REFERENCE

Axelrod, R. (1984). *The evolution of cooperation.* New York: Basic Books.

BIBLIOGRAPHY

Argyris, C. (1973). Personality and organization theory revisited. *Administrative Science Quarterly, 18,* 141-167.

Harris, P. R. (1985). *Management in transition.* San Francisco: Jossey-Bass.

Hofstadter, D. R. (1985). *Metamagical themas.* New York: Basic Books.

Schein, E. (1985). *Organizational culture and leadership.* San Francisco: Jossey-Bass.

Tannenbaum, R., Margulies, N., Massarik, F., & Associates (1985). *Human systems development.* San Francisco: Jossey-Bass.

Issues of Power and Authority in Organization Development

Haywood H. Martin
Catharine J. Martin

Introduction

Imagine that you an are an organization development (OD) consultant who has just been informed by a chief client that he considers one of his key managers a weak leader. The client requests that you conduct a quick assessment of the organization in order to "get rid" of this manager. The client then informs you that your contract has been extended for another year, with a sizable bonus included. What should you do?

This situation is one example of the many complex authority and power issues confronting today's OD consultants. This chapter seeks to highlight some of these issues related to ethics, values, power, and authority, and to offer some strategies for dealing with them.

Consultant authority

One of the first questions a consultant asks when engaging a new client system is "What authority do I have?" The chief client and the consultant must include in their negotiations a definition of the consultant's authority. To understand the type of authority that a consultant really has, we must first review the concept of authority in traditional organizations.

Authority is defined as the power and legal right to decide or act within the scope of a designated position, as generally reflected on an organizational chart. Authority flows from a superior to a subordinate when duties are assigned, and it may be delegated as need dictates. This concept of authority, which shapes the thinking of both clients and consultants who have experience in structured

---

organizations, can result in confusion in OD situations because the consultant's authority does not fit the traditional mold.

For traditional organizations, this "mold" is generally composed of two kinds of authority: line and staff. Line authority refers to the direct and general responsibility of each line position for taking action and achieving organizational goals. A manager with line authority is the unquestioned superior for all activities of the subordinates. The flow of line authority is simple and direct, so that conflicts of authority may be reduced and quick action may be possible. External OD consultants do not have line authority because the consultant's role does not include direct responsibility for achieving organizational goals.

Staff authority is purely advisory to those holding line positions. A person with staff authority studies a problem, seeks alternatives, and makes recommendations, but does not have authority to put recommendations into action. OD consultants do not have staff authority because they do not typically occupy organizational positions that are functionally advisory to the line.

What the OD practitioner does have is a special kind of "consultant authority," which permits one to conduct OD-related activities such as collecting information, counseling, coaching, facilitating, and training. These activities are negotiated with and sanctioned by the chief client.

To put line, staff, and consultant authority in perspective, consider the situation presented at the beginning of this chapter. The chief client, or top manager, has line authority and is therefore responsible for firing or retaining the manager suspected of weak leadership. The personnel officer has staff authority to advise the top manager of the procedures to be followed. The OD consultant could negotiate for authority to conduct OD-related activities to assess the situation and facilitate problem solving. Because the chief client and the consultant have different perceptions of the consultant's authority, however, they must address these differences and seek to resolve them.

The failure to negotiate authority issues can create situations that seriously affect project outcomes and consume the energy of the consultant and members of the client system. Such conflicts may fall into three different categories: inappropriate authority, nonnegotiated authority, and authority versus power.

Inappropriate authority

When the client expects the consultant to perform a task requiring line or staff authority—such as recommending that an employee be fired, or deciding which employee to fire—the OD consultant is being given inappropriate authority. Regardless of the outcome, this prevents the organization from using its own management resources. By usurping line or staff authority, the consultant misses an opportunity to empower the client system to develop confidence in its own abilities. The old Chinese proverb "Give a man a fish, and he will have food for a day; teach a man to fish, and he will have food for life'' applies to this situation.

Another undesirable effect of performing such tasks is that the consultant may be labeled a ''hatchet man,'' possibly causing employees to feel anxious about their job security. This reputation diminishes the trust and confidence the consultant needs to be an effective change agent.

To avoid issues associated with inappropriate authority, the consultant and client should make certain they begin an OD effort with a clear understanding of their roles.

Nonnegotiated authority

Sometimes a client asks a consultant to accomplish a mission without specifically authorizing the consultant to conduct necessary activities. The consultant assumes that the client understands that certain OD activities will be performed, approves of them, and will inform employees accordingly. For example, a client may agree to an organizational assessment, but when the consultant arrives on the appointed day to begin interviews, he or she finds that no interview schedule has been established and none of the organization members knows why the consultant is there. This typical scenario demonstrates the importance of negotiating at the outset for authorization to perform specific OD-related activities, thus ensuring a clear understanding of the related expectations and roles.

Authority versus power

Other issues arise from how members of a client system view the consultant's authority. Because an OD consultant is an ''authority'' in behavioral science, many often attribute to the consultant the power to change operations. For example, some organization members may believe that a consultant authorized to conduct an assessment has more power to make changes than management has. Such a situation may be compared to that of a patient who confuses a medical doctor's ''authority'' to make diagnoses with the doctor's having the power to heal, and does not recognize that the power to heal comes from the patient's decision to be healed and to follow prescriptions. Similarly, organizational change depends on the client's commitment to change and willingness to follow the OD process. Consultants must be clear with themselves and clients about power as it relates to negotiated authority.

Sources of power

Once formal authority issues have been negotiated, power issues may become more clear. The question for the OD consultant changes from ''What authority do I have" to "What authority have I negotiated, and what is my power base?"

Power may be considered a potential source of energy. With respect to OD, power is basically the ability to influence others. Consultants have two major sources of power: chief clients and themselves. French and Raven (1959) have identified five types of power, which we describe below in the context of OD. Legitimate power typically comes from the chief client, and the remaining four—reward, coercive, referent, and expert power—may come from the consultant.

1. **Legitimate power** is based on the acceptance and internalization of OD values by members of the client system. It normally stems from power vested in the consultant by the chief client, and organization members normally become aware of this when the chief client announces throughout the system that the OD program has the ownership and the unqualified support of top management.

2. **Reward power** is based on the ability of an OD consultant to reward members of the client system. Consultants frequently have opportunities to reward members of the client system for behaving in ways congruent with the consultant's values. Complimenting a client for conducting an effective meeting is a typical way of exercising reward power.

3. **Coercive power** is based on the client's perception that a consultant can exact penalties for nonconformity. We have experienced the potential for coercive power in interviews with organization members who expressed their beliefs that those who failed to go along with the OD program would be punished.

4. **Referent power** is based on the client system members' identifying with or liking the OD consultant. A system member who identifies with the consultant may express an interest in pursuing a career in the behavioral sciences, for example, or be especially impressed with the consultant's credentials.

5. **Expert power** is based on the client's perception of the consultant's competence. A certain amount of expert power is normally attributed to the OD consultant unless the consultant demonstrates otherwise by showing a higher or lower level of expertise.

The chief client as a power source. The chief client is a major source of the consultant's power. Beckhard (1969) states that successful OD projects require the support of top management. When consultants lack this support, subordinate-level managers quickly become aware of this and the program fizzles. We saw this happen to a long-term project when the organization's personnel officer convinced the chief client to withdraw support for the program. Shortly thereafter, the project lost its momentum and was terminated.

Schein (1985) suggests that change agents need a power-oriented approach to achieve change. When consultants have no formal base of authority, they are forced to rely on other sources of influence or else terminate the contract. Weisbord (1973) considers an OD project lacking management support to be an untenable contract, likening it to an airplane without fuel: No matter how beautiful it looks, it will not fly.

The consultant as a power source. The other major source of power for the OD practitioner is the consultant's own technical and personal competence.

Technical competence is an important part of the personal power equation. To avoid being perceived as technically incompetent, consultants devote significant effort to "learning the trade"—that is, to using the proper jargon, keeping up with new trends, and attending the right conferences.

Personal power, however, consists of more than mere technical competence. Although members of the client system may not be qualified to judge a consultant's technical skills effectively, they are infinitely qualified to judge one's honesty, authenticity, trust, and level of concern. They notice when the consultant has little energy, is overweight, drinks or smokes excessively, exhibits symptoms of stress, gossips, or cannot handle feedback. Consultants diminish their personal power when they fail to "walk their talk." Clients expect to see consultants act as models of OD values, and begin to tune out when the consultant's behavior does not match the values being expressed.

The following two sections address some strategies for developing technical and personal competence.

Technical competence

Schein (1985) lists several technical power strategies used by change agents. These strategies fall into two categories: noninvolvement and involvement. Depending on the situation, consultants can either use involvement strategies to increase their power or use noninvolvement strategies to avoid power struggles.

Noninvolvement power strategies include the following: presenting a nonthreatening image, conducting research, using a neutral cover, and withdrawing. The advantage of noninvolvement is that it allows consultants to be more objective by keeping them out of the dynamics of organizational power politics. The disadvantage is that the consultants who use only this approach may find themselves hiding from power problems rather than addressing them.

Involvement power strategies include the following: aligning with others who have power, developing liaisons, and making trade-offs. The advantage of involvement is that it allows consultants to participate fully in an organization's power politics and thereby confront issues more directly. The disadvantage is that consultants who use only this approach risk becoming absorbed in their own power needs and losing objectivity.

Consultants sometimes use another involvement strategy we call "acting tough." Those relying on this approach assume that to deal with power politics effectively one must use profanity, work long hours, and be aggressive. A particularly "macho" client organization may even reward such behavior. The disadvantage of this strategy is that it may lead consultants to adopt the old values of an organization that is in the process of change. When organization members see consultants adopting and reinforcing old behaviors and values, they assume these must be valid—and wonder, "Why should we change?".

Power-related issues of values and ego. When using power, consultants need to be sensitive to issues related to values and ego. This section presents some examples of these.

- **"OD values don't match."** The values of OD include open communication, trust, collaboration, empowerment, and responsiveness to human needs. In many organizations, however, individual power and control are often considered subsidiary—or damaging—to efforts to increase productivity. This poses a dilemma for the consultant who seems to be operating from a different value base.

- **"My personal values don't match."** Some organizations have highly stressful environments characterized by prolonged cocktail hours, late dinner meetings in smoke-filled rooms, 12-hour days, and constant travel with little rest. In such circumstances, the consultant faces the challenge of operating under these conditions while modeling values that appear to be in opposition to organizational norms.

- **"Who owns the data?"** OD consultants use their technical and personal power to collect information that might not otherwise be revealed. The consultant promises organization members confidentiality. Some managers, however, believe that they own, and should have access to, these data. In such cases, consultants are confronted with situations in which, if they reveal confidential material so as to satisfy the chief client, individuals or groups may suffer harmful repercussions.

- **"I need the work."** Difficult decisions involving ethics and values must be made when consultants are offered opportunities to extend projects after they should be concluded, or to accept projects calling for them to act contrary to their values (as in the example opening this chapter). Recognizing such dilemmas, and choosing between personal gain and upholding one's values, is never easy.

- **"I need this job for my ego."** Work plays an important role in ego satisfaction. Consultants are particularly vulnerable to meeting their ego needs through their work because of the power attributed to them by members of the client system. Problems arise when consultants use this power to build their own self-esteem at their clients' expense, as when they encourage clients to remain dependent on them. OD projects are less effective when the consultant is unwilling or unable to empower the client.

- **"I'm the guru."** When an organization financially rewards a consultant, admires the consultant's credentials, asks for the consultant's advice, and appears willing to follow instructions, one is tempted to enjoy the power associated with being an expert. OD values suggest, however, that consultants should reject the role of organizational sage and seek instead to enable the organization to discover its own internal sources of wisdom.

- **"I don't have enough power."** Consultants sometimes view themselves as lacking credibility because of their gender, sex, age, race, religion, or any other difference. Such a self-perception results in consultants' becoming withdrawn, reacting defensively, remaining inappropriately silent, exaggerating their expertise, or simply trying too hard. Most consultants must learn to come to terms with feelings that they lack sufficient power, for whatever reason.

Consultants faced with issues of power and authority can use their technical competence to determine the kind of power they need to accomplish their missions. They can then identify which strategies are appropriate for a given situation, while being sensitive to value and ego issues. Following this, they must deliberately seek to transfer their technical skills to the appropriate organization members, thus empowering the client system to solve its own problems.

Personal competence

The most technically competent consultant is ineffective without equally strong personal competence, yet little emphasis is placed on developing this source of power. "Self" power enables consultants to influence others by their mere presence. A strong presence results when consultants strengthen and balance their physical health (shown by energy and stamina), mental health (clarity and alertness), social health (concern and understanding), and spiritual health (inner peace and calmness). In this section we present some strategies for developing power in these four areas.

Physical health. The rigors of the OD process demand that consultants maintain high levels of energy and powerful bodies. These require a healthy diet, regular exercise, adequate relaxation and sleep, and effective stress management. One needs much self-discipline to fulfill these requirements under constantly changing circumstances, including travel.

Mental health. A powerful mind can control its thoughts and emotions, has clear goals and directions, can make decisions, and is open to new information. One can enhance one's mental power by feeding the mind positive information through books, tapes, and affirmation, and by guarding it from the self-defeating negativity of the surrounding environment.

Social health. Powerful consultants show genuine concern for others, feel at ease with many types of people, and do not become "hooked" by games and negativity. They have positive personal relationships and strong support systems. Constant effort is required to love, to give, to accept, and to understand. One must continually uncover and dissolve anger, guilt, and resentment to develop social power.

Spiritual health. The deepest form of personal power comes from knowing who one is in relation to others and having a constant source of power available from within. Inner peace, confidence, and understanding come from faith in a source outside of oneself that feeds one's inner power. Prayer, meditation, connecting with nature, and reading and internalizing the writings of great spiritual teachers are some ways to develop spiritual power.

Summary

Consultants do not operate from a formal position of authority. Their primary source of formal power is the chief client. If this support is not available to an OD consultant, the OD project's chances of success are diminished.

The second major source of power for change agents is the self. Personal power consists of technical and personal competence. Technical competence is the application of the knowledge and skills of OD technology. Personal competence involves a balance of physical, mental, social, and spiritual health.

In this chapter, we present several issues of power and authority. Although we suggest some strategies, we emphasize that no prescribed solutions exist. When consultants face a power and authority dilemma, they may simply wish to consider the solution that will likely produce the greatest good. In the words of Ghandi, as quoted by Attenborough (1982, p. 25):

> ...Whenever you are in doubt or when the self becomes too much with you, try the following expedient: Recall the face of the poorest and most helpless man you have ever seen and ask yourself if the step you contemplate is going to be of any use to him. Will he be able to gain

anything by it? Will it restore to him control over his own life and destiny? In other words, will it lead to... self-rule for the hungry and spiritually starved millions of our countrymen? Then you will find your doubts and your self melting away.

REFERENCES

Attenborough, R. (1982). *The words of Ghandi.* New York: Newmarket Press.

Beckhard, R. (1969). *Organization development: Strategies and models.* Reading, PA: Addison Wesley.

French, J. R. P., & Raven, B. (1959). The basis of social power. In D. Cartwright (Ed.). *Studies in social power.* Ann Arbor, MI: University of Michigan, Institute of Social Research.

Schein, V. E. (1985). Organizational realities: The politics of change. *Training and Development Journal, 39,* 37-41.

Weisbord, M. (1973). The organization development contract. *Organization Development Practitioner, 5,* 1-4.

Organization Development Ethics and Effectiveness: The Disadvantages of Virtue

Gene Boccialetti

In recent years an increasing amount of attention has been paid to the ethical underpinnings of organization development practice. Although this topic is often addressed under the label "ethics" or "values," lately the discussion has also veered into the subject of OD and politics. This has led to many troubling questions. Are OD practitioners behaving in ways congruent with OD's espoused values? Should political—that is, manipulative—means be used to achieve desired ends in change efforts? Are OD practitioners being naive, or considered naive, in their approaches to or avoidance of internal organizational politics? What will happen to OD's image or effectiveness if it becomes entangled in the political subprocesses of organizations?

Such questions often accompany the opinion—sometimes stated, sometimes not—that involvement in organizational politics is at best somewhat unsavory, and may actually represent a betrayal of OD and its goals. The reasoning behind this goes as follows: To become a political actor, one compromises OD's historical identity and ceases to be one of the "forces of light" (Cobb, 1984; Perrow, 1977). This makes OD just another "advocacy group"—a sort of social systems PAC—within a system already overwhelmed with too many such groups. The end result is that no one is left with sufficient credibility or skill to bring together diverse groups and generate consensus for action, renewal, and growth.

Contrast this line of reasoning with another, more startling view. According to this perspective, OD's system of values and ethics is actually a statement of **social ideals,** and as such should never be posited as attainable goals for a real social system. In effect, this system less resembles a gospel than a gyroscope. Efforts to impose these values and ethics on others have boxed OD into a moral-absolutist position and "fixed-rule" mentality. OD has already

---

become—and continues to be—a political actor in organizational systems. Our current concerns about OD and internal organizational politics simply reflect the need to have OD specialists refine their political methods so that they may achieve their desired ends.

Fixed-rule thinking and behavior, however, are incompatible with the **espoused** values of acceptance of others, positive regard, appreciation of diversity, collaborative client-consultant relations, consultation to total systems, learning, and the willingness to be influenced. According to OD's tightly construed perspective, the medium becomes the message—and by operating according to a fixed-rule system, OD practitioners **model** the opposite of OD's espoused values. Further specification of OD's value system and definition of what constitutes ethical behavior should, according to this view, lead to increasingly insistent attempts to enforce values and ethics within the field. The more clearly the parameters of acceptable values and behaviors are defined, the more righteous one may feel in attempting to ensure conformity. This will also mean, however, that practitioners in "good standing" will have less freedom in pursuing goals within a client system. If values such as information sharing and democratic management are to be realized, many alternative goals and means will be inappropriate. Paradoxically, OD practitioners will probably have to use more manipulative and coercive strategies to attain these goals and values, or else face failure. They may find it impossible to achieve congruence with OD's values with respect to both means and ends yet still be effective.

This last point reminds me of the movie "Paint Your Wagon," in which a town appears overnight at a site where gold is discovered. This gold rush town consists entirely of the "fringe elements" of frontier society: miners, prostitutes, bartenders, card sharks, and various hangers-on. Life there is free wheeling, immoral—and a lot of fun. Then a parson appears (on a white horse, appropriately enough). Gripped by moral outrage, he begins preaching to passing residents about the dangerous depths of degradation to which they have descended. He elicits a multifaceted response. Some consider him an amusing curiosity, others an annoyance to be disregarded. Most, however, treat him as an object of scorn and derision. He is too different from them to be understood, and too judgmental to be accepted and integrated into the community. He thus fails to influence people as he wishes, and several of the protagonists actively work (successfully, I might add) to undermine the parson's efforts to "clean up" the town.

Although a comparison to "Paint Your Wagon" might be overdrawn, I wonder if OD is not following the same path as the parson.

Organization development and its values

OD practitioners tend to consider themselves part of the forces of light (i.e., "good guys"). Beer (1980) has stated that the purpose of OD is to help organizations become healthier, more adaptive systems, which usually means helping them to increase diversity, openness, confrontation of differences, and delegation in decision making. Miles and Schmuck (1976, p. 23) refer to "better organizational communication, integration of individual and organizational goals, [and] development of a climate of trust in decision making." French (1969, p. 24) suggests that change agents "tend to be developmental in their outlook and concerned with the long range opportunities for the personal growth of people in organizations," and goes on to cite values related to making work and life richer and more enjoyable, and to giving feelings and sentiment more legitimacy within organizational culture.

Nearly every description of organization development contains some reference to such values. Lately—perhaps not surprisingly—this orientation has received additional support in the pronouncements of Pope John Paul II, who explicitly calls for more worker participation in organizations' decision-making processes. The values of OD, particularly those such as worker participation and improving quality of work life, now seem to have a powerful ally in the Roman Catholic Church. No wonder OD practitioners find it easy to see themselves as part of the forces of light.

Although these developments would seem to augur well for OD's future, I believe they also provoke a more troubling dynamic. In their frequently reprinted article "Democracy Is Inevitable," Slater and Bennis (1978, p. 313) argue that organizational democracy represents "the social system of the electronic era." This assertion not only places OD on the side of the forces of light, but also on the side of fashionable "high-tech." If one views something as inevitable, one should not hesitate to "give a little push" to encourage its arrival. Cobb and Margulies (1981, p. 52) state, "Fundamentally, OD values a democratic workplace and the power equalization inherent in it. . . . [Such values] are generally accepted in our society."

More recently, Sashkin (1984) has written an article entitled "Participative Management Is an Ethical Imperative." Although the text cites reasons as to why participative management **makes sense**, the title and conclusion leave no doubt as to which sort of manager is "ethical." Indeed, Sashkin makes the surprisingly blunt moral declaration that "it is ethically unjustifiable to manage nonparticipatively" (p. 17). He further states that for organizations sanctioning OD-related training, it is "now appropriate to sponsor value focused training for managers" (p. 18). Presumably, such "training" provides little leeway for the committed autocrat.

Cobb (1984) seemingly supports Sashkin's views in his reference to four "basic rights" of individuals within organizations. These are

1. the right to protect one's individual welfare,
2. the right to acquire and use information, and
3. the right to participation, and

4. the right to just and equitable treatment.

Although I do not intend to discuss these "rights" per se, I wish to draw attention to the increasingly close identification of OD with democracy, rights, and morality.

In contrast, Hofstede (1984) has written an article entitled "The Cultural Relativity of the Quality of Life Concept." Based on a multinational study, Hofstede concludes, "Thus, there is a real danger of the humanizers trying to increase the quality of work-life of [clerks and unskilled employees] based on their own [the humanizers'] work values" (p. 392). Hofstede's work suggests that OD's bias in favor of democratization probably leads to inappropriate or irrelevant applications in many cultures outside the U.S. I would extend this notion to include subcultures within the U.S. as well.

Instead of taking a more comparative approach—as I believe it should—OD seems to be moving in the opposite direction. Rather than broadening its values and orientations, the field seems to becoming more narrowly focused.

I agree with Saskin that participative management often—but not always—makes sense, but do not feel comfortable placing this issue into the realm of ethical behavior. From a moral-relativist viewpoint, who has the right or knowledge to make a conclusive definition of ethical management? Moreover, the assumption underlying many such definitions (culminating in the work of Sashkin and Cobb) is that organizations can and should be democratic institutions. I have profound reservations about this assumption. Should we assume that within any organization, particularly one for which membership is voluntary and contracted for, management may "rule" only with the consent of the governed? Should we assume that any "democratic" organization can always generate consensus quickly enough to respond appropriately to all of its daily contingencies? I do not believe we should, and am increasingly troubled by the direction taken by discussions within OD on mentality and morality. Although Beer (1980, p. 8) acknowledges that "OD can legitimately lead to centralization of decisions, more traditional organizational forms, and more directive management styles," these outcomes are rarely pursued or even discussed. With respect to participative management, I believe we should more often ask, "Can it work?" or "Will it help the organization be more effective?" not "Is it right or wrong?"

Such differences and disagreements are not new to OD, or even too problematic. Indeed, a strength of OD is its dialogue over "whither thou goest." Rather, the threat comes from the assumption that OD's espoused values are defined, definitive, and formally sanctioned, and that they can—even **should**—be implemented in all cases.

As such notions become increasingly accepted, membership in the profession begins to be defined in terms of conforming to the values and norms of the group. The nascent certification process represented by bodies such as Certified Consultants International could turn into a vehicle for ensuring conformity rather than encouraging competence, let alone quality.

In addition to the possibility of breeding moral absolutism and an "in group/out group" mentality, I see other disadvantages to this definition of virtue for organization development. Such efforts can impair the consultant-client relationship and harm the chances for success of OD interventions.

The disadvantages of virtue

The OD practitioner becomes irrelevant. Much of the recent discussion about OD and politics arises from a growing sense that practitioners have come to promote the values of openness, trust, and the like within organizations while being naive about the reality of life within them. Many OD specialists fail to recognize that these are social ideals, not characteristics of actual social systems. No social system is **completely** collaborative; each is only more or less so, and either striving or not striving toward this goal. Understandably, clients often consider the untempered promotion of such goals to be unrealistic, unattainable, and evidence of naivete (perhaps worse if they do not even find them desirable to begin with). This produces the following results.

1. The client supposes that the practitioner does not sufficiently understand the client's world to be of much use.
2. The practitioner is more aware of the practitioner's own values, and those of her or his reference group, than the client's.
3. The practitioner sets goals that are unattainable, and learning theorists have long found that goals considered too far out of reach are rarely pursued for long.
4. The practitioner's moral sensibilities keep her or him from grasping other disparate moral elements.

Thus, consulting to the **entire** system, with all its moral and ethical diversity, becomes nearly impossible. Those taking a judgmental starting position either implicitly or explicitly set as their targets for "change" (i.e., re-education) those holding conflicting positions. The practitioner thus acts as a model of someone who lacks respect for other value systems. Those who differ from the practitioner are viewed as "bad guys" who deserve no consideration.

The practitioner neglects alternatives. In any social system, one will find multiple social goods and multiple ways of achieving these goods, all them equally "moral." Generating consensus and taking action requires an open, comparative, pluralistic approach. Viewing the intervention as a "mission" to promote one's values causes the practitioner to ignore the complexities to be addressed. Ultimately, the practitioner will likely reject the less-than-perfect options in favor of the "do-able" ones.

The OD practitioner ceases to learn. I believe that the single most important thing OD practitioners can do for their clients is serve as models of learning. OD practitioners must be excellent learners. Self-righteousness and the nostrums this generates too often take the place of a spirit of thought and inquiry. When confused, the practitioner should set an example for the client and admit to her or his own feelings of disorientation and incompetence. Because this can be so threatening, seldom will practitioners do so if they can instead offer some commandment. Of course, the appropriateness or utility of the commandment is seldom questioned.

I recently witnessed an example of this during a meeting between an executive and a subordinate with whom he was having difficulty. This subordinate ran a separate facility and had brought his own consultant to the meeting. Shortly after the meeting began, this consultant announced that "openness is the name of the game here" and energetically urged his client to tell the executive—who was my client—exactly what he thought of him. When the subordinate balked at doing so, the consultant began to act as the client's "alter ego" and speak as he presumed the client wanted to. I was stunned and frankly rendered incapable by this exchange. This example does more than highlight issues of competence and incompetence: It demonstrates how practitioners can let strong values get them into trouble. Not only did no disclosure (not even a modest amount) occur, but the meeting became quite stilted. The manager and subordinate learned little about each other and failed to make progress in resolving their difficulties; I learned little about any possibilities in the situation; my colleague learned nothing from his intervention. To my surprise, when I suggested to the consultant after the meeting that he had probably tried to do too much too soon, he remarked that he considered the embarrassing situation the **clients'** fault and said, "If they are ever going to get ahead, they have to be open with each other."

OD practitioners can profit from learning about and appreciating the complexities of moral/ethical trade-offs in client systems. In doing so, the practitioner clearly assumes the role of the learner and acts as a model of what practitioners generally insist clients do: Learn from others (particularly the consultants). Closer client-consultant relationships can result when the practitioner identifies with the **clients'** values and perspectives even as the practitioner presents OD's values and perspectives.

The OD practitioner becomes alienated from the client. I have already discussed how the client sometimes, in effect, retreats from the consultant. I now discuss how consultants retreat from their clients.

This occurs when the practitioner resists being drawn into the muddled and muddling arena of middle-ground choices, of short-term responses reflecting questionable ethics, of outright violations of the OD "code." Differences between the client's ethics in operation and the practitioner's own deeply felt and strongly espoused values causes conflict for the consultant. Such circumstances can range from the consultant's engaging in an action that is not "right" according to the tenets of the profession but is considered necessary for achieving stated goals (i.e., effectiveness), to the more subtle situation of the consultant's personally demonstrating processes that are effective but impossible for the client to incorporate.

I myself have increasingly come to feel uneasy about the ways OD practitioners manage information through contracts guaranteeing confidentiality. Under such contracts, consultants promise not to reveal anyone's actual views or statements. This is something the client cannot emulate. Such a process promotes not only a false sense of the consultant's competence, but also a simplistic, either/or means of managing sensitive information. I prefer to tell clients that I do not guarantee confidentiality, but **do** promise to use all my skill in managing information appropriately with concern for the individual, the person's colleagues, and the organization as a whole. Of course, this makes the consultant's job more difficult, but no more difficult than the manager's job with respect to information management. I thus can learn something, and pass this learning on to others in the system. Rather than becoming alienated from the clients' circumstances, I can better empathize with the clients and understand this dimension of their work. I can also develop better decision rules to help clients operate more congruently with their own values. The solutions I offer thus are more realistic and likely to be implemented.

Do nice guys win ball games?

Upon hearing a synopsis of the points I make above, one of my colleagues responded by asking, "Are you saying that nice guys don't win ball games?" That is **not** what I am saying. What I wish to communicate is that nice guys **can** win ball games, but probably not if they (1) are too "full of" a sense of themselves as "nice guys" and (2) think that a sufficient response to unpleasant practical problems is being "nice." The distraction of being nice becomes both a refuge and a means of avoiding difficulties. Even worse, this can prevent one from developing all the skills needed to do a good, thorough job.

Friedlander and Brown (1974, p. 335) state that "the future of OD rests in part on its values and the degree to which its practice, theory, and research are congruent with those values." Tichy's (1974) work cites a high level of "value-action incongruence" among practitioners. Beer (1980) suggests that practice often fails to live up to theory. As OD practitioners' espoused value systems become more finely articulated, this gap will probably widen.

Bowen (1977, p. 387) connects this incongruence to concerns about effectiveness, pointing out that it may be that consultant-client relationships deteriorate over time simply because clients assume that their consultants experience increasing difficulty in behaving in a manner consistent with the values espoused or implicit in the OD techniques employed.

Argyris (1970) warns that consultants seeking to gain experience may be too pushy and controlling in their efforts to achieve change. Such a manipulative approach transforms "normative re-educative" strategies into something resembling the frequently castigated "re-education programs" that many totalitarian countries apply to dissidents. Clearly, such an orientation places OD practitioners in adversarial relationships with clients rather than in collaborative ones.

When viewed in this light, tactics for "overcoming resistance" no longer appear so benign. Once OD's image becomes inextricably tied to moral conviction or forces of light, the OD practitioner feels compelled to "help" reluctant clients overcome their misgivings about OD's values and goals. At this point the consultant has actually ceased working on the **client's** agenda and has begun working on the consultant's own agenda. I have not seen in the literature any acknowledgment that resistance may sometimes stem from a healthy refusal to do something unhealthy—nor have I noted any advice urging consultants faced with resistance to stop what they are doing, quit forcing their ideas on their clients, re-evaluate their methods and goals, get feedback, or the like.

Keeping the above in mind, one can consider the recent discussion of the "political perspective" to be a logical result of OD's persistent failure to address the logical inconsistency within its fundamental tenets. Further specification of ideal states and ethical methodology will, I believe, lead only to more incongruence, confusion, contradictions, mystification of relationships, and ineffectiveness.

This situation has arisen largely because the practice of OD has always had strong political implications that consultants have usually denied and mystified under a cloak of virtue. Its operations are fundamentally opposed to its ideals, a view not generally acknowledged, although expressed by some. Mohrman and Mohrman (1977) found that individuals within organizations considered OD consultants political and considered OD interventions politics. These scholars postulate—correctly, I believe—that OD introduces demands into organizations' political systems for the authoritative (re-)allocation of values. This hypothesis makes ever more sense as OD practitioners are increasingly requested to realize—almost reflexively—the social ideals the profession promotes.

Should we just do whatever works?

At this point a logical question comes to mind: Should OD adopt a "value-free," "whatever-works" stance toward interventions?

I do not believe it should. I personally identify strongly with many of the values of OD, and do not advocate "value-free" applications of any expertise or technology. We in the field, however, ought to do several things to help practitioners and clients develop less mystical, coercive relationships and enable both to learn together as the field of OD develops.

First, **OD practitioners and their sponsoring organizations should stop trying to further specify and delineate the values and ethics of organization development.**

Second, **the OD profession should retreat from some of the specifications already developed.** We should probably get "fuzzier" and more collectively confused as to OD's values and ethics. Perhaps this will make us more receptive to learning and to posing questions about such important issues.

Third, **OD practitioners should explicitly acknowledge their own biases related to values and ethics to their clients, while simultaneously encouraging dialogue about the clients' and others' views and systems.** This will also promote learning.

Finally, **in preparing OD interventions and strategies, practitioners should specifically begin addressing ways of making issues related to values and ethics continuing objects of inquiry.** For example, we should ask whether practitioners should work to enhance the power of those in authority within organizations, rather than seek to "democratize" all client systems.

I wish to conclude by addressing the last point. As we discuss the goals and methods of OD and the ways they relate to its values, we should keep in mind that at all times during an organizational change effort a complex system is in operation. This system includes the consultant's espoused goals and actual goals (including success, survival, continuation, and the like), the client's espoused goals and actual goals—which can be quite diverse, depending on various stakeholders in the client's system—and the espoused methods and actual methods employed by both. I have found that many, if not most, clients' problems could be broken down into "what they **think** they are doing versus what they **intended** to do versus what they are **actually** doing."

Probably no method is more fundamental to teaching a client new skills than that of the consultant acting as a model. OD practitioners should thus seek to empower client systems by setting examples of persons willing to open and sustain dialogue and inquiry into the incongruities of their profession.

REFERENCES

Argyris, C. (1970). *Intervention theory and method.* Reading, MA: Addison-Wesley.

Beer, M. (1980). *Organization change and development: A systems view.* Glenview, IL: Scott, Foresman.

Bowen, D. D. (1977). Value dilemmas in organization development. *The Journal of Applied Behavioral Science, 13*(4), 543-556.

Cobb, A. T. (1984, August). *The use of organizational politics in intervention: Ethical issues and considerations for organization development.* Paper presented to the OD Division at the National Academy of Management Meeting, Boston.

Cobb, A. T., & Margulies, N. (1981). Organization development: A political perspective. *Academy of Management Review, 6*(1), 49-59.

French, W. L. (1974). Organization development: Objectives, assumptions and strategies. *California Management Review, 12*, 23-34.

Friedlander, F., & Brown, L. D. (1974). Organization development. *Annual Review of Psychology, 25,* 313-341.

Hofstede, G. (1984). The cultural relativity of the quality of life concept. *Academy of Management Review, 9*(3), 389-398.

Miles, M. B., & Schmuck, R. A. (1983). The nature of organization development. In W. L. French, C. H. Bell, & R. A. Zawacki (Eds.), *Organization development: Theory, practice, research.* Plano, TX: Business Publications.

Mohrman, S. A., & Mohrman, A. M. (1977). *Organizational politics and development: OD as politics.* Paper presented at the National Academy of Management Meeting, Kissimmee, FL.

Perrow, C. (1977). The short and glorious history of organizational theory. In H. L. Tosi & W. C. Hamner (Eds.), *Organizational behavior and management.* Chicago: St. Clair.

Sashkin, M. (1984, Spring). Participative management is an ethical imperative. *Organizational Dynamics,* pp. 5-21.

Slater, P. E., & Bennis, W. G. (1978). Democracy is inevitable. In J. M. Shafritz & P. H. Whitbeck (Eds.), *Classics of organization theory.* Oak Park, IL: Moore.

Tichy, N. M. (1974). Agents of planned social change: Congruence of values, cognitions, and actions. *Administrative Science Quarterly, 19,* 164-182.

Collusion With Existing Norms: The Intrapsychic Connection

Lee Butler

Introduction

Much of the recent work on organizations as cultures has either compared the organizational cultures of American companies with those of Japanese companies, or has compared effective and ineffective American companies. Similar inquiries have also been made into schools. With respect to the cross-cultural approach, the spark that ignited the inquiry was the decline of America's industrial dominance, which led to an urgent search to determine why Japan is doing better than America in world trade. Lewis and Allison (1982) frame the issue in terms of Japan's winning "the real world war." Perhaps when Peters and Waterman wrote their now-famous book *In Search of Excellence* (1982), they recognized that a true solution to U.S. malaise could not be achieved through cross-cultural analysis, and instead examined American organizations with the aim of extrapolating from their observations those characteristics that give rise to excellence.[1]

Underlying all this is the assumption that if we can identify the things excellent organizations do, and how they do them, we can use this information to train ineffective organizations to "do the right things."[2] The literature, however, largely avoids the issue of how and why the individual organization participant "buys into" existing norms of the corporate culture. What forces operate at this micro level of cultural analysis?

I take the position that people perpetuate existing norms by their collective tendencies to collude with them. This chapter seeks to establish the connection between this collusion and organizational norms, and presents the four characteristics of collusive behavior. That is, I believe that collusive acts are **(1) preconscious,** that they **(2) reinforce pre-existing states and thus help** maintain the status quo, that they (3) stem from a need to protect the self, and that (4) an inevitable paradox is embedded in them.

In his discussion of single-loop learning systems, Chris Argyris (1982) provides the fertile soil for some of the basic concepts presented in this chapter. I thereby refer frequently to his illuminating work.

The preconscious in collusion. The concept of the preconscious comes from psychoanalysis. The preconscious is considered the area of one's psyche containing the mental processes that one is unaware of at any given time, but that are more or less readily available to the consciousness. Although this is difficult—perhaps impossible—to validate empirically, the content of the preconscious is said to develop essentially as a by-product of socialization and other significant experiences of one's lifetime. When a collusive act is done preconsciously, it is virtually impossible for one to recognize it. When helpful feedback enables to make such an identification, however, this is often seen and acknowledged—much to one's chagrin.

Merely pointing out collusion performed today seldom provides an individual with a basis for significantly changing one's behavior in the future. Argyris has pointed out that this very resistance to extinction serves as at least prima facie evidence that people are "undoubtedly **programmed** to behave in this fashion," that we seem "doomed" to behave much the same way under similar conditions in the future (1982, p. 82). This raises the following question: Where does this programming come from?

I contend that one's collusive acts are driven by "replaying the old socialization tapes" that provide us with responses that are ostensibly self-protecting. Throughout one's childhood, one receives continuous remonstrations concerning endless social improprieties. Such parental interventions have been observed among virtually all higher-order species of the animal kingdom. They provide essential information to the young for survival. The messages recorded on socialization tapes and replayed as catalysts for collusion tell us how to "survive" **socially.**

How collusion reinforces pre-existing states. Collusion typically occurs in social situations in which consensus is sought and those participating consider the stakes significant. For example, many contemporary managers find themselves preoccupied with whether subordinates or peers will "buy into" various aspects of tasks. Will they go along with a decision? Will they participate in implementing the plan? Subordinates must weigh the costs of **not** buying into something. Holding a view contrary to that of other members of a group may occasionally threaten one's continued career growth. Such perceived threats inevitably set the stage for collusion.

When one reinforces a pre-existing state, the content of what one says or the impetus for what one does stems from one's replaying old tapes about surviving and maintaining personal safety in such a situation. Subordinates may seek to maintain a margin of immediate personal safety by saying they have bought into a decision, even if they secretly disagree with it. We have all witnessed situations in which someone's taking a position contrary to that held by all others caused that person to become labeled as "not a team player." The price of **expressing** views contrary to those held by an intact work group is often isolation, ostracism, and decreased opportunities for promotion. This reinforces the pre-existing state, for the collusive behavior **sanctions** what is already present—and thus constitutes buying into it.

Are all "buy-ins" evidence of collusion? I answer this with a resounding "no." Collusion only occurs when one's agreement with an ongoing social process has a fundamentally **political** motivation, and, therefore, has little to do with the content of the group process. In this context, the term "political" refers to one's intending at a minimum to maintain a margin of personal safety, or at a maximum to improve one's position. When one buys into an ongoing social process with which one has some deep-seated disagreement that is left unstated, one has contributed to maintaining the status quo, perhaps unwittingly. This dynamic is often innocent enough, but sometimes it can lead to disaster. For example, the Watergate scandal and the destruction of the space shuttle Challenger resulted from situations in which **stated** opposing views either were played down or discounted in the midst of an inexorable quest for consensus.

The self-protecting dimension of collusion. Protecting oneself is a natural selection behavior characteristic of nearly all life forms. Much like most of life's experiences, this occurs at some cost to an individual's continued growth. Collusive behavior is self-protecting because its characteristic short-term outcome perpetuates the status quo, and is the opposite of learning and changing. Collusion reinforces and lends consensual credence to pre-existing circumstances. Such circumstances are often associated with a powerful social norm dictating behaviors that are expected and supported. Swimming against the cultural tide of a decision-making group by stating contrary views is highly risky, and inevitably increases one's personal vulnerability. This is why in most situations people choose to collude, and thus to protect themselves.

What is the paradox embedded in collusion? Each person's preconscious is full of messages indicating how to escape vulnerability in the short term. Replaying old tapes may enable one to avoid personal vulnerability in a given situation, but this leaves the situation unchanged, and thus makes one **more** rather than **less** vulnerable in the long term. The Watergate scandal serves as an excellent example of this.

The paradox embedded in collusion is this: the abyss existing between what Argyris (1982) calls one's intentions and one's outcomes. It is as if one saves oneself from drowning in the short term, only to perish with one's shipmates as the ship eventually goes down.

The formation of collusive centers

Feeling that one is personally threatened is what stimulates collusive acts. Being threatened in social situations means facing the loss of something one values.

Table 1

Some Selected Examples of Collusion Etiology*

Some socialization messages	Some alternative ways these are internalized	Some possible forms of collusion
"Be nice."	"I must mask negative feelings." "I am not a nice person."	Stating agreement although one "feels" disagreement Devaluing and discounting oneself and harboring feelings of low self-worth
"You must work harder" (a message given to women and members of minority groups).	"I am not as good as men in the majority group." "I will never be appreciated."	Underachieving behavior
"Do not question adults."	"I must defer to those with power and authority if I am to be successful."	Not saying what one feels Not threatening or challenging those with power
"It is not nice to fight."	"I must avoid disagreeable situations."	Passive-aggressive behavior ("Don't get mad, get even") Surface agreements ("I'll secretly do what I really want")
"Put others first."	"What I want is not important." "I must manipulate others to get what I want."	Self-deprecating remarks

* I am deeply indebted to my colleagues at NTL Institute and to participants attending my Sunrise Seminar presentation on this topic in July 1985 in Bethel, Maine. The examples provided here are only five of many shared with me at that time.

Without this fear of loss, the psychologically healthy individual feels no threat. At the center of collusive interactions is power. In striving to avoid losing something, we choose not to become less powerful. We would rather win and either maintain our perceived power or else become even more powerful.

Because of this, one of the key goals of collusion is at best to come out on top, or at worst to avoid losing. Indeed, this dynamic is what made the exercise of the Prisoner's Dilemma such a powerful laboratory design.[3] (In this exercise, participants perceive winning to mean losing less than anyone else.)

Our first exposure to power comes at the beginning of the life cycle during interactions with our parents. Table 1 links early messages, the ways they may be internalized, and possible examples of collusion that may result.

Table 1 alludes to many assumptions. One is that we process the socialization messages we receive, and that from this processing comes an associated belief about oneself and a linked belief about some aspect of the social environment surrounding ourselves. Another assumption is that by processing socialization messages, we **internalize** them in some specific way. Another assumption is that messages are internalized in different ways by different persons, and not in the same way by all people. The particular way a given socialization message is internalized, however, is intimately tied to specific ways of responding to the environment. This nearly stereotypical way of responding to situations is what justifies the use of the term ''programmed'' to describe a basic quality of collusive transactions. Figure 1 illustrates the chain of events leading to collusion.

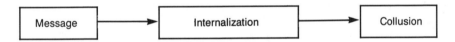

Figure 1. A collusion chain

The programmed dimension of collusive behavior need not be considered an ultimate indictment of our behavior as irrevocably malevolent. Human beings are far too complex for such an outcome. We do know, however, that our tendencies to collude are highly resistant to change. Pointing out collusion today carries no guarantee that one will not commit this again tomorrow; such is the nature of preconscious, socially programmed acts. Yet just as computers can be reprogrammed to handle particular information differently, so can one change one's behavior—usually as a consequence of powerful personal learning. To illustrate how this can occur, I refer to the ''You must work harder'' message.

''You must work harder.'' Little question exists that the Protestant work ethic has historically served to motivate people in the West to work hard. Because this is so entrenched in our culture, any conspicuous success on one's part is considered a reflection of one's having internalized this ethic to some degree. Nevertheless, because cultural minority groups and women are cut off from the network of relationships that often facilitate's one's progress through organizational hierarchies, their parents often implore them from an early age to work even harder. "Get to work before the boss, and never leave before he does" is a credo of many trying to succeed in corporate life, and indicates something akin to a Jackie Robinson syndrome, whereby one feels the need to do superior work to be considered even adequate. Internalizing this socialization message, however, may plant the seeds of collusion with substantial consequences. Many young persons in this category internalize the "You must work harder" message as a parental admonition that they are not as good as men in the majority group. If this were not so, then why else would they need to work harder? Equity demands only equivalent effort, whereas inferiority—or the perception of it—demands greater effort.

When burdened by the notion that one must exert sustained effort to get ahead, a person becomes "set up" to collude in many different ways. Perhaps the most insidious affects one's potential for self-fulfillment. Clearly, our phenomenology lends superficial support for one's internalizing the message as "I am not as good as men in the majority group," for this phenomenology causes young people to see that those holding power in our culture all have visible traits in common: They are white men from the majority group. The general absence of cultural minority group members and women in such esteemed roles reinforces the germination of a notion of personal inferiority.

This silent societal dialogue causes those who are not white men from the majority group to be constantly cautious. Their resulting reticent behavior may be viewed by those in power as a symptom of inherent inferiority and lack of ability. The caution such a person feels is partly driven by a fear that those in authority will discover that one has been masquerading as competent, when one really is not competent at all. This is known as the imposter syndrome, and is the basis for tension and a lack of spontaneity in interpersonal transactions. Hence, events come full circle, for the environment—that is, those with power and authority—perceives the wary behavior as **congruent with the internalized message of inferiority.** At this point a **collusive center** is developed, for the loop is closed and an individual is "programmed" to act in ways inimical to one's own interests, even as one seeks to "protect" oneself in everyday transactions. Figure 2 illustrates this.

The arrows in this figure point in both directions for three basic reasons. First, they are intended to communicate the idiosyncratic way in which people internalize messages. Although many of us receive basically the same socialization messages, we internalize them differently based on our own psychodynamic

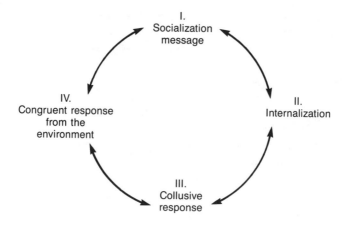

Figure 2. A collusive center

natures. Second, these arrows represent the possible effects of learning and change, which may keep one from closing a circle or help one dismantle a circle as a result of changing one's behavior. (I am reminded of the lead character in the film *Network* crying, "I'm madder than hell, and I'm not going to take it any more!" as a typical example of a collusive center's being dismantled with much anger and energy.) Finally, the arrows indicate that the elements of collusion may be short-circuited at any point in its development, often through the intervention of a significant change in a person's life.

Conclusions

As noted in the introduction to this chapter, much attention is now being paid to organizational change. Inevitably, the technology for accomplishing this task must be directed at changing **norms.** Norms determine the behaviors expected and supported by an organization's culture. Changing ineffective norms to ones that will increase productivity, improve quality, and/or facilitate excellence is a topic of much debate. The link between norms and individual behavior is the internalization of socialization messages, and the extent of the congruity between these messages and an organization's system of norms. Incongruity is the underlying cause of the termination of most women and members of minority groups, which is often attributed to "lack of fit."

Several authors have observed that an individual's failure to survive in an organization is frequently based on that person's inability to understand and appreciate the importance of the organization's culture.[4] Although such persons may work hard at various assignments, they fail to understand the other components of organizational life not related to tasks. These are the important cultural components. The ultimate paradox embedded in this concept may be the final linkage: An individual's survival may be intimately tied to her or his ability to collude with existing organizational norms, yet this may be the least permeable barrier to organizational effectiveness and cultural change.

NOTES

1. See also Deal and Kennedy (1982).

2. The entire saying is: "Tradition-directed organizations are driven to do things right, whereas cutting-edge organizations seek to do the right things." I do not know who first said this. Warren Bennis was observed making this comment during a talk show interview following the publication of his book *Leaders*, and such a statement appears in Rosabeth Moss Kanter's book *The Change Masters: Innovation for Productivity in the American Corporation* (1982).

3. The Prisoner's Dilemma exercise, also known as ABXY, uses mini-max game theory to uncover issues operating in interpersonal and intergroup situations, especially the formation of a climate of trust. I do not know who created this exercise.

4. Tichy is particularly cogent about this point when he makes the following observation:

> The processes that are most central to the organization's culture are the human resources processes. The content of a culture is largely determined by the selection process, [for determining] who gets hired or promoted is in part a cultural decision. The Japanese are very self-conscious about selection and culture. They have all the workers who will be working with an individual involved in the selection process. This is even true for very low-level jobs, so it is clear that the decision is not technical, that they are not spending this time evaluating manual dexterity, etc. Rather, they are seeing "how well the individual will fit in," "how consistent the person is with the culture," etc. By doing this they can select people who best fit their culture. One way to shape a culture is to prevent deviants from getting in the door. Some U.S. companies such as IBM and Exxon recruit MBAs this way. (1983, p. 265)

REFERENCES

Argyris, C. (1982). *Learning, reasoning and action.* San Francisco: Jossey-Bass.

Deal, T. E., & Kennedy, A. (1982). *Corporate cultures: The rites and rituals of corporate life.* Reading, MA: Addison-Wesley.

Kanter, R. M. (1982). *The change masters: Innovation for productivity in the American corporation.* New York: Simon and Schuster.

Lewis, H., & Allison, D. (1982). *The real world war: The coming battle for the new global economy and why we are in danger of losing.* New York: Coward McCann and Geoghegan.

Peters, T. J., & Waterman, R. H. (1982). *In search of excellence: Lessons from America's best run companies.* New York: Harper and Row.

Tichy, N. M. (1983). *Managing strategic change: Technical, political and cultural dynamics.* New York: John Wiley and Sons.

Section IV.
Pluralism and OD

The Wells-Jennings Analysis: A New Diagnostic Window on Race Relations in American Organizations

Carl L. Jennings
Leroy Wells, Jr.

Introduction

In today's unpredictable organization environment, what can applied behavioral scientists working in organization development (OD) do to help create organizations that perform optimally and make the best use of all their human resources? More specifically, what can behavioral scientists do to help organizational leaders and managers retain and best use the skills and expertise of women, blacks, and other minority groups working within the professional and managerial ranks of American organizations?

These questions consumed our thinking and led to the creation of the theory discussed in this chapter.

In 1983, when we put forth our paradigm in "Black Career Advancement and White Reactions: Remnants of 'Herrenvolk' Democracy and the Scandalous Paradox'' (Wells & Jennings, 1983), we were responding to a shared need. That need was to better understand what our feelings, thoughts, and perceptions meant for us as black men and, by implication, all blacks in organizations. We were also concerned about what our perspectives on these issues might portend for American organizations and society as a whole (Kennedy, 1989). We sought to create a framework useful for delineating the distinctive features of racial diversity in organizations and their impact on black managers. Another objective was to provide an angle of vision on racial diversity that pushed beyond the boundaries of describing black advancement in organizations to the creation of a theoretical framework useful for explaining this phenomenon.

At the time we developed the paradigm we decided to focus primarily on the experiences of blacks for two important reasons.

1. The work grew out of organizational and societal dynamics based on the black experience

2. The experiences of blacks have acted as a barometer for unfolding events and trends in American life generally. Witness the present impact of drugs on the nation, a problem once thought to belong to blacks and minorities exclusively. The changes in the average American family structure brought on by the need for mothers and wives to work are also realities identified almost exclusively with black families until now. A generation ago, few mothers of young children worked outside of the home—only 19% in 1960 versus 54% today (U.S. Department of Labor, 1988).

We have adapted our paradigm to OD because we feel practitioners in this discipline should understand the importance of these phenomena for deriving a comprehensive and robust understanding of current organizational systems that have to rely increasingly on a racially and culturally diverse work force. Our analysis thus provides another diagnostic window through which one may view, as well as explain, the issues presented above.

Race-related issues in organizations

On November 29, 1985, the *New York Times* reported that a growing number of blacks were leaving corporate America to pursue entrepreneurial ventures or to work for black-owned businesses (Hicks, 1985). The impetus for their leaving the corporate world was their desire for greater career opportunities, which many minority group members and women said they could not find at the time within corporations. At present, opportunities for women have improved considerably and dramatically in comparison to those for black men. This has resulted, in part, from decreasing numbers of qualified, available men in general and increasing numbers of women, and from the expectation that women will represent the largest group of new entrants into the work force between now and the year 2000 (Hudson Institute, 1987). Although we can find no figures for black professionals who have joined the exodus, the overall number has increased significantly because of corporate restructuring and the stock market crash of 1987 (Farnham, 1989). This trend among blacks represents a significant development with major implications for American business, particularly in new markets and many regions of the world. These changes occurring in organizations across the U.S. have direct relevance for practitioners and theoreticians dealing with minority issues and system-wide organizational change and improvement efforts. Although race relations in this country have improved significantly during the past 30 years, tension and racial strife remain an integral part of American life, and much remains to be done.

OD and race relations

Improving race relations was a seminal aspect of the work of Kurt Lewin and his colleagues, and of the development of applied behavioral science, from which OD emerged. As Morrow (1977, p. 210) states, the Connecticut State Inter-Racial Commission asked Lewin ". . .to help in training leaders and conducting research on the most effective means of combatting racial and religious prejudice in communities." Some applied behavioral scientists, however, felt that improving race relations was not within the province of the field. For example, Burke (1972, p. 6) explicitly declared that "OD does not readily provide a technique or a value system for helping the disenfranchised members of organizations (e.g., blacks, women, persons over 55) gain such things as rapid recognition or equal promotion opportunities." Largely because of such attitudes, a formerly major focus of the applied behavioral sciences (as represented by Lewin) diminished in importance. An issue once considered figural receded into the background.

Exceptions exist, of course. Even though many major works on OD do not emphasize issues related to race and minorities, some OD scholars and practitioners choose to do so, some exclusively and some as a part of their general practice, including Clayton Alderfer and his colleagues (Alderfer, 1983, 1985; Alderfer, Alderfer, Tucker, & Tucker, 1980; Alderfer & Cooper, 1980; Alderfer & Thomas, 1988; Alderfer, Tucker, Alderfer, & Tucker, 1985), Bailey Jackson III and Rita Hardiman (Jackson, 1976; Jackson & Hardiman, 1978), Elsie Cross (1983), Kaleel Jamison, (1978), Rosabeth Moss Kanter (1977), Alice Sargent (1983), among those who have written on these issues, and Ed Nichols, Richard Orange, Janice Eddy, Fred Miller, Judith Katz, Pat Bidol, Edie Seashore, Karen Terniko and Bryant Rollins.

Some may ask: "How can examining race relations through different diagnostic windows lead to a more comprehensive understanding of organization-level phenomena and concomitant strategies for change?" The researchers and practitioners cited above have attempted to answer this question. The most comprehensive effort to understand race relations in an organizational context to date was an eight-year organizational change project conducted by Alderfer (Alderfer, 1985, 1985; Alderfer, Alderfer, Tucker, & Tucker, 1980; Alderfer & Cooper, 1980; Alderfer & Thomas, 1988; Alderfer, Tucker, Alderfer, and Tucker, 1985). Begun in 1976, this project was initiated to improve the working relations of black and white managers in a corporation with more than 12,000 employees and approximately 2,000 managers. According to Alderfer, this intervention

> ...was significantly influenced by behavioral science theories and methods...very little of the program was designed or implemented without explicit attention to how theory related to practice...there was mutual influence among theory, technique, and measurement in all major elements. (1985, p. 2)

The Wells-Jennings Analysis

The Wells-Jennings Analysis focuses on race relations and their influence at the organizational level. This construct, however, can also be applied more generally, and has been used to better understand the treatment of women and of minorities other than blacks, and the behavior of white men in multicultural organizations. The theory provides a framework for better understanding the basis of issues such as quality of work life and organizational productivity (D.L. Ford, Jr., personal communication, 1985; E. Nichols, personal communication, 1984). Frameworks that provide insight into such issues help with the development of healthy organizations embodying democratic values.

Despite public and scholarly rhetoric, our research and analysis revealed that, as far as blacks and women are concerned, the modern organization is not generally a meritocracy, and does not reflect the principles of egalitarian democracy. Rather, the modern organization is a "neo-pigmentocracy" reflecting the remnants of "Herrenvolk" democracy.[1]

Within most organizations, quasi-Herrenvolk democratic culture creates internal dynamics evoking the "scandalous paradox." This concept refers to the ways white anxiety about status leads to barriers restricting black mobility while protecting white privilege and sense of entitlement.

During our ongoing efforts to understand the experiences and treatment of blacks at the organizational level, we reviewed American history dating back to slavery.[2] For the vast majority of blacks brought from Africa to this continent, slavery was their first introduction to American organizational and institutional life; this system accorded them the status of property. The system of governance during slavery has been described by many historians as a "Herrenvolk democracy" (Cell, 1982; Evans, 1980; Frederickson, 1981; Van den Berghe, 1967, 1970; Vickery, 1974; Woodward, 1971a, 1971b, 1974). These ideas are also noted in the work of political scientist Michael Parenti (1983).

Maintaining a quasi-Herrenvolk culture requires enormous amounts of creative human energy. This expenditure of energy can contribute to diminished productivity, work place stress, and human pathos—for blacks, whites, and the system as a total entity. Ultimately, such conditions can retard an organization's ability to achieve or maintain strategic and competitive advantages in the environments necessary for their survival and growth.

Our theory encompasses factors affecting organizations both externally and internally.

External factors. Related to the concept of Herrenvolk democracy is the notion of pigmentocracy, or a society ruled according to skin color (see Lipschutz, as cited by Evans, 1980). In Western culture, particularly in the U.S., pigmentocracy typically refers to a society run by people classified as white. Those in charge maintain the distribution of power by using a system of color values that permits the governing elite to define eligibility for power and privilege in terms of its own physical characteristics (Evans, 1980).

Under Herrenvolk democracy in the antebellum U.S., the exercise of power and suffrage was restricted by law to a dominant group—consisting of white men—structured as a pigmentocracy. Although people at the top of this hierarchical structure may consider it democratic, subordinate groups consider it tyrannical, for equality in political, economic, and other spheres is granted only to members of the ruling group (Cell, 1982).

Because Herrenvolk structure seldom exists in pure form, we characterize this phenomenon in the U.S. as "neo-pigmentocracy" and "quasi-Herrenvolk democracy." The first term indicates that access to power is granted to some blacks and minority group members despite their physical characteristics. The second term indicates that blacks and other minority groups in this country are not oppressed to the degree that they are in such regimes as that of South Africa.

Under neo-pigmentocracy and quasi-Herrenvolk democracy, the government claims to have laws protecting civil rights and equal opportunity. In reality, however, full participation in the democratic process and equal opportunity are generally restricted to members of the ruling elite, although some outside this group may be permitted to partake more fully. By sustaining the illusion of meritocracy and egalitarian democracy, the regime avoids concerted legal action and civil unrest as it maintains the privileged status of members of the quasi-Herrenvolk.

Under true egalitarian democracy and meritocracy, equal opportunity is both protected by law and is a fact of life for all citizens. People have access to organizations, promotions, and privileges based on demonstrated competence, qualifications, and performance. Ideally, this enables people to compete fairly, regardless of race, age, gender, creed, or other such characteristics.

Internal factors. One of the forces influencing the internal dynamics of quasi-Herrenvolk structures is the scandalous paradox. This occurs when someone possessing neither legal rights nor social status receives preference over someone possessing both. During times of slavery, for example, this phenomenon occurred when a slave received some object or privilege normally reserved for

Figure 1 helps one compare Herrenvolk, quasi-Herrenvolk, and egalitarian democracies.

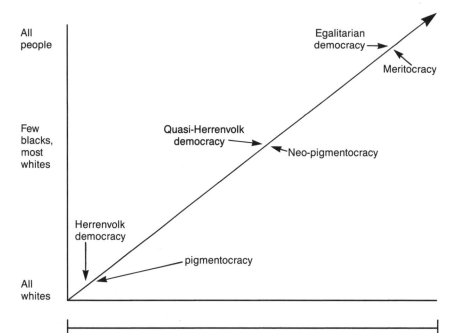

Figure 1. Comparisons of Herrenvolk, quasi-Herrenvolk, and egalitarian democracies

a legitimate member of the household. Today, comparable situations arise when members of the middle quasi-Herrenvolk group believe that the promotion to middle management of someone outside the group, such as a black person, constitutes a scandalous situation.

The legitimist impulse. In reaction to the scandalous paradox, "legitimists"—that is, members of the quasi-Herrenvolk group—feel status anxiety and fear that "their" rightful resources are being given to the undeserving (Evans, 1980). Legitimists defend their privileged position and consider the advancement of those outside their group to constitute encroachment on white entitlement.

Threshold positions. These are the positions the quasi-Herrenvolk consider acceptable for blacks to hold in organizations. When blacks advance

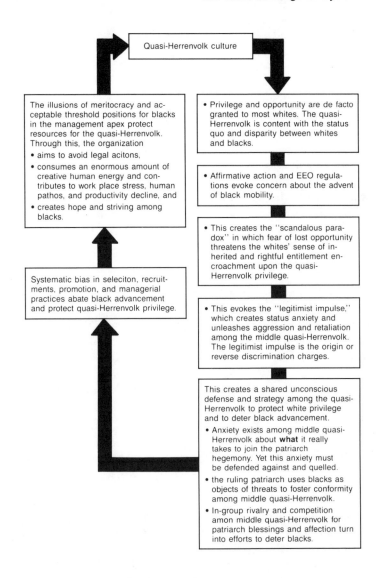

The illusions of meritocracy and acceptable threshold positions for blacks in the management apex protect resources for the quasi-Herrenvolk. Through this, the organization
• aims to avoid legal acitons,
• consumes an enormous amount of creative human energy and contributes to work place stress, human pathos, and productivity decline, and
• creates hope and striving among blacks.

Systematic bias in seleciton, recruitments, promotion, and managerial practices abate black advancement and protect quasi-Herrenvolk privilege.

Quasi-Herrenvolk culture

• Privilege and opportunity are de facto granted to most whites. The quasi-Herrenvolk is content with the status quo and disparity between whites and blacks.

• Affirmative action and EEO regulations evoke concern about the advent of black mobility.

• This creates the "scandalous paradox" in which fear of lost opportunity threatens the whites' sense of inherited and rightful entitlement encroachment upon the quasi-Herrenvolk privilege.

• This evokes the "legitimist impulse," which creates status anxiety and unleashes aggression and retaliation among the middle quasi-Herrenvolk. The legitimist impulse is the origin or reverse discrimination charges.

This creates a shared unconscious defense and strategy among the quasi-Herrenvolk to protect white privilege and to deter black advancement.
• Anxiety exists among middle quasi-Herrenvolk about **what** it really takes to join the patriarch hegemony. Yet this anxiety must be defended against and quelled.
• the ruling patriarch uses blacks as objects of threats to foster conformity among middle quasi-Herrenvolk.
• In-group rivalry and competition amon middle quasi-Herrenvolk for patriarch blessings and affection turn into efforts to deter blacks.

**Figure 2. Wells-Jennings Analysis of maintaining
quasi-Herrenvolk democracy**

beyond threshold positions, this evokes the legitimist impulse and creates status anxiety among white middle managers and "gatekeepers." See Figure 2 for a simplified schematic rendering of the ways in which quasi-Herrenvolk dynamics help maintain a system.

Case examples

The following examples illustrate our application of the framework discussed above.

"She needed the money more." Ms. S., a black supervisor, had worked for ABC utilities—a high-tech corporation—for 10 years. She was a skilled, competent worker known for her diligence, efficiency, and ability to communicate effectively with management, her coworkers, and her subordinates. Performance appraisals consistently recommended her for advancement. When a position became available at a level above her current job, Ms. S. applied for it. She was later shocked to learn that instead of being promoted herself, the position was given to Ms. L., a white woman in her department with fewer qualifications. Ms. S. asked her manager, Mr. B.—a white man—why and how this decision was made. Mr. B. readily acknowledged that although Ms. L. was loyal and efficient, she lacked the skills and competence of Ms. S.; he then explained that Ms. L. "needed the money more." After further conversation, he admitted reluctantly that management had pressured him to select a white candidate.

Analysis. Despite having technical competence, good vertical and horizontal communication skills, and performance appraisals recommending her advancement, Ms. S. was unable to move upward in the corporation. Instead, a promotion was given to a less-qualified woman.

In this case one cannot easily discern the role middle management played in preventing Ms. S.'s promotion. Although Mr. B. may have colluded in this effort, his own part in the outcome is not clear. What is clear, however, is that the hindrances to black career advancement and mobility result from a systemic phenomenon embedded in the corporation. This issue transcends Ms. S.'s technical and interpersonal abilities and Mr. B.'s ability to fully use a qualified employee.

This case also illustrates a tacit, possibly unconscious effort fueled by the legitimist impulse of the ruling members of the system, who represent the quasi-Herrenvolk. These persons consider their behavior necessary to ensure the rights and privileges to which they feel entitled.

In these situations, members of the quasi-Herrenvolk maintain the status quo through covert alliances among those in the middle and upper levels of the organization. Even though white middle managers may comply reluctantly, the effect on those who do not belong to the quasi-Herrenvolk remains the same: They achieve less than what they work and hope for. Such practices "demotivate" employees who are capable of making meaningful contributions. They also contribute to the crisis in human resources we face today (Hudson Institute, 1987).

"In all fairness." Mr. Y, a white man, held the position of department head in an expanding corporation. When he sought to select someone to be his assistant, he identified Ms. H.-J. as the most qualified of the candidates. He felt confident that Ms. H.-J., a black employee, had demonstrated the technical competence and interpersonal skills the job required. Once Mr. Y. made this announcement, however, Ms. H.-J.'s supervisor, a white man named Mr. R, advised her not to take the position, telling her she was "not right for the job." Furthermore, Mr. R. told Mr. Y. that he opposed the selection of Ms. H.-J. for the position. He provided no grounds for his opposition, and did not mention Ms. H.-J.'s seniority or competence, but only told Mr. Y. self-righteously, "In all fairness, I could not do this to the company." Mr. Y. relayed the entire conversation to Ms. H.-J.

Analysis. Although Ms. H.-J.'s department head had approved her promotion, her supervisor worked to prevent it. Mr. R.'s efforts illustrate how the legitimist impulse evoked by the scandalous paradox resulted in a deliberate attempt to deny Ms. H.-J. the opportunity for greater access to authority and power. This is typical of the opposition many blacks face in organizations (see Wells & Jennings, 1983). Such experiences result from a lack of support at the organizational level and the absence of a genuine belief in meritocracy.

Perhaps Mr. R. was acting because of some policy Mr. Y. did not share with Ms. H.-J.; if so, Ms. H.-J. was not given a satisfactory explanation for his attempts to prevent her promotion. She was left with the impression that her advancement was being blocked due to racial motivations.

Mr. R. may have sought to prevent Ms. H.-J.'s promotion because he valued her work and wanted to keep her at her current position so that his staff could remain productive. Such a scenario would suggest that the upper and middle members of the quasi-Herrenvolk had tacitly formed an alliance to prevent Ms. H.-J.'s advancement for the possible betterment of the department.

Being told that your boss has opposed your promotion because "in all fairness, I could not do this to the company" causes pain and disorientation. It sets of a cycle of ambiguity, ambivalence, anxiety, and frustration. Handling issues of race in organizations in this way can result in declining productivity and increased stress.

The illusion of meritocracy. Mr. H., a white vice president for corporate affairs, laughed at the idea of a meritocracy. During an interview, Mr. H. candidly remarked:

> This is something that we've got people sold on. It's the myth that keeps the system going, but everyone knows that the person with the most merit is not the person who rises to the top. Are you kidding me?...I know a man right here in this company who has never been successful at a

single goddamn assignment. He is ambitious and he knows how to kiss the right assess. He has bungled every assignment he's had.

Right now he's in a vital position in the company, and they've given him a strong staff to support him. This is not an isolated example. This is just one glaring example of what I mean. To a lesser or greater degree, it operates all across the board. Everyone knows this.

This meritocracy thing has always been a myth, but a necessary myth. It keeps the troops in line. It keeps them working as if their hard work will get them promoted. I'll tell you that one of the productivity problems in American industry today is caused by the fact that younger troops, white males, know that there's no such thing as a meritocracy. [Laughter]. I think they ought to let more minorities and women in because they work hard. They still believe in the meritocracy. (Davis & Watson, 1982, pp. 60-61)

Analysis. Mr. H. reveals frankly how the quasi-Herrenvolk culture operates in major corporations throughout the U.S., and how the illusion of a meritocracy keeps blacks and women hopeful, earnest, and working hard. Such an illusion pits white men against blacks and women for the coveted resources of the corporate hegemony.

By systematically eliminating blacks from the pool of candidates for managerial positions because they "lack merit," white men ensure their own chances for promotion to the upper ranks. They are, however, unsure of what exactly they should do to reach the top, and only clearly understand that one must conform to the wishes of those at that level if they are to advance. Indeed, the objective criteria for promotion to the upper ranks are usually quite ambiguous—perhaps intentionally. Such ambiguity leads to an environment breeding conformity and dutiful compliance with the perceived cues of the organization's leaders. The net effect of this is that the status quo is maintained, and the privilege of competing for the resources of the corporate hegemony belongs only to white men.

The corporation can publicly pretend to be a meritocracy, and thus get blacks to work harder and whites to defend what they consider to be their exclusive right to the most coveted positions of the corporation. All of this creative human energy is expended to maintain a quasi-Herrenvolk culture. If it were used to solve problems and develop new ideas, American productivity would be enhanced significantly. Moreover, if blacks and whites both understood the benefits they could derive from meritocracy, less tension and more cooperation would exist. Management would present more specific criteria for promotion and advancement, thus paving the way for a healthier and more productive work environment that values and synergizes the unique talents inherent in a diverse work force.

Implications of the Wells-Jennings Analysis for organization development

French, Bell, and Zawacki (1983, p. 3) argue that we need to close "the serious gaps in the technology available" in OD. Our work represents an effort to bridge the gap between what is presently available and what is needed to better understand how to take greater advantage of the unique contributions to organizational life that each of us can make. To the extent that OD is involved with data-based interventions as the basis for facilitating organizational change, our framework offers useful insights.

Much like the environments and organizations to which OD is applied, OD itself is in a state of flux. Given this reality, our framework has important implications for helping us clarify what the conceptual framework of OD is becoming.

Presently, the human resource needs of organizations and society greatly exceed our nation's ability to produce the required expertise. We are not making the best use of the resources we have. Our current crisis is clearly articulated by Warren Bennis (1989), Peter Vaill (1989) and Marvin Weisbord (1987), who detail new strategies and ways of conceptualizing current organizational issues. Our ability to use this information in the best interest of our organizations is, one would hope, being developed. In his recent book, Peter Vaill (1989, p. 19) emphasizes that "some of our best leaders and managers have long since concluded that their own intuitions are the best guides to action," adding, "I think we should understand that, celebrate it and see what we can learn from it." He characterizes the executive role further by highlighting the need to allow expression by "the whole person."

Differences in styles and approaches to work and problem solving have virtually prohibited women, blacks, and other minority groups from thoroughly expressing their "whole persons." For example, Jerry O. Williams was poised to become the first black chairman of the board and CEO of a major Fortune 500 Corporation. Formerly of Chicago's A.M International, he rose to the position of President and COO. Williams earned his promotion one year after his stellar performance on the strategic management team that revived A.M. International and pulled it out of Chapter 11 bankruptcy (Dingle, Edmund, & Hilliard, 1988). Williams reportedly resigned when he and the CEO, Merle H. Banta, "did not see eye to eye" (Edmund, 1988).

With the requisite data, the Wells-Jennings Analysis might yield considerable understanding of this occurrence. Tragically, American business may have lost another excellent resource at a time of critical need. Issues we anticipated in 1983 are currently having a dysfunctional impact on the country's human resource capability at a national level. We are concerned that the influx of women, minorities, immigrants, the elderly, and the physically challenged, as well as the innumerable problems presently confronting blacks, could all have the effect of significantly minimizing the participation of black men in managerial and professional roles in organizations (U.S. Department of Labor, 1988).

We fully realize the need and benefits of including all populations listed above for the success of our organizations. We also think that OD consultants working with managers and leaders are responsible for urging a balanced representation in the use of all our human resources, including qualified and competent black men. This would lend consistency and credibility to the belief that the strategy used with blacks is the right strategy for developing all our human resources (U.s. Department of Labor, 1988).

Practitioners in applied behavioral science need to take the lead in advocating and modeling attitudes and behaviors that are consistent with and uphold the systemic integrity of the pluralistic and multicultural nature of our society and work force, both now and in the future. In so doing, we can expect managers and leaders in organizations to value and uphold these realities as well.

We are convinced that the role of practitioners and theoreticians in applied behavioral science will become increasingly important. These professionals, along with leaders and managers, constitute the group our nation will increasingly look to for assistance in structuring organizations and developing human resources for the future.

The forces of survival and change, characterized by turbulence and tempered by our personal experience, charges and challenges each of us to work with leaders and managers to make their organizations more productive and participative. To accomplish this goal, we must fully use all of our human resources to achieve an outcome fundamental to our nation's principles, one that strives to ensure the survival of our institutions and **all** of its people.

NOTES

1. "Herrenvolk" is a German term referring to the Aryan "master race," and to white men in particular. Hence a Herrenvolk democracy is a regime designed to protect the rights and privileges of white men.

2. For a comprehensive list of the works on which we base our theory, see Wells and Jennings (1983).

REFERENCES

Alderfer, C. P. (1983). *An intergroup perspective on group dynamics* (ONR Technical Report No. 1). New Haven, CT: Yale School of Organization and Management.

Alderfer, C. P. (1985). *Changing race relations in organizations: a comparison of theories* (ONR Technical Report No. 4). New Haven, CT: Yale School of Organization and Management.

Alderfer, C. P., Alderfer, C. J., Tucker, L. M., & Tucker, R. C. (1980). Diagnosing race relations in management. *Journal of Applied Behavioral Science, 16*, 135-166.

Alderfer, C. P., & Cooper, C. L. (Eds.). (1980). *Advances in experiential social processes* (Vol. 2). London: John Wiley.

Alderfer, C. P., & Thomas, D. A. (1988). The significance of race and ethnicity for understanding organizational behavior. In C. I. Cooper & I. Robertson (Eds.), *International review of industrial and organizational psychology* (pp. 1-41). New York: John Wiley & Sons, Ltd.

Alderfer, C. P., Tucker, R. C., Alderfer, C. J., & Tucker, L. M. (1985). *The race relations advisory group: An intergroup intervention* (O.N.R. Technical Report No. 5). New Haven, CT: Yale School of Organization and Management.

Bennis, W. (1989). Why leaders can't lead. *San Francisco: Jossey-Bass.*

Burke, W. W. (Ed.). (1972). *Contemporary organization development: Conceptual orientations and interventions.* Washington, DC: NTL Institute.

Cell, J. W. (1982). *The highest stage of white supremacy: The origins of segregation in South Africa and the American South.* Cambridge, England: Oxford University Press.

Cross, E. Y. (1983). The new work force: Strategies for the 1980s. In R. A. Ritvo & A. G. Sargent (Eds.), *The NTL Managers' Handbook.* Arlington, VA: NTL Institute.

Davis, G., & Watson, G. (1982). *Black life in corporate America: Swimming in the mainstream.* New York: Anchor Press/Doubleday.

Dingle, D.T., Edmund, A., Jr., & Hilliard, S. L. (1988, February). America's hottest black managers. *Black Enterprise,* p. 116.

Edmund, A. Jr. (1989, January). Williams bids farewell. *Black Enterprise,* p. 14.

Evans, W. M. (1980). From the land of Canaan to the land of Guinea: The strange odyssey of the "Sons of Ham." *American Historical Review, 85*(10), 15-43.

Farnham, A. (1989, March). Holding firm on affirmative action. *Fortune,* p. 87.

Frederickson, G. M. (1981). *White supremacy.* New York: Oxford University Press.

French, W. L., Bell, C. H., Jr., & Zawacki, R. A. (1983). *Organization development: Theory, practice, research.* Plano, TX: Business Publications, Inc.

Hicks, J. P. (1985, November 29). Black professionals refashion their careers. *The New York Times,* pp. A1, 2.

Hudson Institute, Inc. (1987). *Workforce 2000: Work and workers for the 21st century.* Indianapolis, IN: Author.

Jackson, B. W., III (1976). *Black identity development theory.* Unpublished manuscript, School of Education, University of Massachusetts.

Jackson, B. W. III, & Hardiman, R. (1978). *White identity development theory.* Unpublished manuscript, School of Education, University of Massachusetts.

Jamison, K. (1978). Affirmative action program: Springboard for a total organizational change effort. *OD Practitioner, 10*(4), 1-8.

Kanter, R. M. (1977). *Men and women of the corporation.* New York: Basic Books.

Kennedy, P. (1989). *The rise and fall of the great powers.* New York: Vintage Books/Random House.

Morrow, A. J. (1977). *The practical theorist: The life and work of Kurt Lewin.* New York: Teachers College Press.

Parenti, M. (1983). *Democracy for the few* (4th ed.). New York: St. Martin's Press.

Sargent, A. G. (1983). Affirmative action: A guide to systems change for managers. In R. A. Ritvo & A. G. Sargent (Eds.), *The NTL Managers' Handbook.* Arlington, VA: NTL Institute.

U.S. Department of Labor. (1988). *Opportunity 2000: Creative Affirmative Action Strategies for a changing workforce* (DOL Publication No. 99-6-3370-75-002-02). Washington, DC: U.S. Government Printing Office.

Vaill, P. B. (1989). *Managing As a Performing Art.* San Francisco: Jossey-Bass

Van den Berghe, P. L. (1967). *Race and racism: A comparative perspective.* New York: Basic Books.

Van den Berghe, P. L. (1970). *Race and ethnicity: Essays in comparative sociology.* New York: Basic Books.

Vickery, K. P. (1974). Herrenvolk democracy and equalitarianism in South Africa and the U.S. South. *Comparative Studies in Society and History, 16,* 309-328.

Weisbord, M. R. (1987). *Productive workplaces: Organizing and managing for dignity, meaning, and community.* San Francisco: Jossey-Bass.

Wells, L., Jr., & Jennings, C. L. (1983). Black career advancement and white reactions: Remnants of ''Herrenvolk democracy'' and the scandalous paradox. In D. Vails-Weber & W. J. Potts (Eds.), *1983 Sunrise Seminars.* Arlington, VA: NTL Institute.

Woodward, C. V. (1971a). *Origins of the New South, 1877-1913* (2nd ed.). Baton Rouge, LA: Louisiana State University Press.

Woodward, C. V. (1971b, August 12). Our own ''Herrenvolk.'' *New York Review of books, 27*(2), p. 11.

Woodward, C. V. (1974). *The strange career of Jim crow* (3rd ed.) New York: Oxford University Press.

Changing Courses and Rocking the Boat: OD and Women

Katharine C. Esty

The story of how organizations have approached the development of women over the past 20 years is the story of a ship that has changed its course over and over. Organization development (OD) practitioners have steered in at least four quite different directions as they have sought to develop women within organizations. In their efforts to develop women, OD practitioners have rocked the organizational boat at times. At other times, these OD efforts have led to some remodeling of the boat itself.

What are the most pressing needs of women in organizations? In addressing this question, OD practitioners have devised four fundamentally different responses:

1. creating an **awareness** of the issues of sexism and sex-role stereo-typing,
2. developing women's **skills** as managers,
3. modifying the **systems and structures** of organizations to provide more opportunity for women, and (most recently)
4. preserving what is valuable in the "feminine" style of leadership and blending it with the best aspects of the typical "masculine" style to develop **"androgynous managers."**

In this chapter, I discuss each of these four approaches.

Creating an awareness of sexism and sex role stereotyping

In 1964, the Civil Rights Act was passed requiring that all employees be treated similarly without regard to race or gender. Most respondents to a survey by

---

the *Harvard Business Review* in 1965 (Bowman, Worthy, & Greyser, 1965), however, believed that this legislation "wouldn't change anything" for women. A majority of the respondents also believed that "women rarely expect or desire authority" and that "women are temperamentally unfit for management." Sixty-one percent of the male respondents and forty-seven percent of the female respondents agreed that "the business community will never wholly accept women executives."

In 1965, of course, hardly any women managers were aboard the organizational ship. Organizations had few, if any, programs for developing the women already on board, and none for increasing the number of women managers. Few executives perceived this lack as a concern or an important issue. At NTL Institute, for example, the only program for women in 1965 was a "special" program for the wives of the senior executives attending the two-week Human Relations Training Laboratory. Few women attended NTL's regular programs for middle managers. Even as late as 1979, an NTL Senior Managers Program's with about 30 participants included no women.

New ideas were stirring, however. Friedan (1963) had sparked the rising of the women's movement. The media began to pay considerable attention to the issues of sexism and sex-role stereotyping in the work place. In the late 1960s and early 1970s, hundreds of thousands of women joined grassroots consciousness-raising groups to explore together women's issues and sex-role stereotypes in particular. They often saw themselves in a new light—as part of a sisterhood—and they examined together how women had colluded with society in limiting their choices and lowering their aspirations. In the 1970s, several books appeared describing the lonely life of the woman manager, the unwelcome reception many women received upon entering organizations, and the need to recruit more women for entry-level management positions (Hennig & Jardim, 1977; Gordon & Strober, 1975; Loring & Wells, 1972).

OD practitioners, spurred on by the growing interest in women's issues, designed a variety of programs to heighten an awareness of these issues in the work place. By 1975, for example, NTL Institute was offering four programs for women's development. The core program (a prerequisite for the other three) was designed "to provide a context where women can explore at length personal, interpersonal, societal, and political issues around the sex-role stereotypes which affect their self-image, feelings, behavior and goals." Forward-looking corporations such as Digital Equipment Corporation and Connecticut General Life Insurance (now CIGNA) sponsored awareness programs for women as part of their management development effort.

Some programs included men as well as women, such as the "Male-Female Awareness Program" sponsored by Northwestern Bell Telephone Company in 1977 and 1978. Participants in this program were told that the objective was "to provide an opportunity for you to become aware of your own attitudes and feelings around male/female communication and interactions on the job" and "to help arrive at a common understanding of what we mean by the word sexism, sexist behavior, and individual and institutional sexist practices." During this four-day program, participants read numerous articles, viewed films on the socialization of men and of women, and talked at length in small groups— sometimes in "mixed sex" groups, sometimes in "same sex" groups.

In the mid-1970s, the prevailing mood concerning women's issues was optimistic. Many assumed that as the numbers of women in entry-level management positions continued to increase dramatically, only a decade or so would pass before women would rise to top leadership positions in corporate America. Moreover, some thought that sexism and sex role stereotyping might possibly be vanishing phenomena.

Learning the ropes: Developing women's skills as managers

In the 1970s, while some OD practitioners focused on awareness and attitudes, others concentrated on teaching women new skills enabling them to "catch up" with their male counterparts. The socialization of women was a recurrent theme of many articles and books, ranging from serious conceptualizations (e.g., Miller, 1976) to more pragmatic works (e.g., Harragan, 1978). Numerous authors described how women had been socialized to be passive, accommodating, and subordinate. Because women typically had not played competitive sports when young, many argued, they lacked certain skills—such as competing, knowing how to move beyond a loss or to accept a win, or functioning as team players— useful for the world of work. For example, Harragan's (1978) first chapter is entitled "Working Is a Game Women Never Learned to Play." OD practitioners tended to agree that women needed to learn the ropes if they wished to board the organization ship, and that this meant developing programs to teach women the skills they had missed along the way. Such efforts clearly indicate the commonly held assumption that if women were to succeed, they had to become more like men. As Harragan put it (p. 66), "You're in the ball game—fight, team, fight!"

In the mid-1970s, much attention was focused on the effects of the "old boy network" on women's advancement. Success in the corporation, people were repeatedly told, depends as much on who one knows as on how competent one is. Even as late as 1985, middle managers in a large Boston bank reported that to get ahead in the bank one needed to have gone to Harvard or Dartmouth, to play golf, and to live in a suburb beginning with the letter "W." Women were encouraged to be more political in their work relationships and to recognize, at last, that attention to detail and conscientious fulfillment of their work responsibilities alone might not get them too far.

OD practitioners in the 1970s designed various skills programs for women to help with this process. For example, in 1975 NTL Institute offered three such programs. One called "Skills in Action" was aimed at helping women "translate their new perspective into behavior." The brochure describing the program stated that it addressed topics such as life planning, career development, conflict utilization, risk taking, creative problem solving, assertiveness training, issues of sexuality and body, power and powerlessness, rejection, feedback, and ambivalence about success. The second program, "Women and Management," focused on some practical skills such as problem solving, supervising, decision making, and running meetings, but still retained an emphasis on changing dysfunctional, self-limiting attitudes such as deference and dependency.

The third skills program, "Women and Power," had the stated goal of sharpening "power skills." The brochure claimed, "For years women have been denied real power in their personal and professional lives and have been taught to believe that needing power is inappropriate for women, that seeking and using power are somehow un-feminine." The program was advertised as an opportunity for women to deal with their feelings about power. Although the description discussed skills, the actual focus was on helping women change their attitudes and perhaps become better able to rock the boat when necessary.

These programs differed greatly from the 10-week management development program for women initiated by Margaret Hennig and Anne Jardim at the Simmons Graduate School of Management. Since 1977, this program for women has featured the study of financial management, mathematics, and economics. It is geared toward middle managers who have acquired budgetary and supervisory responsibilities, but have not been trained for them. In short, as Hennig and Jardim put it, their target is the "quantitatively disadvantaged woman." This program, however, also includes the study of interpersonal skills, such "managing for influence," how to maneuver politically in organizations, and how to manage one's career, as do the four-week and one-week versions of the course.

Redesigning the ship: Modifying organizational systems and structures

The third basic approach to developing women in organizations has made the structures and systems of organizations the targets of change efforts. Kanter (1977) persuasively argues that the job makes the person. She claims that if women in organizations appear passive, unmotivated, and lacking in drive, this is because they typically hold positions with little opportunity and power. Anyone "stuck" in a low-level, dead-end job would tend to behave this way and thus seem uncommitted, incompetent, and unpromotable. When women are placed in jobs with long career ladders and greater opportunity, Kanter asserts, they tend to behave differently, becoming more active, more involved, and more effective. According to this reasoning, organizational systems must be changed to provide more opportunity for employees—especially for women.

OD practitioners who accepted this structural theory approached the development of women from a new angle. For example, in the mid-1970s, the managers of General Electric Medical Systems were concerned that so few of the women they hired for sales jobs remained with the firm longer than three months, and hired some OD consultants to address this problem. The data the OD team gathered suggested that one of the key factors in the success of the men in sales force was the informal day-to-day training they received from the more experienced sales staff.

Rather than focusing on how the female sales representatives differed in style or attitude from their male counterparts, the consultants examined how the women's opportunities and experiences differed from the men's. They found that, in the usual course of events, when a woman joined the sales force, she rarely received the kind of casual but consistent on-the-job training and support accorded to men. Based on this finding, the team recommended a new extended program to offer the kind of training and support the women had been missing. A pilot program was launched, and the number of women who stayed on the sales force for more than 90 days increased significantly. The consultants had intervened at the systems level rather than directed their efforts at ''improving'' the women or changing the men.

In the mid-1970s, OD practitioners seeking to modify organizational structures so as to give women more opportunities suggested various structural changes, including ''mentoring'' systems, career development programs, redesigned career ladders, cross-training, and incentive systems. Advocates of this structural approach believe that the beauty of these kinds of interventions is that they not only develop women in organizations, but they help develop all employees. And beyond that, they do not blame anyone for the past.

Steering toward androgyny

In the 1980s, perceptions about the needs of organizational women began to shift again. In many quarters the optimism evident 10 years ago has diminished, and people now wonder whether time alone will really close the gender gap, especially in the ranks of top management. Although a great many women became managers in the 1970s, few had risen to the top by 1986. In 1985, only one *Fortune* 500 company had a female chief executive, and no women were in the wings. At IBM in 1973, for example, women represented fewer than five percent of all managers and fewer than two percent of the senior managers (Much done, 1984). A decade later, the overall percentage had increased considerably—at that time approximately 26% of all IBM managers were women—yet the number of women in senior management had only increased to 5% (this small increase represented an improvement, yet was also disappointing). Furthermore, the climate has changed regarding an awareness of problems related to gender. "Sexism is no longer a legitimate issue," one woman consultant to a *Fortune* 500 company recently told me.

The issue in the mid-1980s was that women had begun leaving corporations. In 1984, the leaders of four *Fortune* 500 companies expressed concern to one organizational consulting firm that their fast-track women were quitting at just about the time they were to be promoted to senior management positions. In April of that year, *Fortune* magazine highlighted the issue with a vivid illustration: A woman was depicted grasping for the top of a ladder whose highest rungs were broken.

Attitudes about women managers have changed during the past 20 years. A 1985 replication of the *Harvard Business Review* survey of 1965 found some dramatic shifts (Sutton & Moore, 1985). In 1985, only nine percent of the men surveyed and four percent of the women believed that "women rarely expect or desire authority"; this is good news considering that a majority held this view in 1965. At the same time, however, 20% of the male respondents to the 1985 survey and 40% of the female respondents believed that "the business community will never fully accept women executives." This was not the only bad news presented in the *Harvard Business Review*. The same issue reporting the survey results also presented an advertisement for the Harvard Business School's Program for Management Development, which included a photograph of 15 persons in a classroom. This group, identified as the "next generation of senior managers," consisted of 15 men—and no women.

Some new winds have begun stirring, though. In her book entitled *In a Different Voice* (1982), Gilligan argues that women's value systems are typically quite different from men's, explaining that women generally emphasize relationships, whereas men tend to emphasize rules and justice. For example, she notes that if a group of girls are playing a game and a disagreement arises, they usually will stop the game to preserve the harmony and relationship; in a similar situation, boys will refer to the rules to settle the conflict. Gilligan asserts that these values typical of women should be considered different from— rather than inferior to—those of men.

In *Feminine Leadership,* Loden (1985) states that women's leadership style typically differs from men's along four dimensions. That is, women usually prefer cooperation rather than competition, rely on intuition as well as rational thinking in solving problems, emphasize the long-term health of the organization rather than focusing on short-term gains, and usually favor team and participative approaches. Gilligan's positive assessment of women's contributions is being applied to organizational life and has provided a different perspective on the developmental needs of women.

In 1985, NTL Institute offered a program for women that, according to the catalogue, focused on factors that "separate and unite" black and white women. This sense of sisterhood has diminished; the word sounds almost anachronistic in 1989. The 1986 NTL brochure listed "sustaining a feminine identity" among the objectives for its sessions on professional and personal skills for women managers. At the 1985 OD Network Conference in San Francisco, these evolving ideas of the 1980s were expressed by many practitioners. One description of a workshop stated, "Men and women are raised with different experiences, assumptions, beliefs, and values. These differences may contribute to a different way of being in the world and a different approach to working in organizations." Another workshop outline took this idea a step further: "Feminist process will be demonstrated [in the workshop] as being key to a smooth running and peaceful organization and world."

Conclusion

Clearly, programs at training institutes and in corporations shift with the prevailing winds; as the "hot" issues for women change, so do the programs offered. Fewer corporate programs on gender issues are available now than in the 1970s, and in 1986 CIGNA presented no "women's programs" at all. Does this decrease reflect a lack of special needs for women? Or does it indicate a lack of concern for existing problems? The answer probably is a bit of both. Women as a group have made some progress in their development, so in many cases a special track no longer seems appropriate. Indeed, the new breed of women managers might actually consider some of these programs sexist or condescending and want no part of them.

One cannot deny, however, that at the federal level commitment to affirmative action has diminished. How this has affected the commitment of corporate America to developing women and increasing the number of women managers can only be estimated now, but many OD practitioners have noted a reduced interest in women's issues across the board. According to *Bricker's International Directory* (1985), only 11% of those who attended management development programs lasting two weeks or more in 1985 were women.

Moreover, although the idea that the "feminine" world view has something valuable to offer is "in the air," acceptance of this has not yet reached the corporate training room. The subtitle of Alice Sargent's book *The Androgynous Manager* (1981) is *Blending Male and Female Styles for Today's Organization*. In the future, instead of OD programs for women, we may see organizations changing their course once again by seeking to transform themselves into androgynous organizations. Others may move toward valuing the differences between men and women. "Managing diversity" has already emerged as a new focus and way of addressing the topic of women in the work place.

Look back on events of the past 20 years, one can see substantial shifts in how OD practitioners have perceived the needs of women managers and in the kinds of programs they have designed to meet those needs. From the vantage point of 1989, we can safely conclude that real progress has occurred since 1964. An awareness of the issues of sexism and sex-role stereotyping has increased dramatically. Efforts to develop women's managerial skills have also improved, with considerable resources spent both to provide special skills programs for women managers and to enroll increasing numbers of women in traditional management development programs.

With respect to attempts to modify the systems and structure of organizations to provide more opportunity for women, the results are far less conclusive. The organizational boat was rocked a bit in the 1970s, but the fundamental structures of our corporations have remained essentially unchanged. Organizations are still designed as if all employees were married men whose wives stay at home. Although women now generally receive a more congenial welcome to organizational life than they did in the past, they are usually rewarded only for adapting to the prevailing structures, which many consider procrustean beds. The work in feminine leadership is interesting because it implies that organizations can benefit from incorporating the "feminine" perspective, and suggests that some structural changes may occur in the future.

As we move into the uncharted waters of the 1990s, a new set of women's needs are taking precedence: child care, parental leave, permanent part-time jobs, and flexible schedules. If these issues are successfully addressed, we can take the next step in enabling women managers—as well as their male counterparts—to develop their full potential in the organizational context. To accomplish this, however, we may have to rock the boat as well as chart a new course.

REFERENCES

Bowman, G. W., Worthy, N. B., & Greyser, S. A. (1965, July/August). Are women executives people? *Harvard Business Review, 43*(4), 15-28, 164-178.

Bricker's international directory: University executive development programs (1985). South Chatham, MA: Bricker Publications.

Friedan, B. (1963). *The feminine mystique.* New York: W. W. Norton.

Gilligan, C. (1982). *In a different voice.* Cambridge, MA: Harvard University Press.

Gordon, F. E., & Strober, M. H. (1975). *Bringing women into management.* New York: McGraw-Hill.

Harragan, B. (1978). *Games mother never taught you.* New York: Warner Books.

Hennig, M., & Jardim, A. (1977). *The managerial woman.* New York: Doubleday.

Kanter, R. M. (1977). *Men and women of the corporation.* New York: Basic Books, Inc.

Loden, M. (1985). *Feminine leadership.* New York: Times Books.

Loring, R., & Wells, T. (1972). *Breakthrough: Women into management.* New York: Van Nostrand Reinhold.

Miller, J. B. (1976). *Toward a new psychology of women.* Boston: Beacon Press.

Much done, more to do. (1984, May-June). *Think: The IBM Magazine.*

Sargent, A. G. (1981). *The androgynous manager: Blending male and female management styles for today's organization.* New York: Amacom.

Sutton, C. D., & Moore, K. K. (1985, September/October). Executive women—20 years later. *Harvard Business Review,* 63(5), 43-66.

The Cultural Awareness Hierarchy: A Model in OD Interventions in Cross-Cultural Settings

Robert Chasnoff
Peter Muniz

Organization Development (OD) practitioners increasingly find themselves intervening in cross-cultural work settings, both at the international level and intranational level.

At the international level, corporate activities such as buying, selling, and producing products and services cause many "home office" personnel to come into contact with people of different cultures. Until a few years ago, the home office was almost always in the U.S., but now it may be located in some other country, with its subsidiary located in the U.S. The activities of public-sector organizations also frequently cause their members to work with people from other cultures.

At the intranational level, Equal Employment Opportunity/Affirmative Action legislation has increasingly brought members of the dominant culture into contact with those of other cultures within the same work setting. The successful recruitment of foreign professionals and scientists who receive their degrees from U.S. educational institutions is also contributing to the multicultural nature of the U.S. work force (Masterson & Murphy, 1986). Mergers, acquisitions, and organizational moves often bring persons from widely separated—and thus culturally unique—geographic areas into a common work setting. Moreover, the increasing movement toward globalized corporations is amplifying the multicultural component of those organizations.

Cross-cultural work settings challenge people to work effectively with one another despite their "cultural differences." Sometimes these differences act as barriers that prevent people from achieving results and positive interpersonal relationships, and other times they act as masks or smoke screens that

---

prevent organization members from identifying and resolving the real factors impeding effectiveness and communications.

Note this example of a situation from a multinational organization. Two persons, each of a different culture, were members of the same work team. These persons were in conflict with each other, and this was adversely affecting the team. Both insisted that this conflict stemmed from irreconcilable cultural differences. During a team building meeting, a consultant (one of the authors of this chapter) sensed that the cause of the conflict actually lay elsewhere, and said to the warring individuals, "Look—if the two of you were of the same culture, you'd still have the same conflict!" The individuals glared at the consultant, stared at each other in shock—and eventually proceeded to confront and resolve the real source of their conflict. Similar episodes have occurred in other organizations.

To work in cross-cultural settings, OD practitioners must be able to apply certain critical factors that are necessary for fully understanding such settings. Figure 1 presents The Cultural Awareness Hierarchy, a conceptual model outlining these important factors as a series of steps and conditions needed for an individual to understand, relate to, and work productively with members of other cultures. One must consider these in the order presented for every step of the OD process. For example, to attain the knowledge and understanding needed for Level IV, one must first have attained the knowledge and understanding required for Levels I-III. The model is universal. It is applicable in either a highly heterogeneous country or in a country whose cultural base tends to be homogeneous.

If the members of one culture treat members of another culture in a condescending manner, conflict is inevitable. Sometimes expatriates arrive in a host country lacking knowledge of the nation's culture and bringing instead biases and stereotypes. For example, they may think, "These people are dumb, slow learners, and primitive." Such opinions get communicated to employees of the host country and eventually affect organizational relationships and outcomes.

In one company, as soon as someone from the home office was assigned to work in a foreign subsidiary, the kidding and teasing began. Some would say that the person was "being sent to the boondocks" or was being punished for committing some gross error; others expressed concern and sorrow for the person who would soon be working with "that primitive group." Some of these comments were made in jest, but most were serious. Such behavior demonstrated the negative view the home office staff had of the employees of the foreign subsidiary—a view that was often ill founded and built on stereotypes and rumors rather than actual data. It caused the person being transferred to arrive at the new location already biased against the host country nationals. Members of upper and middle management contributed to such teasing until

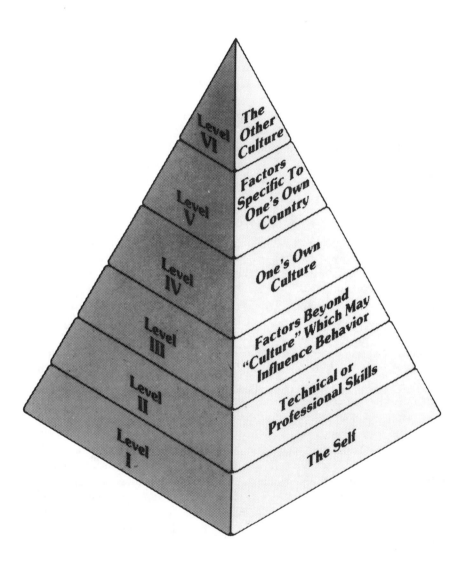

Figure 1. The Cultural Awareness Hierarchy™
© Robert Chasnoff and Peter Muniz

This chapter discusses the six levels of The Cultural Awareness Hierarchy, states why each factor was placed at a specific level within the model, presents examples related to each level, and describes how the OD practitioner can use The Hierarchy.

Beware, however, that **focusing on "cultural differences" could be a trap.** The first challenge facing the OD practitioner and client in a cross-cultural setting is that of erasing the notion that differences related to culture must be a major factor influencing the organization. In truth, cultural differences have a much smaller impact on work settings than people generally wish to believe. Batdorf (1980) argues that frequently people call something a "cultural problem" when it actually is a problem of a different sort. We recognize that cultural differences **do** matter, and thus include this factor in The Cultural Awareness Hierarchy, but only at a proper level in relation to other factors influencing results and interpersonal relationships.

The Cultural Awareness Hierarchy

Level I: The self. At the base of The Hierarchy is knowledge of one's self. People must be aware of their own interpersonal abilities and understand their roles and behaviors as members of their own cultures. One's self-awareness, interpersonal ability, experiences, background, education, values, and attractiveness as a person constitute aspects of the self that are crucial at this first level of The Hierarchy.

When trying to determine the underlying causes of negative results and interpersonal difficulties in a cross-cultural work setting, one should begin with Level I of The Hierarchy. For example, when conflict occurs among persons of different cultures, the facilitator should consider the individuals first. Some persons sent to work in cross-cultural settings cannot work amicably even within their own cultures; obnoxious individuals usually remain obnoxious no matter where they go. People who lack self-awareness and will not accept feedback or try to change their behavior in their native cultures will most likely cause conflict in any culture, notwithstanding their technical/professional expertise or their knowledge of the other culture. Such persons continue their counter-productive behavior when they and those around them focus on "cultural differences" rather than confront individual behavior as the major cause of conflict and other problems.

Level II: Skills. At this level, one directs attention to technical or professional skills important for success in one's own culture. All the appreciation and understanding in the world will not suffice if one lacks the basic tools of competence. Thus, this level calls for an honest assessment of skills.

If a person is technically or professionally incompetent, or if others have a low regard for that person's competence, difficulties will arise when the person works with members of another culture—regardless of how much that person knows about the other culture. For example, in a foreign subsidiary of a large multinational company, the employees from the host country often complained about having to work with expatriates and "helpers" from the headquarters who lacked necessary technical/professional skills. They also suspected that in some cases cross-cultural training was substituted for technical competence. Moreover, some questioned top management's motives in sending incompetent employees to the foreign subsidiary; one wondered, "What are they telling us when they send us their discards?"

Carefully selected international assignments for developmental purposes can contribute significantly to a person's career progress and the company's results (Callahan, 1989). But sending employees to another country to gain on-the-job experience that they could well gain at home causes problems. Instead of being assets from the headquarters, they represent burdens to the foreign subsidiaries. Thus, technically or professionally incompetent persons and those lacking experience lead to difficulties. A person with appropriate expertise, however, will more easily gain acceptance in another culture—provided, of course, that the other levels of The Cultural Awareness Hierarchy are addressed satisfactorily.

Level III: Factors beyond culture. This level emphasizes the importance of factors beyond culture that may influence behavior. These include poverty, racism, international relations, organizational health, and sexism. Each can result in behavior too often ascribed incorrectly to culture.

In our experience, conflicts and problems related to Level III occur more often in cross-cultural settings than those related to the other levels. The placement of these factors at this level enables one to focus on people in a generic sense before specifically addressing the cultures involved.

If the members of one culture treat members of another culture in a condescending manner, conflict is inevitable. Sometimes expatriates arrive in a host country lacking knowledge of the nation's culture and bringing instead biases and stereotypes. For example, they may think, "These people are dumb, slow learners, and primitive." Such opinions get communicated to employees of the host country and eventually affect organizational relationships and outcomes.

In one company, as soon as someone from the home office was assigned to work in a foreign subsidiary, the kidding and teasing began. Some would say that the person was "being sent to the boondocks" or was being punished for committing some gross error; others expressed concern and sorrow for the person who would soon be working with "that primitive group." Some of these comments were made in jest, but most were serious. Such behavior demonstrated the negative view the home office staff had of the employees of the foreign subsidiary—a view that was often ill founded and built on stereotypes and rumors rather than actual data. It caused the person being transferred to arrive at the new location already biased against the host country nationals. Members of upper and middle management contributed to such teasing until the OD consultants notified them that this was a major influence on the cross-cultural work setting in the foreign subsidiary.

Allowing home office staff to use a host country as a vacation "paradise" can wreak havoc in the foreign subsidiary. In one company, unnecessary field trips by U.S. personnel to the foreign subsidiary caused such problems for the host country plant that the general manager obtained an agreement with his subordinates and U.S. counterparts that all such trips had to be cleared by him. Immediately afterward, the number of field trips decreased significantly!

Organizational factors such as culture, norms, policies, and economic conditions are addressed at Level III in The Hierarchy. The relationship between a member of the headquarters staff and someone in a line position in a foreign subsidiary may be influenced more by the roles they fill in the organization (Muniz, 1981) than by their different cultures. In addition, the political climate affecting the countries of the people in a cross-cultural work setting may affect their relationships and productivity. Finally, minority group members experiencing institutional racism may become angry—sometimes violently so—not because of their culture, but because of the treatment they receive from institutions representing the dominant culture.

The next three levels of The Hierarchy discussed below focus on culture.

Level IV: One's own culture. At this level, attention is directed to one's own culture. The major focus is on understanding and accepting the behaviors, passions, and motivations based on one's own culture. The rationale behind this is that only when a person understands culture-general concepts and her or his own culture is that person ready to understand and deal with people from other cultures.

Most of us take our own cultures for granted. This poses no problem as long as one never leaves one's culture, or that culture is not infiltrated by outsiders. As soon as persons enter another culture or experience the influx of people from another culture, however, they must analyze the culture they previously took for granted so that they can study and understand their own behavior and that of people from the other culture.

Benedict (1959) warns that one should resist the temptation to analyze other cultures by using one's own culture as a standard. This temptation proves particularly strong when people fail to understand their own cultures, leading them to judge other people's behaviors while using themselves as models of what is correct. In such cases, when faced with others who behave differently than they do, these people become judgmental and may even reject members of another culture whose behavior is "incorrect." Such a lack of understanding of culture in general, and of one's own culture in particular, may, for example, lead people to describe themselves as "patriotic" while they accuse foreigners of being "nationalistic."

Once people gain an understanding of culture-general concepts, they become better able to understand and accept cultural differences through a knowledge of the many determinants of culture and the reasons underlying differences among cultures. Given this conceptual base and an understanding of their own cultures, they become less self-centered about their own cultures and more open minded about other cultures as different ways others have developed for coping with or responding to the various situations in which all humans find themselves, regardless of geographic location.

When they analyze their own culture—including the nation's history and geography—many U.S. Americans "discover" that Mexico and Canada are also part of North America, and that Central America and South America share the same hemisphere with the U.S. Furthermore, such analysis enables them to gain insight into the resentment other "Americans" feel toward the U.S. when its citizens use the term "American" to refer only to themselves and their nation. Thus, many of the beliefs and behaviors subsumed under the term "culture" lend themselves to better scrutiny when tested against reality. Moreover, confronting the myths we accept helps us to identify more easily the similarities and differences among our own cultures and those of others.

Level V: Factors specific to one's own country. This level of The Hierarchy emphsizes the need to understand elements specific to one's own nation. For example, some countries are monocultural, others are multicultural, and some may be considered "melting pots," as the U.S. used to be called. One can expect more consistent behavior among the citizens of a monocultural nation than among those of a multicultural one.

For many years, immigrants to the U.S. were forced into a mythical melting pot. Many decided they had to bury cultural features from their native lands as part of the price of assimilation into the American culture. Often these immigrants, whose descendants are now members of the majority culture in the U.S., survived by leading dual lives, one acceptable to the dominant culture and one acceptable only in their well-insulated ghettos.

In the cross-cultural training programs we conduct, second-and third-generation Americans frequently describe experiences and family stories they thought they had forgotten about children's being told to avoid speaking their "native" language outside the home, or to dress or behave in ways acceptable to the dominant culture (Muniz & Chasnoff, 1983). These recollections often are touched by rage, a sense of inferiority, or shame related to these persons' cultural ties to their ancestors.

Naisbitt (1982, 1984) predicted that people throughout the world would become more assertive about preserving their languages and cultures—and this is now happening. In the U.S., minorities have been doing this for years, at no small price. Increasing numbers of minority group members are saying, "Yes, I am proud to be an American, but I am also proud to be a member of my minority group. I refuse to reject this group's culture, and I will behave according to both cultures, even to the point of using two languages.'' Such a stand often evokes a negative response from second- and third-generation Americans, who remember the pain associated with giving up their own cultures of origin to gain acceptance in the U.S. Some even changed their names, a practice reminiscent of black slaves' being forcibly stripped of their African names and assigned Anglo-Saxon ones. Some blacks have asserted their culture of origin by adopting African names, an action other Americans sometimes find difficult to understand or accept.

Most persons in the U.S. have finally come to recognize that the U.S. is neither monocultural—as Japan tends to be—nor a melting pot. The realistic, correct view is that the U.S. is a multicultural country.

This level of The Hierarchy also addresses such circumstances as Puerto Rico's relationship to the U.S., Belgium's dual-language situation, and the political-religious controversy in Ireland.

Level VI: The other culture. After acquiring the knowledge and understanding represented by the previous levels, one can profitably pay attention to another culture with the expectation of gaining a more productive understanding of what makes the members of that culture ''tick'' and being less likely to stereotype, judge, or scorn them.

When people work in cross-cultural settings, knowlege about one another's cultures can help bridge major gaps. Running the risk of offending someone because one lacks the necessary knowledge of or sensitivity to that person's culture is foolish. The literature on this subject consistently warns us about the dangers associated with cross-cultural blunders, including losing business deals, low productivity, conflict, and poor interpersonal relations.

Language sometimes impedes communications and results (Metge & Kinlock, 1984; Muniz & Chasnoff, 1985). Learning the language of another culture is important because this increases cultural understanding. Making some effort to learn the other culture's language, no matter how rudimentary one's knowledge is, conveys a positive message to members of that culture. A refusal to even try conveys a negative message. Americans working in cross-cultural settings often face language barriers because of their refusal to learn another language. This frequently supports foreigners' view of Americans as self-centered and arrogant. Furthermore, some Americans become impatient when dealing with persons from other cultures who do not speak English well, leading these persons to resent Americans and possibly think, ''Here I am struggling to speak English, and the American is still dissatisfied.''

How to apply The Cultural Awareness Hierarchy

Before intervening in cross-cultural work settings or applying The Cultural Awareness Hierarchy to others, you must apply the model to yourself. Initially, you must determine the extent to which you possess the personal characteristics required to work in cross-cultural settings (Level I). Some would argue that self-awareness and interpersonal ability are cornerstones of the OD profession, and perhaps a significant majority of OD practitioners possess these attributes, but you must still address this level of The Hierarchy. Next, you must confront yourself as a professional, determine your strengths and weaknesses, and decide what changes you must make before intervening in a cross-cultural work setting (Level II).

You must also focus on your contributions to and ability to address factors beyond "culture" that may be influencing you and the client (Level III). Following this, you must come to understand your own culture (Levels IV and V). We have found that many Americans use hyphenated cultural designations to identify themselves (e.g., African-American, Italian-American, Mexican-American, Spanish-American). You must identify and analyze every component of your culture(s). Finally, you must learn about the other culture(s) represented within the client organization (Level VI). This includes making an effort to learn the language of that culture.

We offer the following tips for OD practitioners planning interventions in cross-cultural settings.

1. Do not focus on cultural differences initially.
2. Apply The Cultural Awareness Hierarchy at each step in the OD process. This includes ensuring that your interventions are not ethnocentric and that they do not violate the norms of anyone's culture.
3. If cultural cliques exist in the organization, avoid joining any of them. Maintain neutrality and deal with all cliques equally. You must also avoid becoming identified with the company headquarters by those in a foreign subsidiary, which usually begins when home office personnel tell a consultant about their problems and experiences with "those people" in the overseas division. Similarly, you should prevent those in the home office from perceiving that you have been "co-opted" by members of the foreign subsidiary. This can be difficult, because whenever you explain the point of view of one cultural group to the other, you may be perceived as identifying with the group whose position you are trying to relate.
4. Be sure to confirm whatever data you gather about a cultural group. Research involving cross-cultural settings has produced a plethora of hints and tidbits, but some of this is simplistic, incomplete, or misleading. Although you may start by reviewing such findings, verify this information with your own research and experience.

5. Do not forget about the individual. Knowledge about a culture provides generalities; the individual provides specifics. Moreover, within any culture, variations occur among individual members—even in homogeneous countries. Do not let cultural information act as a barrier to understanding individuals.

6. Remember that you do not have to abandon your own culture. You must understand the other culture and ensure that you do not violate its norms, but do not try to become a member of the other culture. When persons from different cultures relate to one another successfully, they do so through a process permitting each party to use behaviors and skills appropriate for temporary, productive interactions among themselves. This enables the parties to maintain their own cultural integrity while working with one another. Of course, persons who interact successfully for long periods with members of another culture may eventually internalize elements of that culture. In such cases, one either becomes bicultural or develops a third culture comprising elements from both cultures involved.

These six guidelines have proven useful in our work in cross-cultural settings. We hope that they, along with The Cultural Awareness Hierarchy, will also be of service to others engaging in these efforts.

REFERENCES

Batdorf, L. L. (1980, August). Culturally sensitive training. *Training and Development Journal,* pp. 28-41.

Benedict, R. (1959). *Patterns of culture.* Boston: Houghton Mifflin.

Callahan, M. R. (1989). Preparing the new global manager. *Training and Development Journal,* pp. 29-32.

Masterson, B., & Murphy, B. (1986, April). Internal cross-cultural management. *Training and Development Journal,* pp. 56-60.

Metge, J., & Kinloch, P. (1984). *Talking past each other: Problems of cross-cultural communication.* Wellington, New Zealand: Victoria University Press.

Muniz, P. (1981). Diagnosing and resolving line-staff conflict. In R. Chasnoff & P. Muniz, *Managing human resources: A practical guide.* Somerset, NJ: Laboratory for Applied Behavioral Science.

Muniz, P., & Chasnoff, R. (1983, October). The Cultural Awareness Hierarchy: A model for promoting understanding. *Training and Development Journal,* pp. 24-27.

Muniz, P., & Chasnoff, R. (1985). Teambuilding in organizations: An approach to improve productivity. *Revista de Ciencias Comerciales, 7*(1/2), 15-21.

Naisbitt, J. (1982). *Megatrends.* New York: Warner Books.

Naisbitt, J. (1984). *Megatrends* (2nd ed.). New York: Warner Books.

The Use of Group Relations Methods in the African-American Community

Jimmy E. Jones
Jean Thomas Griffin

Two issues faced by the A. K. Rice Institute since its inception have been the inclusion of so-called "minorities" (which usually includes African-American persons) in its Group Relations Conferences and the application of the tools, methods, and knowledge gained from these conferences to "everyday life." That these issues are often linked is no accident, because minority groups are frequently thought to have high stakes in psychosocial and political change in the functioning of U.S. organizations, institutions, and government. This thinking partly stems from others' viewing African-Americans as the persons who will gain the most from such change. In reality, however, African-Americans and other so-called minorities are often unfairly treated as the objectified targets of the urgent need of society as a whole for change and growth. Thus, other groups end up "working out their thing" through the experiences of African-Americans with respect to change, both inside and outside Group Relations Conferences. This situation led us to explore the issues involved in using group relations methods in the African-American community.

Methods

Our major method of approaching this topic was analyzing our own experiences and formal educational backgrounds as these related to past and possible uses of group relations methods in the African-American community. Our particular perspective is based on the following.

1. We are both African-American persons interested in actively seeking change and development for the African-American community and the broader community.

2. We are both trained to use group relations methods and have done so extensively, both within the institutions in which we work and as external consultants.

3. In addition to our informal education and experiences leading to an understanding of the psychosocial/political dynamics of change in the African-American community, we have both been formally trained in the disciplines of education and psychology.

Thus, to collect data for this chapter, we met regularly to define and refine our concepts about the use of group relations methods in the African-American community.

Results

Our work led us to three major findings.

1. Group Relations Conferences are valuable for understanding organizations and basic organizational change. This leads us to focus in this chapter on the philosophy and methods of Group Relations Conferences that we consider particularly valuable for helping the African-American community and broader community move toward change.

2. Group Relations Conferences are valuable for understanding the psychosocial and political relationship between the oppressors and the oppressed. We believe that often this crucial issue is not fully understood or explored with respect to its impact on positive change.

3. Group Relations Conferences and methods can be used effectively in the African-American community only if they are modified extensively. Given our first two findings, we considered it helpful to offer concrete suggestions for change. The following section presents reflections on these suggestions for change to make the methods more accessible and useful to the African-American community.

Organizations and basic organizational change

Group Relations Conferences can provide valuable experiences for understanding basic organizational concepts. Although we do not necessarily recommend that all community leaders and workers attend these conferences, we do feel that their conceptual framework would probably help many develop better knowledge of and approaches to community organizations. "Tavistock"

Group Relations Conferences have their philosophical basis in psychoanalytic and social systems concepts that we consider valuable for understanding the complexity of organizational change, change in the African-American community, and change in the broader community. Two basic constructs of Group Relations Conferences are relevant to this point.

First, the psychoanalytic approach is helpful because community change agents must become more aware of the dynamics of the individual psyche if they are to work effectively on the more complex levels of groups, organizations, and communities. Although we disagree with the degree to which Freudian concepts and the therapeutic approach are adopted by some staff members of Group Relations Conferences, we do consider an intrapsychically based model—such as that of psychoanalysis—valuable.[1] The **technique** of psychoanalysis—which serves as a primary determinant of the role of the consultant with respect to "here-and-now" events—is appropriate for addressing an individual's feelings and fantasies about important concepts of authority (the right to work), leadership (the ability to get people to follow someone), power (all the resources at one's disposal), boundaries (internal and external limits), and primary tasks (the work that must be performed for a group or organization to exist). To move organizations effectively, one must understand and deal with these issues at some overt conceptual level. That is, one cannot move organizations if one cannot move individuals.

Second, because of their broad social systems orientation, Group Relations Conferences represent an education model providing insights clearly applicable to everyday life. Although this point seems rather obvious, our experience has indicated that people tend to think either that the training model should be transposed totally to the "back-home" job site (which for most participants is a therapeutic or educational setting) or that its concepts should only be used for thinking about one's job and its related institutions. Clearly, however, lessons from the Group Relations Conferences have tremendous implications for political change in the larger society. Although we are not necessarily suggesting a "super" Group Relations Conferences for the NAACP or the U.S. Congress, we do believe that **applying conference-influenced** ideas about authority, representation, and other issues to social change efforts and the political arena would have a strong impact on the way this nation functions. Imagine what would happen if people came to care as much about what elected and politically appointed officials do on their behalf as participants typically care about the other Group Relations Conference participants who represent them during the intergroup or institutional event. For example, grasping and using concepts such as authority, role, and boundaries certainly would clearly help parents and community members negotiate more effectively with large urban public school systems that fail to carry out their wishes adequately.

The primary method of Group Relations Conferences—that of offering a residential, bounded, experiential, "here-and-now" event with discussions—is highly effective. It provides participants with the chance to create a micro-society in which they can examine social systems issues in depth, explore new behaviors, step back and reflect, experience the pull of dynamics, and confront authority. These are only a few of the learning opportunities available. Much of what participants learn does not become readily apparent or firmly conceptualized during the conference itself. The model is too dynamic to present "cut-and-dried" objectives, and generally the full impact of a Group Relations Conference is still felt six to twelve months afterward. Participants have reported learning about themselves and others, about large-group, small-group, intergroup, intragroup, organizational, and systems phenomena. In particular, their lessons were about the concepts of authority, power, leadership, and "followership" as these relate to themselves and their interactions with others.

Because of the above, we feel that Group Relations Conferences are valuable for understanding basic organizational change.

The psychosocial/political relationship between the oppressors and the oppressed

This crucial issue often is not fully understood or explored with respect to its impact on positive change in groups, institutions, and society at large. In Group Relations Conferences, the small study group event and large group event are especially helpful for observing this phenomenon.

For the conferences, consultants adapt methods based on psychoanalytic theory for working with group members. One of the consultant's tasks is collaborating with the group in examining the members' feelings about and understanding of the member-consultant relationship. The psychoanalytic orientation of the consultant's role contributes to members' fantasies of being oppressed or manipulated by the consultant. Typical situations related to this include the following.

- Group members act as if the consultant were forcing them to remain in a difficult or painful learning situation. In reality, though, they have several options, ranging from working constructively with the consultant to physically leaving the group.

- Group members believe that they need "permission" from the consultant to behave in a particular way, or that the consultant knows of a prescribed behavioral mode they should follow. Therefore, they collude in maintaining their "oppression" either through inaction or by acting counterproductively.

- Even though they consider the consultant an oppressor or manipulator whom they want to avoid, the group members still find themselves identifying with and wishing they were like—or liked by—the consultant. Sometimes they express these desires by assuming the mannerisms and speech patterns of the consultant.
- The group members begin to deny that they have any power (i.e., resources) at their disposal or any responsibility (i.e., accountability) for influencing the situation. Outside of the Group Relations Conference, however, the participants use their resources to conduct their lives and manage the lives and resources of other persons, and most of these resources are still available to them during the conference.

We find similar behaviors all too often in our work for change in the African-American community. Elucidating issues such as these gives African-American persons some insight into understanding the relationship between the oppressors and the oppressed.

Similarly, based on social systems theory, the intergroup or institutional event of Group Relations Conferences provides a framework for understanding the psychosocial/political relationships among groups. Such dynamics include the approach/avoidance behavior participants display toward the conference staff members, which almost immobilizes them. Participants strongly want to obtain consultation from the staff, and just as strongly want to avoid the staff. In the African-American community, evidence of similar immobilization includes the difficulties African-American groups have in organizing themselves to negotiate for positive change with local officials, members of Boards of Education, city planners, and the like.

Participants perceive and experience an oppressor/oppressed relationship in most Group Relations Conferences. Both inside and outside of conferences, psychological and political boundaries between the oppressors and oppressed are often unclear and difficult to identify. Understanding this lack of clarity is useful for people engaged in working toward positive change in the African-American community. This is why Group Relations Conferences are valuable for helping us understand the psychosocial/political relationship between the oppressors and the oppressed.

Modifications needed
for the African-American community

Despite the value of Group Relations Conferences, the model must undergo some changes if it is to remain dynamic, constructive, and educational. The parent organization—A. K. Rice Institute—must lead the way in altering this model to make it more valuable and applicable to a more diverse population.

Modification should address three primary areas: recruitment and "intake," the structure (or methods), and follow-up applications. Although we specifically focus on how the model can be used in the African-American community, many of the modifications we suggest would also benefit the broader community.

The recruitment and **intake** process for Group Relations Conferences must adopt new techniques for increasing the diversity of the participants and staff. Currently, the lack of communication, sponsorship, time, and money appear to be inhibiting recruitment in the African-American community. Communication is usually directed only at small populations of health workers and educators. This is understandable, for the model was imported by psychologists and psychiatrists from England, and members of these professions are not trained to advertise their services aggressively—and in some cases they are explicitly prohibited from recruiting clients for their institutions or practices. Such concerns and ethical traditions, however, are not applicable to Group Relations Conferences, and can have a negative influence on intake procedures.

Group Relations Conferences are usually sponsored by and presented within institutions controlled by whites. Many of these organizations are alien to the African-American community, some even blatantly hostile. In such cases, these institutions foster suspicion or avoidance among African-Americans. The cost and time required to participate in the conferences also inhibits recruitment. In this society, African-American persons at all levels generally earn less than their white counterparts; therefore, most cannot afford to pay for themselves to attend either residential or nonresidential conferences. Moreover, many have employers who would not permit them to take the time to engage in such educational activities.

Broadening the participant base of Group Relations Conferences so that it becomes a more heterogeneous, interdisciplinary body also requires a simultaneous broadening of the staff and management. Innovative and aggressive intake procedures are needed, along with sponsorship by more African-American educational and community organizations and the presentation of conferences at low cost and at sites accessible and acceptable to the African-American community.

One of the serious drawbacks related to modifying the **structure of the methods** is the conferences' emphasis on Freudian concepts. This tends to place the focus on evidence of pathology during the conference rather than on possibilities for positive, collaborative learning experiences. Staff members should seek to make conferences educational activities rather than parodies of mental health practice, and should emphasize a social systems orientation rather than a psychoanalytic one. Issues-oriented conferences (e.g., those addressing relations between men and women, family relations, and racial concerns) should also be considered as a vehicle for expanding the use of this method in the African-American community. Current methods of preparing documentation should be altered so that these are written in a clear, explanatory style. The concepts addressed are difficult and complex, and the more clearly they are described, the better the participants will understand the learning contract.

Other possible structural changes include those allowing for conferences to be presented as evening workshops, weekend classes, daily classes, college courses, and special one-week classes or courses. Such educational methods would involve teaching the principles in both an experiential and didactic manner in periods varying from one hour a week for six weeks to one weekend a month for six months to a year. African-American community members could thus attend workshops without jeopardizing their employment or finances.

Finally, a real weakness in the model—as conducted in the United States—is that too often **follow-up** involves perhaps some consultant jobs by individual staff members rather than a systematic intervention. Most conferences call for ''application'' groups holding terminal discussions. Other professions, including physicians, teachers, trainers, therapists, and carpenters, have methods of encouraging and teaching people to apply what they have learned. Residencies, apprenticeships, mentor relationships, internships, role playing, co-consulting, observation, and recording are all techniques that could facilitate follow-up for Group Relations Conferences and help participants begin the process of application. Application could also be furthered by encouraging participants to come to conferences prepared to apply what they learn to a particular situation, whether this involves one's job, family, group, or organization. Ongoing post-conference discussion groups might also prove valuable. Follow-up and application efforts are most effective when presented during the intake process along with the presentation of the primary task and role. This encourages the idea that the learning does not stop when the conference ends, and that participants are expected to apply it beyond the conference.

Conclusions

The African-American community can benefit from the principles, concepts, and model of Group Relations Conferences. The intake process, model, and follow-up process must be modified, however, if these conferences are to be accepted by the African-American community. Recruitment efforts must become more aggressive and expansive so that the conference staff, management, and participants become more diverse and heterogeneous. More accessible and acceptable sites must be identified for the African-American community, and the structure must be altered to accommodate the schedules and income of working-class people. Follow-up and application processes must be developed to encourage the practical application of the skills, knowledge, and information participants glean from the conferences. The Group Relations Conference is a valuable educational tool, but must exist as an open system if it is to avoid the entropy and ultimate death occurring in closed systems.

We realize that the scope of the work reported in this chapter is limited by our own imaginations and experiences. We wish to see the changes and innovations set forth above carried further than our vision now allows. We also note that work must be continued in the African-American community to ensure that Group Relations Conferences do not become another tool of oppressive groups.

The issues we address relate primarily to the conferences sponsored by the A. K. Rice Institute, and deserve further study and clarification. For example, although the model is a tool for understanding the dynamics of change, it is not in and of itself a revolutionary tool, but rather an educational one. The boundaries and overlap among education, therapy, and politics should be clarified.

Group Relations Conference methods are valuable and should be shared with the African-American community. The majority of the persons with the necessary skills to do this, however, are not African-American. Because issues of trust, language barriers, and community commitment problems have not been resolved among the races, non-African-Americans have difficulty being accepted by the African-American community. This dilemma must be resolved. The simplest strategy calls for the A. K. Rice Institute to train as many African-American as as possible, and for these persons to return to their communities to continue the teaching/learning process. Only through efforts at collaboration can the oppressor-oppressed chain be broken. Both must want change and freedom, or else the chain will remain.

NOTE

1. Some would argue that psychoanalysis is not an appropriate intrapsychic model, but this chapter does not provide sufficient space for an extended discussion of this.

Section V.
Thoughts on the Practice of OD

Three Gifts of the Organization Development Practitioner

Daryl Funches

Introduction

The topic of professional development for organization development (OD) practitioners is receiving wide attention in increasing numbers of graduate programs, conferences, and workshops offered by various organizations. The literature on diagnostic models and types of interventions also is increasing, although research on the impact of OD work is still inadequate. With this generation of knowledge and technology, occasional attention has been given to the internal experience of consulting. The growing use of terms such as "effective use of the self" and "the self as an instrument of change" indicates a recognition of the importance of understanding the internal factors affecting the ability to use our knowledge, skills, and emotions in supporting the development and change of client systems.

This chapter addresses three of these internal factors—three gifts of the OD practitioner. I became aware of the importance of these gifts as I participated in a personal growth workshop for practitioners in the helping professions. This workshop, entitled "Holding On and Letting Go" was developed by Bob Tannenbaum and Bob Hanna through NTL Institute. Throughout my career, I have felt the desire to understand more about the effective use of self in the change process. This desire has been related to the belief that learning about changing and "growing" myself, so to speak, would ultimately be crucial for developing my own frames of reference for and abilities to facilitate growth and change in working with organizations, groups and individuals. Perhaps my insights from the workshop and other experiences will prove meaningful for others struggling to develop their abilities to use themselves effectively in serving client systems.

The insight

As I emerged from one of the most emotionally expressive and draining moments of my life, I began to see things differently. I felt as if I had traveled into the core of my being, looked at the most fearful truth, and painfully mourned myself into a state of relief, peace, and joy. The relief came from releasing pent-up thoughts and emotions, and from knowing that one can express these yet still remain intact. The peace came as I recognized that the "uniqueness" of my experience was universal. The joy came from experiencing the depths of my pain, of the reality of not being loved as I wished to be. This joy was not the jubilant type that would have led me to chatter and rave about what had just happened, but rather caused me to exalt my experience through meditation, prayer, and praise for the gifts allowing me to know this part of myself—which enabled me to move on.

I knew at that moment of awakening that what I had been seeking to reflect in my work could be expressed in terms of three gifts: the gift of discernment, the gift of presence, and the gift of heart. Within them lie the blend of the rational and the intuitive; the integration of the body, mind, emotions, and spirit; and the courage to act according to one's beliefs, convictions, knowledge, and feelings. During the week's journey, I had been blessed with seeing these gifts in myself, in others, and in our guides on the journey. The technology I had emphasized throughout the earlier part of my career paled in comparison to these three gifts. Indeed, I saw how my own history demonstrated both support for and interference with my ability to manifest these gifts in my work.

The gift of discernment

The gift of discernment is two-fold. The first part is the ability to distinguish between work and nonwork in client system behavior. The second is the ability to frame and focus the nature of clients' activities in ways that enable clients to understand their behavior better and the choices they can make to achieve their goals. In using the gift of discernment, the practitioner recognizes which of the client's activities serve the work of the individual, group, and/or organization, and which ones either subtly or blatantly hinder the client's attaining needed growth or learning. To do this, I am continually working on multiple levels by:

- attending to client system behaviors, noting recurrent themes,
- identifying assumptions and the related affect underlying these behaviors,
- ascertaining the connections among the above behaviors and assumptions and goal attainment, learning, and growth,
- tracking my own internal responses to situations, and

- selectively sharing observations and judgments so as to focus clients' attention.

The gift of discernment thus requires us to rely on our perceptions and to exercise judgment, in addition to using our knowledge and technical skills. It also demands the constant examination of our internal experience and the selective, responsive, and responsible expression of that experience in service of our work. The clear sight afforded through discernment is gained from the perspective of seeing the system (and oneself) as an indivisible whole. From this perspective of awareness, one can see what is being created and limited, and how.

When working with clients, I often have the occasion to determine that some activity the clients are performing is not "real" work—that is, work serving the organization's purpose. Rather, the activity is conducted as a defense mechanism against the anxiety the real work is causing, or as an attempt to get some other significant human need met. For example, recently the top manager of one of my client organizations recognized the occurrence of such an activity. A list of issues had been generated during a meeting of persons from the two levels of management reporting to him, and he reacted to the list by saying, "These are matters that any one of you could spend 20 minutes back in the office resolving. We didn't come together to work on rat **** issues!" Everyone in the room knew this was true, but only the top manager had dared to acknowledge this. During its previous meeting, the group had experienced substantial discomfort because some members had expressed intense feelings about the difficulty of the change process the organization was undergoing, raising issues of trust and commitment. This was so frightening to the group that at the next meeting it sought to avoid the process issues and focus on technical issues—"real work"—instead. The group had not yet come to understand that the process issues, such as a high level of vertical conflict and a lack of coordination across functional work units, were also manifest in the technical problems confronting the group. In getting its most recent product developed, the company had the same problem in the technical arena: no vertical integration and poor interfaces with different hardware environments.

Our consulting team intervened occasionally as the process issues were raised implicitly during the second meeting, but the group did not consider these interventions meaningful at first. We occasionally felt undervalued and useless, yet were committed to staying engaged in whatever ways we could until the group was ready to work. In our judgment, the group members would have indicated their readiness to work by acknowledging either that their relationships did indeed affect the technical aspects of the organization's work—even if they did not understand how—or that their current path was not leading to their goals.

Had we sat back and said nothing, we would not have been "earning the right to work" with them (Bridger, 1986, discussion at conference entitled "Rethinking Change," Tavistock Institute). Our preoccupation with being accepted and valued was potentially debilitating. Had the client group never acknowledged or faced its own similar preoccupation, it would not have earned the right to work with us. Expressing the gift of discernment is a key to earning the right to work in a consulting endeavor.

In this situation, I was struck with the recognition that the entire consulting team—which was composed of an African-American woman, a white man, and a white woman—all simultaneously experienced the same phenomena. This was no mere idiosyncratic response to a situation based on one's need for acceptance, security, or approval. The organization members, for all their persistence in pursuing the company's work, had also begun to feel less valuable, less certain, and even impotent in their attempts to address the organization's needs. Had none of us, client or consultant, been willing to share our perceptions or express our judgments about the situation, we would have been engaged in a rather collusive pact.

Expressing the gift of discernment sometimes requires substantial courage from a consultant. One's comments may produce defensiveness, justification of the activity's legitimacy and necessity, attacks on one's own utility, and the like. Even worse, one's comments may be ignored, or at least not acknowledged. A preoccupation with this, however, hinders the ability to be present and thus to work with the client system. Instead, one should use such feelings to inform oneself of one's own needs and motives, and perhaps the underlying needs and processes of the client system. In the situation described above, the consultants learned that their feelings of impotence, uncertainty, and inability to make a difference at the particular moment were shared by the group members. Discernment requires us to trust our internal experience as a potential source of useful information for the client.

When I am using the gift of discernment, I do not fold when my comments produce dismay, defensiveness, or no verbal response. Early in my career, a teacher advised that I needed to find ways other than verbal responses and direct implementation of my ideas to determine the impact of my work with groups. Only after some time have I come to understand what this advice means. One must accept one's own judgments as legitimate, while accepting the client's judgments as well. Staying engaged in the face of one's own or the client's resistance enables a person to remain in contact with the work being done.

The combination of having conviction in your judgment and staying engaged with a client and the client's experience poses a creative dilemma for OD consultants. You must be willing to examine your own motivations and needs related to your perceptions, and to consider those of the client. You must have conviction, yet must not become so locked into one way of working or expressing yourself that you no longer make yourself heard by the client system.

Consultants can use reactions to their judgments in creative ways that prove meaningful for the system's work and development.

As with any other gift, one should use the gift of discernment responsibly. This means consultants should not withhold discernment to gain approval or acceptance or to punish the client. Consultants punish clients when they withhold what they believe should be said because they are angry at the clients' inability or unwillingness to use their insights. Serving one's own ego by "beating up" the client is not a responsible use of discernment. When your ego is overly affected by a client's response to the work performed, this means you have an opportunity to learn from the experience about your own internal needs and motives. Doing so enhances discernment.

Perhaps it is the fear of failure, rejection, or of not being loved or valued that sometimes disables us when we try to exercise this gift—particularly when expressions of discernment may appear to be harsh, critical, or insensitive. In such cases, the recipients of these expressions may not consider discernment a gift. Discernment, however, can be expressed in succinct, constructive, and potent ways, enabling oneself and others to do the work that needs to be done. At its best, discernment is accompanied by the gift of heart, which magnifies the system's ability to use the consultant and the consultant's ability to support the system.

The gift of discernment clearly involves using one's cognitive powers to sift through vast amounts of data to frame issues in ways that better enable the consultant and the client to work. Consultants must also use their affective experience to gain their understanding of the situation at hand, relying on their strengths and "shadow sides" for perception and judgment.

Consultants have no more monopoly on the gift of discernment than clients have on feelings of insecurity, impotence, and need for acceptance and approval. Therefore, not only must we ourselves grow in terms of the gift of discernment, but we must help our clients do the same. This is part of both the client and the consultant's earning the right to work with one another, the right to consult and be "consulted to." When clients begin to demonstrate more ability in this area, this signals that they and the consultant can become partners in the OD work.

The gift of presence

The gift of presence is two-fold. First, it is the ability to exist fully in the "here-and-now" situation with a client system. From this here-and-now perspective, one assists the client in taking into account or tuning into different levels of reality as needed: what is actual, what is desired or potential, what is possible, and what is probable, given current plans and actions. Through attention to the here-and-now, the past can be understood as it affects the present; moreover, in the present the future is created.

The second and equally important aspect of the gift of presence is the ability to use one's style, identity, and beliefs congruently with one's theories and models so that the client system grows and learns in part from the change practitioner's ways of doing, being, and seeing the world. Related to this second aspect is the significance of the intervenor's role in providing "a presence that is otherwise lacking in the system, (so) it follows that an effective intervenor should be able to move from one presence to another. This is an ideal that at best can only be approximated by most practitioners" (Nevis, 1987). The key is to develop a presence that integrates your theoretical frame of reference and person so that you become the embodiment of your message about learning and change. A broad use of presence can be found in those who are change leaders or practitioners in a given system.

In the context of the definition above, the gift of presence is then both a space or place in which to work and a quality of integration of the self that allows for clear movement along various continua, providing the push or pull, the validation, or challenge needed to support learning and/or goal attainment. Presence provides a consultant with the awareness used in discernment and with the courage and range of behaviors needed to act on what is discerned. With this courage a consultant is willing to be present "right here, right now" and rely on oneself as a primary instrument for working with others. Developing this gift requires continual examination and stretching your own boundaries, allowing for the integration over time of who you are with what you believe and what you do. It requires that you become more whole and gain access to and the courage to become more and more of who you are as a unique person—to change and grow from within.

How often do consultants or managers of a change effort search for that one magical thing to do or say that can be recalled later as the act that saved the day, the moment to be remembered and described with a dramatic flair that glorifies the consultant and perhaps the group? If we have mentors or role models whom we admire from a distance, we may even ask ourselves what these guides would do in a situation facing us. At such moments, however, the key lies not in one's ability to reach consciously backward to old techniques or forward to future glory or success, but instead in the gift of presence. Projection and reflection have respected places in our work. The essence of what the intervenor can make of these, however, is in the moment, if we rely on the fertile ground of the unconscious to bring forth whatever is needed from the past, and on faith in ourselves to allow the future to create itself from the potency of action in the here and now.

In the personal growth workshop mentioned at the beginning of this chapter, practitioners guided us through psychologically difficult journeys with no apparent fear for psychological safety—either ours or theirs. If they were fearful, they were also courageous. Throughout this journey, however, they demonstrated a superb ability to attend to the here and now, and in doing so supported our growth, learning, and insight. The journey was not full of advice and prescriptions, nor of complex steps for reaching goals. Rather, the methods were simple yet profound. We could choose to go forward or retreat. The practitioners were present for those who wanted to work and moved away from or confronted those whose words or actions indicated that they were engaged in "pseudo-work."

Courage regarding the psychological safety of others must be coupled with respect for others' defenses and boundaries. We cannot be driven by a need to crash through others' defenses in the service of our own needs. To understand the client's limits, a consultant must trust her or his own intuitions while also using data from the client's behavior and statements. The consultant must know how to use presence to influence others.

In this regard, we can consider two basic modes of influence in using the power of our presence: the provocative mode and the evocative mode. According to Nevis (1977, p. 126):

> The provocative mode draws on a belief that system outcomes are what count if one is to be influential in actuality, and that nothing of real consequence can occur unless the intervenor causes, or forces, something to happen. . . . In the evocative mode, the consultant strives to get the system interested in what is being attended to by the system: the goal is creation of fresh awareness and the education of the system to be more effective in its awareness processes. There is greater willingness on the part of the intervenor to allow the client system to remain at the awareness stage. . .and to let client actions emerge. The aim is for the intervenor to be arousing but not unsettling.

There are certainly degrees of freedom along the continuum from evocative to provocative, and we could probably all find examples of each in our behavior as consultants to or leaders of change efforts. The evocative mode can be as "passive" as being there and witnessing the work of a system in a way that evokes a certain sense of safety and ability to work and disclose, or as active as sharing your observations without interpretation. Beyond this, we move into the provocative arena by confronting boundaries, interpreting behavior, acting in ways that are counter to the culture, structuring interventions that are likely to produce particular reactions or outcomes, or forcing or coercing action in some way, potentially including assault. Nevis defines modeling and elicitation as two types of evocative behavior and confrontation and assault as two types of provocative behavior (see Table 1).

Table 1.
Examples of provocative and evocative
modes of the use of self in change efforts

Evocative mode		Provocative mode	
Modeling	Elicitation	Confrontation	Assault
Buddha's life style	Confucius' *Analects*	Evangelical preaching	Coercive persuasion
Ghandi's ascetic life	Tao Te Ching		Draft card burning
Utopian communities; social experiments that may be observed by others; trendsetting, new lifestyles	Client-centered counseling	Boycotts and sit-ins (e.g., Ghandi, King's bus boycott)	Terrorist acts such as bombing, kidnapping, airplane hijacking
	Teaching through the lecture method	Techniques of S. Alinsky	Wildcat strikes, Clamshell Alliance break-ins at Seabrook Nuclear Facility
	M.L. King's speeches	Peaceful demonstrations	
Apprenticeship learning arrangements	Use of rich language: metaphor, imagery, poetic modes, gestures	Strong rhetoric; propaganda	D. Ellsberg's release of the Pentagon papers to the press
President Carter wearning a sweater, walking to the White House on Inauguration Day		M.L. King's protest marches	Synanon therapy
	President Reagan saying "there is no energy shortage in this great land of ours" (paraphrase of his remarks)	Sadat's historic trip to Jerusalem (1977)	Rolfing
		Encounter groups	est programs
President Reagan wearing Western-style clothes and riding a horse		Assertiveness training	Acts that browbeat or "rape" others into responding; any act of hostility or an act that strongly violates an agreement
	Asking questions or making remarks that gain the attention of others	Tavistock Group	
		Confrontation meetings	
Being attractive in manner/style, so as to draw attention, interest	Awareness-enhancing techniques, such as those used in Gestalt therapy, psychosynthesis synectics, body therapies (Alexander, Felldenkrais, etc.)	Bioenergetics	
		Third-party intervention	
Vicarious learning, observing without trying or simply by being in the same space with another		Interpreting another's behavior to them	
		Statements to clients that stretch, or go beyond, established boundaries	

Organization development practitioners often bring the power of their presence through modeling, elicitation, and confrontation. Assault may be limited to those change efforts in which managers have imported into the organization something of a training "cult" that uses assault methods to deliver its messages.

When client systems struggle with facing the old order or past difficulties, and attempt to create a new order, change practitioners need to use their presence to attend to the pain, fear, joy, and excitement of transition and change. In the face of visions, constraints, desires, and resistance, pressure can be used to explore, push, stretch, and/or affirm boundaries. Most of us have experienced the gift of presence from friends when we needed someone to "be there" for us; we have all needed someone to be present to hear and see what comes up, speak words of reinforcement, encourage us to dig deeper, challenge us when we retreat or lie to ourselves about what is happening, or give us space to retreat when we have struggled enough. Although we may often feel as if we must provide some special answer to help someone in need, we should remember that sometimes the gift of presence is best expressed by our ability to witness others, attend to them, and reflect on their experience. At other times, when the call for action is urgent, our presence may best be used in a confrontational manner.

When we use the gift of presence, we can see when someone has gone too far or may need to go further. If we cannot see this, we can at least recognize what we need to ask. We are not limited by a lack of a road map indicating exactly what type of psychological disturbance is occurring. We do not need a code book of disorders or a checklist of interventions when people express certain behaviors. What we need is attention to the here and now and a range of ways we can use ourselves to support awareness and/or action.

We cannot be present, however, when we are preoccupied with how we are being seen or experienced, or with determining "the right thing to do." We can be present only when we are in touch with our feelings, thoughts, and intuitions in the moment. The gift of presence gives consultants access to an area of "creative indifference" (Zinker, 1977), enabling them to work with clients without predetermining how things should be and what they should do. Any magic in the consulting process, if such a thing exists, is often attributed to this type of stance—that of an evocator—not from one's investment in a predetermined set of actions. The magic is that the influence seems invisible until the system begins to learn more explicitly about the process of change.

The gift of presence requires change practitioners to become more "whole" in the work they do. Although they must recognize the appropriate role to fill in relation to the client, they must also integrate themselves as whole beings into that role. If this role is considered substantially distant from one's own personal identity and experience, work becomes a form of personal death, as opposed to an experience of growth and vitality.

When I began practicing OD consulting, I sometimes felt and behaved as if my role called for me to operate from the right hand, but I operated from the left hand. As soon as I left the client's presence, I seemed to become an entirely different person seeking expression and relief, as if my concept of the role and the work did not allow for the presence of this other being. Over time, the two have come closer as I have learned to honor my internal experience while engaging in the practice of consulting. Using the gift of presence calls for us to honor our internal experience as much as we honor the role we have chosen. The tensions existing between one's role and one's self are akin to the tensions in the client system between individual needs and task demands.

In the practice of OD consulting, we ask client systems to attend to the process and content of their work, to the task and nature of relationships, and to their technical and social systems. Doing this requires them to actively use their experience in the present, reflect on the past, and anticipate the future in terms of likely outcomes. Consultants must do the same. Yet in my work in developing OD practitioners, I am struck by how frequently we are so preoccupied with performance and/or acceptance that we miss the many opportunities available to take advantage of our competence for the client system.

For example, consultants frequently are unaware of how their internal experience and the client's observations at a given moment exemplify the very essence of the issue the client is talking about. We can miss using what goes on right in front of us as an opportunity to enhance the client's awareness of the organization's dynamics. Awareness, growth, and change are exciting and vital, yet they also produce anxiety for both the consultant and client. In the midst of these ambivalent experiences, consultants and clients are challenged to stay engaged with one another rather than raise their defenses and flee from the intensity of the work that is to be done.[1]

Presence involves attending to the symbolic realm in an organization as it relates to one's own identity. For example, I consult to many organizations having a predominantly white male culture. As an African-American woman, I have sometimes experienced confusion within myself and the system when I enter a new client organization for the first time. A voice from the past may say: "What am I doing in here? This is a mistake. This is not safe." An unconscious collective or conscious individual voice in the system may ask what I am doing there as well. I have learned that being present requires me to face and work out any limitations I experience as a result of internalizing the oppression of my past, including what may have happened yesterday. In addition, I must also understand what I symbolize in the system because of my identity. Rather than run from the symbolism, I can use it and explore it in ways appropriate for the service of the work.[2] I recall one case in which a client said, "They will expect you to be tough and confrontational and intimidating since you're a African-American woman." This is consistent with what Dumas (1983, pp. 122-123) points out:

> The mythical image of the powerful castrating black matriarch pervades contemporary organizations and poses a critical dilemma for black females that makes competition for, and competent performance in, leadership positions a costly endeavor. There are increasing efforts to resurrect the black mammy in today's ambitious black women. There

are negative consequences for those who succumb as well as for those who dare to resist.

My first impulse when the client painted the picture above was to explain how false this stereotype was and to differentiate myself from it. I did not think until later how this representation of who I am could occasionally be helpful in working with the system. On many occasions, I am aware that as an African-American woman, I can be alternately experienced as an intimidating force, or as an earth mother or a shaman, with powers to nurture, protect, be clairvoyant, and heal, depending on the needs of the system and my responses. Developing the gift of presence has required me to acknowledge my own vision of who I am in relation to systems and to acquire and/or cultivate the range of behaviors helping me manifest that vision. I can now appreciate why I work where I work and what I have to give and learn.

To use presence as a gift in your work, acknowledge and affirm that you are in the right place right now to learn what you need to learn, and to support the system as it learns what it needs to learn. Presence not only moves us closer to understanding more about our own dynamics, it also provides useful information about being engaged with a particular client. Responsible use of the gift of presence requires us to know ourselves and show ourselves in the service of the work to be done. As we do this, we are earning the right to work by staying engaged with the client. Clients earn the right to work by being willing to be so engaged. We all have the option of being detached or being split—separated from what we teach and speak—but these occurrences should not be confused with using the gift of presence. As we help leaders align their own behavior with their visions, we contribute to the power of their presence as well.

The gift of heart

The gift of heart is the ability to attune and connect oneself to the system in which one is working. Into this gift I assemble those qualities of compassion, humanitarianism, grace for others, passion for one's craft, and the will to extend oneself in the service of the work of learning and growth. This gift involves the inherent struggle of giving versus withholding of the self, recognizing people's infinite capacity to love and the finite capacity of our physical selves.

Using the gift of heart requires one to face one's own pain, struggles, and joy and to connect with others through what we know about the process of living, learning, and growing. It is not a gift given lightly, for in expressing it we make indelible marks on others' lives and draw ourselves into more and more relationships with others. We are connected to the universe through this gift; it is at this level that we are one.

Whether we do so through models, concepts, music, movement, words, or touching, we can give of this part of ourselves to others. The gift of heart represents a leap into others' lives, showing one's desire to be with them in their struggle. It is not always welcomed or accepted, yet consultants must bring this gift to clients. Otherwise, why bother to engage in OD work? When practitioners examine the reasons for doing the type of work involved in organizational growth and change, they always indicate—despite the occasional rewards of recognition, money, and accomplishment—that the heart is involved at some level.

Clients often comment on what they perceive as my high energy level and its usefulness in supporting them in their work. I believe that the source of this energy is often centered in the heart, drawing upon energy in the universe and putting it back out in ways that demonstrate connection. This is particularly important when we are working on issues of separation—such as conflict or diversity—within organizations.

The gift of heart can also be expressed just as much when one negotiates a contract as when one makes an intervention. It must be a part of the business as well as the practice, the role as well as the person. With this gift, we give meaning to our work and our lives; without it we turn into stone. Through the gift of heart we pump our life's blood into our actions and our words. Perhaps we should not offer advice without the gift of heart. How many of our statements to clients would we take back if we applied this criterion?

Through the gift of heart we become attuned to the mission, purpose, or vision of a given client system. Through the gift of heart we can best see manifestation of the notion that work is love made visible. Choices concerning the client systems with which we work and the nature of our work enable us to discover which paths have heart for us. This gift enables a consultant to recognize the connection between her or his own values and sense of purpose and those of the client system. Although the client's values may not represent your own, you can learn more about your willingness and ability to influence those systems, and answer the question "toward what end?" In working with a particular client, a consultant faces the ways in which the system is both similar to and different from one's perceptions of it. We discover in our hearts the extent to which we can join the system and care about its mission and its internal experience in accomplishing its purposes. In some cases, a sufficient bond is lacking. Thus, the gift of heart enables us to belong, although marginally, to some systems and not at all to others.

Once a consultant is in a given system, this gift influences the nature of what one does. In my work, I have occasionally thought, "Something else is needed here, and it's not on an intervention checklist or in the book." Often what is needed is a higher order of work—a level of healing, a different consciousness of what is happening and of what can happen. With the gift of heart, we can support and lead this order of work. First, however, we must know how the work connects with one's own sense of purpose and meaning in life.

We don't attain the gift of heart by reading one more article on sociotechnical systems, morphogenesis, or strategies for change in systems. Perhaps we can read about interventions that failed or interventions that succeeded, but rarely do authors write about the experience of connecting or not being able to connect with a client system and the nature of its work.

Joining the three gifts

Together, these three gifts affirm the importance of determining with whom we work and what we do. When they flow together, the gifts represent a higher order of doing, being, and knowing, into which we can integrate the theoretical and technological frames we use in our work. Together, they are similar to the brain, heart, and courage that were so essential for Dorothy to find her home in "The Wizard of Oz." "Home" really does rest in effective use of self.

The heart provides the very basis for doing the work needed and being with a particular system. It also provides the connection through which one can have sight of the whole. Discernment provides the sight with which to see oneself and the system clearly. Presence integrates thought, action, and emotion together in ways that symbolize what we desire to create. Without the gift of presence, discernment would be experienced as being "out there, not in here." Together, I think the three gifts provide significant symbols for facilitating and creating change at deeper levels. Indeed, the gifts are essential if we are to help create new ways of seeing and knowing in organizations that are necessary to move forward into the next century.

In teaching and developing OD practitioners, I have noticed that some persons misinterpret the importance of the three gifts by devaluing knowledge and skill development. The knowledge and skills of the OD practitioner are assets that must be seen in their proper place in the business of growth and change. The mechanisms that we use to "grow ourselves" stay with us and increase our ability to work with clients. The gifts that we can bring as a result of developing ourselves are with us in every consulting situation, but knowledge and skills vary in their applicability to particular situations. Knowledge and skills are necessary, but not sufficient for the work of supporting the growth and change of others. Knowledge and skills provide ways of helping clients learn about learning; they enable us and clients to understand more about what clients are experiencing in the process of growth and change. But when we can blend knowledge and skills with the three gifts, we have the most that we can bring at any given moment to a client and to ourselves.

In a sense, the confluence of the gifts along with other knowledge, techniques, and feelings is a part of becoming whole in our work. A variety of streams in our lives join in this endeavor. Acknowledging the importance of the three gifts in one's work is simple; the challenge is to embrace and integrate these gifts firmly into the foundation of what one does as a practitioner.

The path to the three gifts

The swiftness with which I gained insight into the three gifts was matched only by the elusiveness of clarity about tapping into these gems. Thus far in my journey, I can point to only one path to learning to share them with clients.

Immediately after the personal growth workshop described in the beginning of this chapter, I was committed to perform in a trainer role with three colleagues, conducting our own laboratory experience for 40 participants. I did not know how I would conjure up the physical, emotional, and mental reserves for doing this. I simply told my colleagues, who I knew would understand, that I was emotionally exhausted, spiritually uplifted, and ready to work. I knew I would not have the energy to experience my usual anxiety about preparing lectures, my usual preoccupation with whether I was doing "the right thing" in small group sessions, and the like. I trusted that I would be able to do whatever needed to be done during the seven-day period. During the laboratory, I was able to assume the stance of creative indifference described earlier in this chapter. The gifts were present in me throughout the week; indeed, I did some of the best work I have ever done, and had a newfound appreciation for the provocative and evocative ways of using myself.

In reflecting on other such peak experiences in my practice, I became aware of a common thread. In each case the professional work came after I had performed an exceptional amount of work on myself, whether this lasted an hour or a week. This practice of reflecting upon and envisioning my own patterns of practices clearly had a positive effect on my work. In these peak experiences, the gifts have been the grounding forces of my work, allowing for effective use of self. The knowledge and skills I brought were resources I brought into this broader framework.

Consequently, I argue strongly that practitioners should work on the self constantly and recognize that personal growth is the same as professional development. I believe that all OD practitioners know this to some extent, although we vary greatly as to how we act on this knowledge. The quality of what we do when working with colleagues on our own behavior also has immense value for developing the three gifts. In a sense, we must earn the right to work with one another, exploring the motives, needs, and assumptions reflected in our behavior with one another and with the client systems. This is part of earning the right to work with the client and with other consultants. Those of us who are involved in graduate programs and professional development programs for OD practitioners should ask ourselves how our work contributes to the development of the three gifts. When we work with clients and colleagues, we should ask how our work expresses these gifts and helps others develop them.

The path to the three gifts is one of challenge, confrontation, support, grace, and the discipline to engage in continual examination of oneself, of others (clients and colleagues), and of one's relationships with them. This examination requires vigilance, and is simultaneously loving, exciting, frightening, painful, and rewarding (Peck, 1979). Negotiating a contract with a client may give a consultant the formal right to work, but the consultant and client must also earn the right to work with one another in behavioral and psychological terms. We must be willing to examine ourselves and one another with the same scrutiny we apply to client systems.

I have begun to practice developing the gifts within myself by using the same change model (a subject for another paper) that I use with my client systems. This is not a surprise, as the model itself came out of work I did on my own process of creating change. My reflective work in this regard has increased the quality of my work in consulting to change processes in organizations. I have also come to recognize that the gifts are as applicable to leaders of change efforts in organizations as they are to OD practitioners.

Paradoxically, developing the three gifts thus relies in part on using these gifts in the service of the work of our own development and that of our clients. We develop them by acknowledging their existence and using them. This paradox raises another question about the path to the three gifts: What are their origins? The term "gifts" implies some form of endowment. This endowment does not come from other people, however. It is the legacy of one's own creation and "re-creation" in the struggle to become whole. This legacy is the trust, so to speak, that we can use as we do the work and grow in the discipline that enables us to claim the legacy.

Underlying each of the three gifts, then, is a sense of self-authorization, self-empowerment, unconditional love, and entitlement. These cannot come from other people; if they could, others could take the gifts away. The origin of the three gifts is in the spiritual domain, transcending yet incorporating valuable assets from other domains in our work and lives. Hence, the path to the three gifts is essentially a spiritual journey requiring us to recognize another order of our existence. In doing so, we must face the unpleasant aspects of ourselves along with the "good" parts. The insight that I describe above is based on such an encounter with the self. The beauty of this process is that it lets us realize that the creation of and effective use of the self is truly a work of art.

NOTES

1. I do not wish to imply that all defense systems are inappropriate; indeed, they are necessary for protecting us from elements in our environment that might harm us. Some defensive responses, however, disable clients and consultants as they seek to perform the work needed to allow the system to more fully accomplish its purposes.

2. The symbolic meaning of presence as it relates to identity is one of the reasons that race and gender diversity of consulting staff is so significant in change efforts. A diverse staff sends a message that we are willing to engage client systems in ways meaningful to the changes they face currently and in the future.

ACKNOWLEDGMENTS

I thank the following colleagues and friends for listening to and supporting me when I developed these ideas: B. Tannenbaum, B. Hanna, L. Wells, J. Katz, B. Marshak, C. Brantley, M. Weisbord, D. Tucker, P. Parham, A. Mayas, G. King, R. Anderson, N. J. Anderson, and E. Lowry.

REFERENCES

Dumas, R. (1983). Dilemmas of black females in leadership. In R. Ritvo & A. Sargent (Eds.), *NTL manager's handbook*. Arlington, VA: NTL Institute.

Nevis, E. (1987). *Organizational consulting: A Gestalt approach*. Cleveland: Gestalt Institute of Cleveland Press.

Peck, M. S. (1979). *The road less traveled*. New York: Simon and Schuster.

Zinker, J. (1977). *Creative process in gestalt therapy*. New York: Vintage Books.

Future Search: Toward Strategic Integration

Marvin R. Weisbord

> On the way to the moon the Apollo astronauts made tiny "mid-course corrections" that enabled them to land at an exact predetermined spot. The corrections were small, but because the moon was far away they made a big difference. It is like that with us. Some of the changes we make in society, in our lives, or in our organizations seem insignificant, but over the years they can have major impact. (Lindaman & Lippitt, 1979, p. 4)

A productive work place is one in which people share the risks and rewards, working together on economics and technology. They improve their social relations by confronting the "outside" world more often and confronting each other less so. They accept responsibility for themselves and for the community. This happens only when people unite over common values and purposes and achieve a more complete vision of their work system.

Planner Russell L. Ackoff (1977) of the University of Pennsylvania once observed that corporate planning is like rain dancing: Whether or not it brings rain, it makes the dancers feel better. Extending past trends to predict the future has become an exercise in futility. Economists cannot do it, politicians cannot do it, scientists cannot do it, nor, alas, can you and I.

Discovering alternatives

What are modern rain dancers to do? Is this a practical problem or a philosophical one? In the late 1950s, social scientists Eric Trist and Fred Emery (1960) were asked by an English aircraft engine company to help it resolve a marketing crisis. Uncertain what to do, Trist and Emery asked that all relevant parties—the engineers, accountants, marketers, and executives—be assembled. In that historic conference, a diverse group of persons looked together at changes in the "environment" and the implications of these for managing. This did not constitute rational problem solving, but rather an exercise in creative integration, intelligence, wisdom, and mutual discovery.

This was a creative extension of the legendary social psychologist Kurt Lewin's (1948) insight that you steer a ship using feedback from the **outside,** not according to how the rudder, engines, or crew are acting. Lewin invented a new form of inquiry—action research—whereby organization members join the "experts" in a systematic study of their problems, and thus become active participants rather than passive recipients in the effort. Emery and Trist extended the method to invent a new group orientation helping people integrate economics and technology—the whole open system—in a fast-changing environment. In computer science terms, this was the equivalent of dumping all relevant data into a system's RAM (random access memory) and making it quickly available to all parties, who could then use it to bring their own data bases up to date and to write a better program together. The company undertook a strategic reorientation and turned around a serious crisis.

This search—dubbed an "environmental scan"—became an integral step in sociotechnical work design. Trist and Emery began to use this design broadly to create a strategic umbrella for communities of interest with disparate "stakeholders," such as corporations, cities, towns, industries, unions, trade associations, and professional societies. Variations were used in Scandinavia, Great Britain, Australia, and Canada, although rarely in U.S. corporations before the 1980s.

Inventing the future

Biologist Ludwig von Bertalanffy, author of general systems theory, once observed that the same ideas spring up in parallel in diverse fields. From the late 1940s on, Ronald Lippitt—Lewin's American colleague and a cofounder of NTL Institute—had sought along with Emery and Trist to extend group dynamics learning to large organizations, networks, and communities. Lippitt too had moved from small-group problem solving to future-oriented conferences for huge networks. What started Lippitt down this road were audiotapes he secured of 30 planning groups in action.

Researchers pinpointed how the groups built long problem lists from which they selected items to be analyzed and solved. Most notable was how the voices grew more depressed as people attributed problems to causes beyond their control. They used words such as "hopeless" and "frustrating." Action steps tended to be short term, designed to deal with symptoms and reduce anxiety. The motivation, noted Lippitt (1983), was to escape the pain induced in part by the method itself—the piecemeal listing of problems, of which the solution of any one might create still more problems.

In the 1950s, Ronald Fox, Lippitt, and Eva Schindler-Rainman (1973) began speaking of "images of potential," envisioning what could be instead of lamenting what was. In the 1970s Lippitt teamed with futurist Edward Lindaman, who had directed the planning for the Apollo moon shot. Lindaman believed that the future was created by our present ways of confronting events, trends, and developments in the environment. The "preferred future"—an image of aspiration—could be a powerful guidance mechanism for making far-reaching course corrections. Lindaman and Lippitt found that when people plan actions for the present by working backward from what is really desired, they develop energy, enthusiasm, optimism, and high commitment.

"Futuring" thus focuses attention **away** from interpersonal relationships and toward the experiences and values affecting everybody. Lippitt adapted the insight to national voluntary organizations such as the YMCA, and to conferences for several states and more than 80 cities and towns (Schindler-Rainman & Lippitt, 1980). Diverse interest groups could jointly envision desirable futures simultaneously for, for example, the PTA, manufacturers' associations, doctors, community activists, juvenile authorities, the chamber of commerce, the school board, and so forth. Searching together gives organizations more dependable anchor points for their own planning. It ties everybody to reality through taking joint snapshots, and becomes the basis for a more truthful "movie" based on mutual interests.

People learned to think of the future as a condition created intentionally out of values, visions, and what is technically and socially feasible. Such purposeful action gently increases the probability of making the desired future come alive. Repeating the process over and over again with relevant others, which Ackoff (1974) calls "interactive planning," could become a way of life for corporate planners if they could bring the whole system into the room.

An integrative strategy conference

For several years my colleagues and I have experimented with a future search conference, integrating ideas from Fred and Merrelyn Emery, Fox, Lippitt, Lindaman, Trist, and Schindler-Rainman (Weisbord, 1984). We have used variations in the steel, textile, and financial services, medical education, service organizations, schools, colleges, and an agricultural cooperative in Sweden. We have managed search conferences as short as half a day (an unsatisfying experience) and as long as three days (an exciting one). We have witnessed little or no follow-up, and extensive activities carried forward for a year or longer. We have worked with as few as a dozen people (too few) and as many as a hundred (a hard but manageable number). We have found that within 48 hours people often generate important new learnings that influence their organization's future course for years.

Search conferences excite, engage, produce new insights, and build a sense of common values and purpose. They have been especially attractive to organizations facing significant change, such as that associated with markets, mergers, reorganizations, new technology, new leadership, and the wish for a coherent culture and corporate philosophy. We have used the conference to set the stage for work design. We also have used it at turning points when people knew they had to do something new, but were not sure what.

Assumptions

We base the future search conference on three assumptions.

1. Change is so rapid that we need **more,** not less, face-to-face discussion to make intelligent strategic decisions. Teleconferencing will not do. John Naisbitt (1982, p. 46) notes in *Megatrends,* "Talking with people via television cannot begin to substitute for the high touch of a meeting, no matter how rational it is in saving fuel and overhead."

2. Successful strategies—for quality goods and services, lower costs, more satisfying ways of working—come from envisioning preferred futures. Applying problem solving to old dilemmas does not work under fast-changing conditions. Each narrow solution begets two new problems.

3. People will commit to carrying out plans they have helped develop. Lewin and anthropologist Margaret Mead showed that during World War II, when they found that housewives were more likely to change their food habits through discussion than through exhortations by nutritionists.

Community, common sense, and self-control are always more satisfying than a forced march dictated by authority. Self-motivation, not some technique, provides the intangible energy source for making organizations succeed. An investment of hours or days in searching may reduce misunderstanding and speed up commitment by weeks, months, or even years. It may also uncover new possibilities that cannot emerge in any other forum.

A typical conference brings together 30-60 persons for 2-3 days. Together they do a series of structured tasks, looking at the organization's past, present, and preferred future. The tasks are cumulative. Each session builds on previous ones. The last even involves everybody in action planning for the future.

Below I describe one typical version. My goal is not to present a "cookbook" for the conference, but rather to indicate some ingredients and to encourage diverse menus.

What's good for the goose. . .

In 1983 the late Ronald Lippitt helped Block-Petrella-Weisbord organize a future search with client managers from AT&T, Bethlehem Steel, McNeil Consumer Products, Smith Kline & French, Soabar Corporation, Warner Cosmetics, and consulting colleagues from the United States and Sweden. Together we looked at the future of the work world, and the meaning for clients and consultants alike.

Our decision to open a private meeting to clients and friends was triggered by a startling statement in *Megatrends* (Naisbitt, 1982): Producers fear losing control if they invite consumers into strategy and policy discussions. "Too many corporations that should know better are terrified of this whole idea," Naisbitt writes (p. 178). "I do not think it an oversimplification to state that producers can only become more successful by learning how to better satisfy consumers."

In our conference we compared notes on major trends reshaping business firms. All noted the need for constant retraining, the emergence of a world marketplace, fewer jobs at the middle and top. The ways in which our company's future scenario must take account of these trends became plainer to us. My confidence in participative work design and reorganizations was greatly strengthened by managers' comments during this conference.

Getting organized

How? You cannot "wing it." You have to spend a day or more in planning, and another day preparing materials. The search is best planned by those who will manage it and a group of four to six potential participants. They decide on the participant selection method, place, schedule, meals and breaks, group tasks, and goal focus (e.g., "designing the corporation for 1995"). Each task is structured to support the overall focus. Work sheets are provided to enable small groups to organize their tasks without special facilitators.

You must find a room large enough to contain the group comfortably, one that has plenty of wall space for posting newsprint. It must be well lit, preferably with windows on at least one wall. The only thing more depressing to a group than problem solving is working in a dark, windowless "dungeon" of a room.

Who? We seek to involve only people with a stake in the sponsoring organization's future. They must be active participants. Any group important to implementation should be there. Top management always participates, with people from as many functions and levels as feasible. The guideline is diversity, and the whole system to the extent possible. Business firms, for example, should consider having participants representing customers, suppliers, union leaders, all dimensions for the gender, age, and racial and ethnic backgrounds of employees, and all functions and levels of management.

We prefer groups of 50 or 60 persons, which permit great diversity of views, knowledge, and experience, a higher potential for creative solutions, more likelihood of follow-through, and more linkages with the outside. For logistical reasons, an organization may run a series of conferences or parallel groups of 50. A few volunteers from each then meet afterward to sort through the data and ideas and prepare a combined scenario or discussion paper.

Schedule. I like Merrelyn Emery's (1982) idea that the conference start with dinner on a Wednesday evening, followed by the first work session. This makes use of the Zeigarnik effect—that is, the tendency to recall unfinished tasks—and ensures a fast start the next morning. I find it desirable to end a future search on a Friday afternoon, as that gives people a weekend to collect their thoughts, review key events, and digest important ideas rather than plunge into paper work at the office.

Prework. People are invited to bring newspaper and magazine clippings describing events and trends they believe are shaping their organization's future. These clippings will be displayed on a bulletin board and used in the discussion. Sometimes a planning group will request artifacts and mementos from the past—old ads, news clips, uniforms, photographs, awards, brochures, posters, trophies—that symbolize and embody history. People display and discuss these materials, making them a foundation for imagining desirable futures.

Start-up. People usually sit at tables in groups of six to eight persons, each with its own easel, colored markers, and tape. During the two days, no more than three groupings will be made—one by function or common interest, another with maximum diversity of levels, functions, ages, and so on, and perhaps a third of self-selected volunteers—in addition to the total group.

A few ground rules are established at the start.

1. This is **not** a problem-solving conference. It is an exercise in learning, awareness, understanding, and mutual support.

2. Every idea and comment is valid. People need not agree with it. Every contribution is written on newsprint in words as close to the speaker's as possible.

3. This is a task-focused meeting. Every task has "output," and all output is recorded and discussed.

4. We stick to the time schedule. Groups are responsible for completing tasks on schedule.

5. The consultants manage time and structure tasks. Participants generate and analyze information, derive meanings, propose action steps, and take responsibility for output. Consultants may add their own "two cents," but only as another contribution to the discussion. No lectures are given.

The conference's success depends on uncovering important shared values and building congruent action plans. It has four or five major segments, each lasting as much as half a day and requiring participants to

- build a data base,
- look at it together,
- interpret what they find, and
- draw conclusions for action.

The last task includes generating action proposals and a structure—including task forces and assignments—for carrying them out. All of this is discussed at the start.

The past. The first activity focuses on history. Participants examine their collective past from three perspectives: the self, the company (or industry or town), and society.

Task: Alone, make notes on significant events, milestones, highlights, or activities you recall from each decade. When ready, take a magic marker and transfer your memories to the appropriate sheets on the wall.

About 30 minutes is needed for everybody to write on the newsprint scattered around the room. With two sheets provided for each topic for each of the three decades, 18 persons can write at once (see Figure 1). Simple contributions make a potent whole. As the data go up, reluctance turns to interest, then surprise, as participants rediscover and interpret how much change they have lived through together and how much this influences the present. The activity is a powerful community builder. Participants see that for a long time they have been in the "same boat." Younger participants learn much that they never knew about the past, older participants learn much about youthful values and commitments.

Each table analyzes one theme across three decades—one looks at all the items listed under "myself," another under "company," a third under "society"—for patterns and meanings. As the tables report on this, a consultant notes emerging trends. The whole group then interprets good and bad trends and the direction of movement of each, which is a way of discovering important values. Those who brought mementos say a few words about them, adding to the sense of continuity some anchor points in the sea of change.

The present—from the outside and inside. The present is examined from two perspectives. One is provided by a list of external events, trends, and

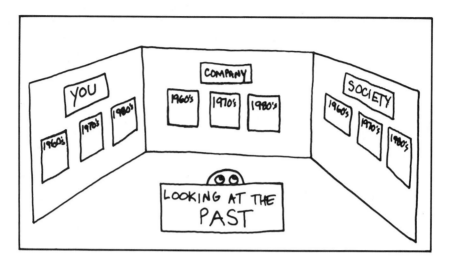

Figure 1. Focusing on history

developments shaping the future right now. This analysis is helped by the news clippings and articles. We ask each participant to tell the group why her or his clipping is important. A recorder notes each person's remarks. Then the participants set priorities for items on the group's list. A poll of priorities reveals several common themes shared by all groups. Pooling these creates a map similar to what Emery calls "the extended social field," or relevant outside network of forces and institutions demanding attention. Group analysis reveals what these trends and forces mean to us, and what we believe will happen in the future that we cannot ignore now. Figure 2 depicts an example of how a group presents this.

We also look at the present from an internal perspective, using a simple Lippitt exercise that surfaces values. Participants are asked to generate lists of "prouds" and "sorries"—the things going on right now in their organization about which they feel good and bad. This leads to a shared appreciation of present strengths, needs, and hopes. It also results in a mutual "owning up" to mistakes and shortcomings and builds commitment to do something about them.

Participants cast votes for the "proudest prouds" and "sorriest sorries." These are totaled, displayed, and discussed. This step often leads to a productive dialogue across levels, and the sharing of a good deal of new information in the large group. Conference managers actively probe, summarize, and note key statements on newsprint during the dialogue.

Devising a preferred future. Now is the time to generate future images. Participants either form new voluntary groups based on their own needs or work in groups set by the steering committee. They are given one to two hours to create a rough draft of a "preferred future scenario." They are asked to imagine the most desirable, attainable future five years later. The more imaginative the method, the better the scenarios. People have described themselves as riding magic carpets or rocket ships into the future, floating on clouds, writing newspaper stories or producing television documentaries. Having plenty of media—crayons, colored paper, scissors, and tape—stimulates new ideas. Background music helps. One conference ran a "county fair," with each group building a booth to display the future. Others have developed segments for "60 Minutes," cover stories for *Time* magazine, or features for the *New York Times* Sunday business section.

As a final step, participants are asked to reflect on what they have learned and to make three lists suggesting actions for themselves, their functions, and the whole organization. The suggestions are reviewed and discussed during a two-hour lunch break on the last day of the conference. Department personnel sit together, review participants' functional proposals, and decide on the next steps. Meanwhile, the steering committee or top manager group engages in

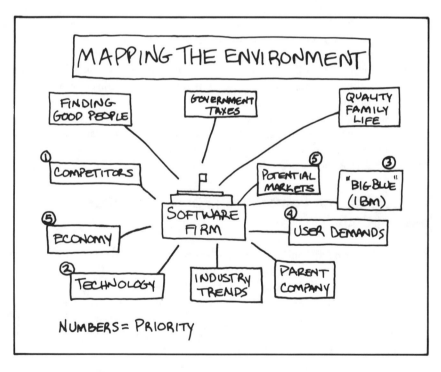

Figure 2. Focusing on the present and future.

an intense work session, recording "action proposals for the organization"—that is, matters related to policies or systems that cut across departmental lines and cannot be handled within one group. Before closing, volunteers are recruited to document the meeting, communicate to others, and carry forward the next steps. In one search conference, a dozen task forces were organized to search for new markets and explore new technology. In another, a group undertook an effort to merge future scenarios into a philosophy and proposed plan of action for an entire company.

Search conferences build community

One way to appreciate the future search conference is to compare it to traditional business conferences. Some organizations, for example, organize three to five days' worth of guest speeches by experts to stimulate top executives. The speakers are picked for their charisma, ability to entertain, or reputation as authors of best-selling books. Their audiences like to be amused and inspired. They do not expect to do any work, and might resent being asked without warning to become active. They enjoy watching the dance and do not expect rain.

Or consider the statistical business review, a two-hour slide show devoted to budgets, costs, product lines, and variances. Of course, data help meet people's needs for feedback and information, but a "data dump" gives them too many numbers and too little time to digest them. The people become overloaded, their circuits clogged. Rarely is time given for discussing ways to make the numbers come up differently.

Neither expert "input" nor data dumping takes advantage of the significant resources present in the room. Neither taps into the thoughts, ideas, perceptions, attitudes, and reactions of the audience. If future action is desirable, better ways exist for using 50 persons' time.

A future search conference is based on different assumptions

Search conference participants receive advance briefing as to their involvement. They know that they are to be both audience and actors. True, the work is paradoxical and seems confusing at first. But as people sort out the past and present, they become more focused and purposeful. By devising whole future scenarios, they create a new perspective on optimistic, value-based action. Traditional meeting formats subtly reinforce dependency and passivity. The search conference promotes dignity, meaning, and community.

A few years ago I organized a search conference as part of an NTL laboratory in Bethel, Maine. Townspeople, lab participants, and NTL staff joined in looking at their mutual interests—from the standpoint of stores, restaurants, churches, schools, medical facilities, hotels, and banks. NTL's summer workshops provide local income and jobs, and the community offers important support services. Among the problems noted was a "culture gap" between NTL's participants and the people providing service in stores and restaurants, leading to tension and misunderstanding.

Several good ideas were proposed, not just for reducing the tension, but for creative steps that would benefit everybody. One central insight was that the townspeople had lived for years with persistent rumors that NTL planned to pull out of Bethel. NTL's leaders realized that this chronic headache could be cured only by a policy of commitment. NTL took a public stand on remaining in Bethel, and since has invested in improving its conference facilities—a key ingredient of community building. Townspeople have taken over the writing of the participants' guide to summer services. A joint committee of townspeople and NTL staff has continued to build a productive community of interest. Only in a face-to-face discussion of the future by many stakeholders could this new spirit be infused into an old relationship.

The future search conference fits any organization and strategic situation—whether this involves manufacturing, sales, volunteers, retail, government, health care, education, staff, or line. It does not matter whether the participants see each other once a day, once a year, or have never met before. Given a few simple tools and instructions, they are able to search for a desirable future together. The governing board of a prestigious medical specialty group, for example, meets only once a year. Using a day and a half of time from their annual meeting to conduct a future search, they established policies that unified curriculum development efforts in many medical schools. Two years later, the participants continued to build on the work done in that conference.

Community building

The search conference has proven to be a powerful tool of productive work places. Far from requiring conformity in thought and action, it provides a forum and norms that respect individual differences. Personal attitudes, thoughts, feelings, and styles are honored. People sometimes fear that past disagreements will intrude and prove disruptive. Under the guidance of experienced consultants working with a committed steering group, this does not happen. A major strength of the search conference is its unifying effect on people even when they fear divisiveness. It is a sort of town meeting structured toward output and creativity.

The conference is not interpersonally threatening, for it does not focus on how people feel about one another, but rather on how they feel about the future. It tends to bring people closer together in their goals and attitudes, rather then heighten their differences. Instead of gazing inward or being problem-centered, the participants seem to link strong personal feelings to external realities—the events, trends, and developments shaping the world. Problem solving, as Lippitt's research showed, depresses people. A future search conference energizes them. It creates hope and optimism. Many people have reported this pleasant surprise.

Projecting a "big picture" into the future also gets people to think about product end use. My partner Tony Petrella witnessed a dramatic consequence of this when, following "futuring," one company decided to reduce its manufacturing of silicone breast implants—a product employees felt ashamed of—in favor of brain shunts, which are life-saving devices based on the same technology. On another occasion, I saw the biodegradability of disposable products escalate from a minor technical matter to a central strategic issue in a manufacturing firm as several groups (unexpectedly) flagged the issue. It was not "just an R&D problem," but eventually became the core of one scenario in a proposed reorganization.

Conclusion

Each of us is a repository of experience, skill, knowledge, gossip, new developments, old techniques, war stories, legends, myths, colorful characters. Moreover, we all have visions and aspirations, sometimes only half formed, for what we want most. These fertilize productive work places. In traditional conferences this sense of community often comes alive only in the bar after hours. That is why people say that social time is the best part of business meetings. Only over drinks or dinner do we become fully ourselves with one another. That is because typical conferences do not call on us to work and learn together, only to listen and react. No wonder the "real work" happens afterward.

The future search conference links values and actions in "real time." It promotes community by using more of each person's reality. It joins people who need one another, yet rarely interact, in a new kind of relationship. It stimulates creativity and innovative thinking. It offers a unique springboard for planning and goal setting. In the last half of the 20th century, few media exist that are as powerful as this one for raising an awareness of who we are, what we are up against, what we want, and how we might work together to get it.

REFERENCES

Ackoff, R. L. (1974). *Redesigning the future: A systems approach to societal problems.* New York: Wiley.

Ackoff, R. L. (1977). The corporate rain dance. *The Wharton Magazine*, 1(2), 36-41.

Emery, M. (1982). *Searching: For new directions, in new ways for new times.* Canberra, Australia: Centre for Continuing Education, Australian National University.

Fox, R. F., Lippitt, R., & Schindler-Rainman, E. (1973). *The humanized future: Some new images.* La Jolla, CA: University Associates.

Lewin, K. (1948). *Resolving social conflicts: Selected papers on group dynamics* (G. W. Lewin, Ed.). New York: Harper & Brothers.

Lindaman, E., & Lippitt, R. (1979). *Choosing the future you prefer.* Washington, DC: Development Publications.

Lippitt, R. (1983). Future before you plan. In R. Ritvo & A. Sargent (Eds.), *The NTL manager's handbook* (pp. 374-381). Arlington, VA: NTL Institute.

Naisbitt, J. (1982). *Megatrends.* New York: Warner Books.

Schindler-Rainman, E., & Lippitt, R. (1980). *Building the collaborative community: Mobilizing citizens for action.* Riverside: University of California Press.

Trist, E. L., & Emery, F. E. (1960, July 10-16). *Report on the Barford Conference for Bristol/Siddeley, Aero-Engine Corporation* (Document No. 598). London: Tavistock Institute.

Weisbord, M. R. (1984). Future search: Innovative business conference. *Planning Review*, 12(4), 16-20.

Basic Principles of Change

Walter Sikes

Organization development implies change, and most OD programs include planned change efforts. Even attempts to stabilize certain factors in an organization can benefit from applying concepts of change. Therefore, understanding the theory and practice of change is essential for influencing organizational behavior.

This chapter presents ideas related to change processes I have found useful in my own work. It does not summarize the vast literature of the field, nor present everything I consider helpful. Rather, it focuses on those concepts I have found most helpful. The following are seven principles I feel are **most** important for understanding personal and organizational change.

1. You must understand something thoroughly before you try to change it.
2. You cannot change just one element of a system.
3. People resist anything they feel is punishment.
4. People are reluctant to endure discomfort even for the sake of possible gains.
5. Change always generates stress.
6. Participation in setting goals and devising strategies reduces resistance to change.
7. Behavioral change comes in small steps.

I am indebted to the many persons whose knowledge I have blended with my own to arrive at these seven principles. I particularly depended upon the work of Chris Argyris (1982), Warren Bennis (1969), Rosabeth Moss Kanter (1983), Jack Lindquist (1978), Ronald Lippitt (Lippitt, Watsen, & Westley, 1958), Douglas McGregor (1960), Everett Rogers (1983), and Goodwin Watson (1967). My seven principles clearly do not represent the scope of these scholars' work, but are consistent with the concepts they present.

1. You must understand something thoroughly before you try to change it

Change projects have buried change agents who ignored this principle. Many of us have attempted to do good works for or on behalf of others, only to discover too late that our agenda did not fit the needs and realities of the situation. We often have difficulty remembering that for an intervention to succeed, it must be based on a good diagnosis of the client's situation, not the change agent's needs and values.

Examples abound of the failure to abide by this principle, including the following.

- Faculty development committees have devised programs to improve instruction, without first determining from faculty members what they need, want, and are willing to do.
- Managers have established quality circles without first understanding the impact they will have on the complex relationships among supervisors, workers, technicians, and representatives.
- U.S. Marines were stationed in Lebanon in 1983 before the administration fully understood the culture into which the Marines were inserted or the likely consequences of the intervention.
- Social workers sought to get residents of a Peruvian village to boil their drinking water, but they did not realize that the villagers' culture promoted the belief that hot food was appropriate only for ill people.

Even when we gather data by surveys, interviews, or observations, they still may not be sufficient for understanding the dynamics of a system. Several reasons for this exist. One of the more fundamental, I have found, is that the data gatherer's conscious or unconscious biases may result in an interpretation of the information supporting the intervention that person can make. Thus, OD practitioners tend to see things in terms of individual responsibility rather than system responsibility. For example, we help establish programs to teach women living in slums to keep their children from eating lead-based paint chips, rather than addressing the systemic problem of eliminating the lead-based paint.

Another example is that of a quality of work life program that trains company and union officials in group leadership—something that can be done readily—without addressing the suspicions of the foremen and union representatives that block the formation of problem-solving groups. Usually, if a problem is defined in terms of individual behavior, we find it more manageable than if it were considered a consequence of system dynamics.

Frequently, if an individual, group, or organization truly understands the dynamics of a situation that is to be changed, the change will come about with only a minimum of planned action. This is particularly true of behaviors related to organizational norms. If the persons perpetuating the norms clearly perceive (1) what they desire, (2) which norms are dysfunctional, and (3) the behaviors supporting the dysfunctional norms, change will "automatically" begin to move in the desired direction. Even answering such a core question as "What makes people working here want to leave early?" can start the change process.

2. You cannot change just one element of a system

People who are to undergo change function in organically whole systems, meaning that change in one element affects many others. Therefore, much of the risk and many of the failures of change efforts stem from unintended or unanticipated consequences of the interventions. For example, the developers of mechanized tomato harvesting systems did not anticipate that the new technology would reduce the number of commercial tomato growers in California from 4,000 to 600 within nine years, and the number of workers in the industry from 50,000 (mostly men) to 18,000 (mostly women). Moreover, the tomato-growing region moved from Joaquin County to Yolo and Fresno Counties. The innovators of the new harvesting systems did not prepare for or moderate these enormous social impacts, because they had not considered how the change would affect the entire system.

Systems are generally biased against change. Individuals wishing to change their roles or behavior tend to encounter much pressure from the system to remain as they are, no matter how unsatisfactory this is. Most persons who have attended programs to learn interpersonal skills have experienced overt and subtle pressure from others in their systems to return to the behaviors they exhibited before they underwent training.

When one's behavior remains unchanged, the other members of a system do not have to make changes themselves to adjust to new behaviors. Furthermore, undesirable behaviors of others give one an excuse for not resolving one's own problems. For example, if one can blame all one's difficulties on having an alcoholic father, one can thus avoid feeling responsible for one's own behavior. This may lead one to act in ways that encourage one's father to continue drinking.

Another example of the difficulty of changing one's role involves my own family. A few years ago, my youngest daughter—a member of the U.S. Army Nursing Corps—was stationed in Fort Lee, Virginia. One weekend she came to Ohio to pick up a car, and spent much of her time visiting friends. By Sunday afternoon her mother and I began worrying about her driving back to Virginia that night, bothered by visions of robbers and rapists lurking in the West Virginia mountains our youngest (i.e., baby) daughter would have to go through. When she finally got ready to leave, I asked the standard parental question: "Do you need to go to the bathroom before you leave?" She responded, "Dad,

I can't believe this. Mom just asked me the same question. Look—I am a mother, a wife, a college graduate, a nurse, and an officer in the United States Army. I can decide for myself when I need to go to the bathroom.''

Of course, in our family system she is none of these things. She is the youngest kid—and always will be. If we cannot eliminate the rapists and robbers, we can at least try to ensure she faces them with an empty bladder. After all, what are parents for? Other systems are as resistant to change as families.

3. People resist anything they feel is punishment

People almost always find change uncomfortable or punishing. How does change cause discomfort? At a minimum, change makes one exert additional energy, either in making the change oneself or adapting to it. People also tend to put their self-esteem on the line when dealing with change. For example, if an executive plans to turn his work group into an effective team that communicates openly, is trusting, generates creative ideas, and is supportive of its members, he and others will judge his competence by how well the team achieves these goals. Such an evaluation is clearly stressful, threatening, and punishing for most people. One should therefore not be surprised that many people are reluctant to initiate this experience. Trying something new means testing the limits of one's competence, which is scary.

The punishing aspect of change can be lessened by reducing the challenge to one's sense of self-worth. Limit the judging—which tends to be severest when one judges oneself—and the sense of feeling threatened will diminish. That then makes one freer to try more change.

The motivation to change and a sense of reward from the effort to change can be strongly supported by emphasizing what one can learn from the experience. Teams and individuals find learning satisfying if they do not feel a loss of self-esteem because of perceived incompetence while trying to learn. For several years, I worked with change teams on many college campuses engaged in various efforts to improve their institutions (Sikes, Schlesinger, & Seashore, 1974). The teams used different means of reaching their goals, but one thing happened consistently: They all felt excited and rewarded by the opportunity to learn things about themselves, their institutions, education, and the change process. Those teams were specifically designed and trained to support learning. I have observed the same phenomenon occur with other work groups—such as quality of work life committees, or groups in an architectural firm—when the legitimacy of using the experience to **learn something** was highlighted.

4. People are reluctant to endure discomfort even for the sake of possible gains

As I note above, when dealing with any type of change, one must assume that the person or group undergoing the change will consider it at least somewhat punishing. Overcoming this disincentive is difficult, particularly if the benefits resulting from the change are long-term and/or uncertain.

Consider the problem of getting people to reduce cholesterol in their diets. One is told to give up many of the foods one may enjoy eating—such as steak, butter, eggs, bacon, cheese, and ice cream—and switch to less-familiar, perhaps unappealing foods. The payoff from this change may not occur until 20-50 years later, if at all (some people with low cholesterol levels still have heart attacks and strokes).

Some change involves actual physical pain, such as giving up something one is addicted to. When one quits smoking, using heroin, drinking alcohol, or even overeating, at least some discomfort results, and often deep agony. To reach long-range, possibly tenuous goals, people must persevere through unpleasant periods of adjustment, and we all find this stage difficult.

The hindrances to social or organizational change resulting from this principle are powerful. For example, most of us prefer to maintain an unsatisfactory relationship in a work group rather than expend time, energy, and anxiety to improve it. This is especially so when we are not sure improvement will result anyway, and if it may occur only in some distant future after much hard work. In light of how often organizations move personnel around, we should not be surprised that a common strategy is to let problems persist rather than confront them.

Even in situations specifically designed for learning, one tends to use existing skills rather than undergo the discomfort associated with trying new ways of doing things. In T Groups, those who consider themselves competitive compete, those who consider themselves supportive of others give support, those who consider themselves collaborative collaborate, and those who consider themselves loving love. The same phenomenon occurs in executive team-building sessions, even though they are held so that persons can learn new skills. We are reluctant to go beyond the limits of our known, tested abilities.

For most persons, overcoming this requires an environment that recognizes and rewards short-term gains, accepts missteps, legitimizes learning, and offers strong social support. Also helpful is the view that resistance is necessary for learning. For example, I need to confront dominating team members so that

I may learn to deal with dominating team members. To extend my skills in that area, however, I also need team members who support my efforts to make required changes, and a clear view of what I want to accomplish and what resistance I will face.

5. Change always generates stress

All change, pleasant or unpleasant, causes stress. The most stressful tends to be change one feels one cannot control. The person initiating a divorce usually feels less stress than that person's spouse. Any change in employment is stressful, but getting fired produces more tension than resigning does. Deciding on and taking action to alter one's interpersonal style is stressful, but not as stressful as being told by one's boss that one must change to keep one's job.

Two strategies arise from these observations. The first is to enable those undergoing the change to maintain a sense of control. NTL Institute's policy that no one be required to attend an interpersonal skills workshop is consistent with this. The second strategy is to make certain that those undergoing change can manage the related stress because they have effective support systems, relaxation techniques, health practices, and the like.

6. Participation in setting goals and devising strategies reduces resistance to change

One of the most highly researched theories of behavioral science is that participating in setting goals and devising strategies reduces one's resistance to the resulting change. Whether the change involves diet, using contraceptives, accepting new technology in the work place, or making a strategic plan for the company, involving those who will be affected in diagnosing the need for change and planning for action will make them more likely to accept the innovation.

Gathering data through interviews, surveys, observations, or experiments and giving feedback to those involved is a common and effective first step in planned organizational change efforts. Following this, the next steps typically involve personnel in analyzing the data and devising action for correcting the problems they define.

For personal change, a similar process calls for the individual seeking to change to receive information about her or his behavior and its consequences. This person can then decide what to change and how to do this.

Either organizational or personal change can be greatly aided by skilled consultants. Frequently, however, the problem of "client ownership" of the change process arises. Clients demand answers and solutions, even though they rarely accept or use what consultants tell them without making some adaptations of their own. Moreover, persons in most organizations have difficulty accepting that outsiders can contribute anything useful.

Another difficulty is the consultants' need to appear competent, both to themselves and to their clients. After all, they were hired as experts, and experts are supposed to have answers. Consultants have difficulty maintaining the position that what they are experts in is helping clients identify and solve their own problems.

Thus, although the research results seem clear, many barriers exist to involving people in a change effort. A paradox is that the statement "participation reduces resistance to change" is itself an "expert opinion" that clients resist unless they participate in reaching that conclusion. The principle's truth can best be demonstrated through experience, which requires trust. Perhaps the key skill of effective OD consultants is their ability to get clients to make a leap of faith and to help them learn from it.

7. Behavioral change comes in small steps

When one gives someone feedback about behavior one dislikes, one generally does not want to see that person act that way again—even though one may make pious statements about being nonevaluative or giving the recipient of the feedback the choice of what to do with the information. This is especially true if the person giving the feedback is in a more powerful position than the recipient (e.g., is a boss or parent). If a father catches his child bouncing on a bed and tells the child to stop doing this, the father means "no more bouncing." Wanting to feel in control of its life and to maintain its self-concept—and to have fun—the child may bounce a few more times. Although parents find this response frustrating, it is a healthy reaction for a child.

We often prevent ourselves and others from changing by having unrealistic expectations about the magnitude or speed of the change. People have difficulty being satisfied with small changes that move them in the desired direction, and thus—lacking big changes—do not move at all.

A client of mine who was the senior partner of architectural firm wanted to travel less frequently because this was adversely affecting his personal and professional life. In a discussion with me, he vowed to reduce his traveling by half. I told him I did not think he could do this immediately, and suggested that during the next three months he try to spend one more weekend at home per month. He did this, and after a few months had substantially reduced his traveling. A year later he told me that my notion that change comes in small steps was a great insight to him, as he had been prevented from acting by the assumption that he had to deal with a problem by making a big move all at once. Whenever he could not do that, he made no change whatsoever.

Helping a person or organization make small changes or "experiments" that move them toward a goal can be useful. To do this, the person undergoing the change must consider gradual progress legitimate,even when addressing large problems. The phrase "avoid abrupt changes" is generally good advice, as such changes tend to be stressful and short-lived.

Conclusion

I hope that these principles—as do all good ideas of social science—cause you to have "ah-ha" reactions and to recognize something you have known all along. After all, you have been observing organizations and people, too, and should have had reactions similar to mine. Perhaps organizing these observations into principles will help you apply them more easily to change efforts. For practitioners, the ability to use what is known and to help others use what they know is what makes a difference.

REFERENCES

Argyris, C. (1982). *Reasoning, learning and action*. San Francisco: Jossey-Bass.

Bennis, W. (1969). *Organization development*. Reading, MA: Addison-Wesley.

Kanter, R. M. (1983). *The change masters*. New York: Simon & Schuster.

Lindquist, J. (1978). *Strategies for change*. Berkeley, CA: Pacific Soundings Press.

Lippitt, R., Watsen, J., & Westley, B. (1958). *Planned change*. New York: Harcourt, Brace and World.

McGregor, D. (1960). *The human side of enterprise*. New York: McGraw-Hill.

Rogers, E. (1983). *Diffusion of innovations* (3rd ed.). New York: Free Press.

Sikes, W., Schlesinger, L., & Seashore, C. (1974). *Renewing higher education from within*. San Francisco: Jossey-Bass.

Watson, G. (1967). *Concepts for social change*. Arlington, VA: NTL Institute.

Sociotechnical System Design in Transition

Abraham B. Shani
Ord Elliott

Introduction

Sociotechnical system (STS) design is becoming an increasingly popular cross-cultural organization design approach for examining and changing the work place environment. Published reports of STS methods of organization design indicate that they have had more success in improving productivity and the quality of working life than have traditional work designs (cf., Davis, 1983; Golomb, 1981; Pasmore, Francis, Haldeman, & Shani, 1982; Pava, 1983; Trist, 1982). Although STS approaches to organization design have been tested in many experiments in innovative work organizations during the past 35 years, however, research has produced little empirical evidence concerning the specific design principles used and their relative importance. Moreover, some authors have begun to claim that the "current state" of STS design theory is "questionable" (Miles, 1980), "vague" (Hackman, 1982; Shani & Pasmore, 1983), "diverse" (Cummings, 1985; Margulies & Colflesh, 1985), and not responsive to the challenging environment of businesses today (Elliott, 1984; Pava, 1986).

This chapter addresses these issues. Following a brief overview of the sociotechnical system work design theory, we examine the design principles advocated by 21 STS scholars and designers. The complex relationship between design principles and strategic planning has emerged as one aspect leading to the somewhat contradictory and disjointed body of knowledge. Today's turbulent business environment demands that STS design elements be integrated with strategic management elements (Shani & Elliott, 1988). We ourselves argue that the technical, social, and strategic elements of an organization must be put to optimum use if the organization is to be effective—or even survive.

Sociotechnical systems design

Managers and scholars alike appear to agree in general that the purpose of work design is to maximize productivity while minimizing costs. Numerous work design paradigms have emerged, each offering a particular definition of productivity and a specific approach for resolving major issues (Shani & Stebbins, 1987).

The concept of sociotechnical systems emerged from the studies and consulting work of the Tavistock Institute in England (Trist, 1951, 1982). This approach essentially sought to develop a better fit between the technology, structure, and social interaction of the work place so as to achieve desired organizational and human objectives. STS design has emerged as a prescriptive model for organizational change at the operational level, especially in manufacturing. Although a large body of literature now exists addressing STS interventions and design factors, the array of views promulgated by researchers, theorists, and practitioners obscures the extent to which they share a common conception.

The role of management in the optimum use of organization design. Because the goals of an organization are considered a form of interdependence between the firm and its environment, the organizational entity may be loosely classified as an ''open system'' striving to attain a steady state by achieving optimum growth (Thorsrud, Bjorg, & Bjorn, 1976). Although the commitment of the leaders and members is crucial to maintaining the desired steady state, an organization's ability to adjust to environmental fluctuations is a function of the flexibility of the technical and social subsystems. The STS solution attempts to weld the behavioral subsystem with the mechanistic (technical) subsystem to integrate the whole organization, with the goal being to achieve overall effectiveness while harmonizing the conflicting objectives of the subsystems.

In general, scholars agree that the primary task of managers is strategic management. In the sociotechnical system, management strives to have the organization attain the optimum fit with its environment. The basic philosophy underlying STS design is that informed decision makers, attempting to make the best investment decisions, should facilitate the efficient allocation of the organization's resources by adhering to the concepts of ''joint optimization'' and of controlling key variances at the lowest level at which both the technical and social subsystems operate (Emery & Emery, 1978; Pasmore, 1988; Taylor, 1975). The technological demands of the production process and the social/psychological needs of employees are considered the factors most important to work design success. Thus, joint optimization often requires a compromise between the goals of optimum technical rationality and optimum employee satisfaction (Cummings, 1978).

The key concepts of joint optimization and controlling variances at the lowest level of meaningful interaction between the social and technical subsystems provide the guidelines for STS intervention designs. Our review of the contemporary literature suggests that although many versions of STS interventions have been attempted, these have been based on three major clusters of design factors. Moreover, our selective review reveals that these interventions have relied on some design principles more than others. Table 1 presents a list of these design principles.

Table 1
Sociotechnical Systems Design Factors

General design factors
1. Organization as a system of social and technical subsystems
2. Organization as an open system
3. Compatibility with organizational context
4. Variances controlled at the source
5. Minimal critical specification
6. Congruency supported
7. Information system
8. Management facilitates boundary spanning
9. Management role focuses on strategy and policy

Task design factors
10. Each job comprises various tasks
11. Individuals use multiple skills
12. The job results in a completed product
13. Facilities augment tasks
14. Direct feedback given

Structural design factors
15. Parallel structures
16. Autonomous work groups that
    (a) create complete products,
    (b) have members with multiple skills,
    (c) control the scheduling of their own tasks,
    (d) provide their own maintenance and service,
    (e) receive direct feedback on their performance,
    (f) are ongoing learning systems, and
    (g) are involved in strategic planning
17. Reward systems congruent with social system design
18. Ongoing organizational learning process

Although this list is somewhat arbitrary and is not exhaustive, we believe it is well suited to serve as the basis for a survey of STS design studies.

The characteristics of sociotechnical system design elements

Our survey of the literature examined the writings of 21 STS scholars and practitioners. Our selection is by no mean exhaustive, and our final choices reflect two main goals: to provide a list representing a range of different fields of STS research, and to include only those authors who have sought to specify, refine, or develop the STS design principles.

Our survey revealed references to 18 different STS design factors (see Table 1). Of these factors, we found high agreement among the authors as to the importance of one-half (see Table 2), whereas one-third were idiosyncratic (i.e., each noted in only one work studied). We found agreement for the importance of underlying design philosophy of general system theory (Factors 1, 2, 3, and 6), the specific task design principles (Factors 10, 11, 12, and 14), the autonomous work group design principles (Factors 16a, b, c, d, e, and f), and the principle of designing a reward system congruent with the social system design (Factor 17). This congruity reflects the primary and widespread emphasis of STS as a mechanism for enhancing the performance of the social system at the operational level through the creation of autonomous work groups. The idiosyncratic design factors focus on the parallel structural design principles of the structural design cluster (Factor 15), the information system design principles (Factor 7), and the strategic formulation and planning, both at the team involvement level (Factor 16G) and the management level (Factor 9).

Observations

Autonomous work groups. Of the works we examined, 82% reported the employment of design principles involving autonomous work groups. Most STS systems are designed around the creation and development of highly cohesive teams as basic subunits of the organization. Theoretically, the highly interdependent nature of most process operations seems to indicate that they are best managed by such teams—a correct assumption when the work is technologically complex, with high levels of interdependence among persons across different functions. Not all technology within an organization, however, requires teams. Simple, highly manual forms of technology requiring little interdependent work seem to call for an alternate work unit design. For many, however, sociotechnical system design has come to mean the development and evolution of autonomous work teams. In many cases, this goal has largely been achieved. The problem with autonomous work teams, however, is that in becoming autonomous they

Table 2
Design Factors of Sociotechnical Systems: A Consensual Summary*

Authors	General design factors									Task factors					Structural design factors										
	1	2	3	4	5	6	7	8	9	10	11	12	13	14	15	16	16a	16b	16c	16d	16e	16f	16g	17	18
Albrecht (1983)	X					x									x								x		
Bartlett and Villagomez (1981)	x	x	x					x							X	x		x		x		x		x	x
Cherns (1978)	x	x	x	x	x	x	x			x	x	x	x	x			x	x	x	x	x	x	x		x
Cummings (1985)	x	x	X	x	x			x		x	x	x	x	x	x	x	x	x	x	x	x	x	x	x	x
Davis (1978)	x	x	x	x					x	x	x	x		x	x	x	x	x	x	x	x	x	x		
Elden (1979)	x		X			x									x	x									
Elliott (1984)	x	x	x	x	x	x	x		x	x	x		x	x			x	x	x	x	x	x	x		
Emery (1959)	X	X	x										x		X										
Golomb (1981)	X	X				X					x	x	x		x	x		x	x	x	x	x	X	x	x
Hanna (1988)	x	x	x	x	x	x		x							x	x	x	x	x	x	x	x	X		
Herbst (1974)	x	x	x	x			x	x		x	x	x	x	x	X	x							X		X
Macy (1982)	X	x								x	x	x	x	x	X	x							X		x
Margulies and Colflesh (1985)				x	X	x		x	x						X	x	x	x	x	x	x		x	x	x
Palmore (1988)	x	x	x	x	x	x		x		x	x	x	x	x	x	x	x	x	x	x	x	x	x	x	x
Pava (1986)	x	x	x	x					x	x	x	x	x	x	x		x			x	x				
Shani (1985)	x	x	x				x	x		x	x	x		x	x	x	x	x	x	x	x				
Susman (1975)	x						x	x	x	x					X	x			x	x	x				
Taylor (1986)	x	X	x	x	x	x	X				x	x		x									x		
Thorsrud, Bjorg, and Bjorn (1976)	x	x	x	x	x	x			x	x	x	x		x	x	x	x	x	x	x	x	X	X	X	x
Trist (1982)	x	x	x							x	x	x			x	x	x	x	x	x	x		x	x	x
Walton (1982)	x		x	x						x					x	x	x	x	x	x	x		x	x	x

* The numbers across the top of the table correspond to those assigned to the factors listed in Table 1. An "x" beneath a number indicates that the author(s) alludes to this design factor, but does not highlight it. An italicized "X" beneath a number indicates that the author(s) explicitly highlights this design factor.

insulate themselves further and grow less willing to cooperate across teams. Although interdependence within teams may be increased, interdependence across teams is often minimized by the formation of autonomous work units.

Even more problematic is the explicit assumption that team development is synonymous with desired business results. Perhaps the energy once directed toward matching individual needs and business objectives has unconsciously been transferred over time to toward developing autonomous work teams. Thus, teamwork and its various refinements may have caused the melting pot take the place of satisfying individual career objectives and achieving business results.

This does not mean that STS design prevents either individual or organizational development. In those systems attempting to pursue the original design intentions, technicians demand increasing amounts of information about the business. That is, for them to attain business results, they must know more about the business, and for them to pursue individual development, they must expand the scope and complexity of their work.

Parallel structure. Of the works examined, 14% reported the use of parallel structures to facilitate both the collaborative design process and ongoing organizational learning. The parallel structure consists of multiple groups whose tasks are to inquire into the state of the organization, recommend design modifications, and occasionally help implement the design. The word "parallel" refers to functioning outside the normal chain of command and serving as a pipeline for collecting, sharing, and acting on ideas and knowledge concerning the organization; the word "structure" refers to a particular division and coordination of labor. The parallel structure design has the following characteristics: It is a knowledge-seeking, problem-solving design for recommending action to the formal organization (Zand, 1981), it promotes non-hierarchical relations among organization members (Bushe, 1984), it creates complex role sets (Rubenstein & Woodman), and it functions outside the normal chain of command yet is strongly linked to the formal organization. Although they seem to have great potential, surprisingly little is reported about the principles of parallel structure (Bushe & Shani, 1988).

Multiple skill requirements. Although 59% of the works examined cited a requirement that individuals possess multiple skills, only 54% reported multiple skills within teams. Inherent in the team concept is the notion that technicians should learn more than just one skill. In general, the flow is thought to move in the following direction: learning basic process skills as part of the team's operations, then understanding and using maintenance skills, and finally developing administration and team coordination skills. Ideally, "dirty," manual, or dull work should be combined with more interesting and complex work in forming individual jobs.

Sociotechnical systems tend to overemphasize the promise of interesting and challenging work, and to play down the performance of relatively undesirable work. This may produce difficulties: For example, if automated packing machinery breaks down and makes hand packing necessary, the supervisors may be unable to get their subordinates to perform this task and may have to make contracts outside the organization to have the work done. A faster rate and clearer direction of growth occurs as an individual moves from using operating skills to developing coordination skills. Once team coordination skills are developed, however, the concept of individual growth and contribution to the organization becomes less clear. A deliberate effort is made to prevent an individual from developing into a specialist in a craft or function. Theoretically, STS has no operators, mechanics, or electricians per se, for all of these functions require skills each technician is capable of learning and using. Specialization is considered a malfunction of the principle of multiple skills, and possibly a prelude to the unionization of the work force.

Within mature sociotechnical systems, however, a handful of specialists do tend to emerge, even though the existence and labeling of such specialization is formally denied. Typically, they are found in the electronic or computer areas, where it seems impossible for multi-skilled generalists to also possess the necessary in-depth knowledge of minicomputers, microprocessors, and other electronic equipment. From an industrial relations perspective, the presence of specialists undoubtedly increases the potential for union activity, but specialization does not automatically lead to unions, especially when only a few such individuals work for the organization. Moreover, a firm may enhance its retention of sophisticated and mature individuals with high levels of technical competence by acknowledging their expertise. Clinging inflexibly to the principle of requiring multiple skills prevents an organization from making practical design changes that meet real business challenges (Kolodny & Dresner, 1986).

Information system design. Of the works examined, 27% reported the incorporation of information system design into the redesigned organization. STS's emphasis on open systems has led to the notion that the greater the amount of information flowing in the organization, the more effective the organization will be (considered literally as a high degree of openness and a high volume of communication in all directions—up, down, laterally, diagonally). The optimum amount, nature, and direction of information, however, depends on the types of specific technology employed within a work unit. For example, warehouse trucklift operators do not need to communicate frequently with one another to perform their jobs successfully.

Moreover, as a team evolves toward greater autonomy, its information needs change as the team matures and becomes more successful. For example, a team once content simply with knowing the results expected of it may now want cost and profit data for different functions, including advertising, which is external to the plant. Many managers believe that teams should not be allowed to have such information—for reasons ranging from security to the opinion that knowing certain things is a management prerogative—and thus retard the flow of information. Therefore, the premise that sociotechnical systems are characterized by a greater degree of communication is not entirely valid. The information needs of various types of work units do differ, and the level of openness is frequently limited by managers of functional groups outside the plant.

Open systems and strategic planning. Although 23% of the works examined addressed the issue of strategy as part of STS design principles, only 18% reported cases in which autonomous work groups participated in strategic planning. Strategic planning is generally considered an activity occurring in the upper levels of the organizational hierarchy. Because an overwhelming number of STS applications have occurred in manufacturing, it is not surprising that the design processes have generally failed to incorporate strategic planning. Figure 1 depicts the traditional STS design focus. The technical system has most often determined the ultimate organization configuration, which also primarily results from applying STS to the manufacturing setting rather than to the entire organization.

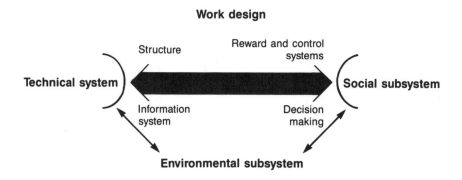

Figure 1. Sociotechnical system design: The traditional view

Strategic thinking and sociotechnical systems

Applications of sociotechnical thinking at the upper levels of an organization should naturally focus more on issues of strategy. Furthermore, to the extent that STS involves the entire organization, strategic planning must begin with the strategic situation rather than technical prerequisites. Although most of the organization design literature addresses the optimal internal organizational design, the strategic management literature deals with the "matching," "align-ing," or "fit" of organization resources with environmental opportunities and threats (Chandler, 1967; Schendel & Hofer, 1979). Andrews defines the role of fit within the strategy paradigm as

> ...the ability to identify four components of strategy—(1) market opportunity, (2) corporate competences and resources, (3) personal values and aspirations, and (4) acknowledged obligations to segments of society other than stockholders....(1971, p. 38)

This and other such statements indicate that the concept of fit, which is at the heart of strategic management, ignores organization development elements and their potential causes and effects.

Although the notions of fit and joint optimization both have been used by many consultants as normative concepts when highlighting the importance of synchronizing complex organization elements (cf. Venkatraman & Camillus, 1984) and arguing that congruence among several elements is a prerequisite of organizational success (Peters & Waterman, 1982), these notions lack precise definitions. Furthermore, Van de Ven (1979) argues that considerably more theoretical work is needed if we are to incorporate fit into a theory of organizations.

In a recent work, Smircich and Stubbant (1985) propose that organiza-tions' environments are enacted through the social construction and interaction processes of organized actors. As such, the merger of organization design elements with the elements of strategic management has been considered a natural solution and a topic deserving further inquiry.

A broader-based framework incorporating STS design with strategic think-ing would likely provide a more holistic explanation of organizational dynamics. A framework incorporating the strategic, technical, and social elements of the organization and considering their degree of joint optimization, fit, and/or match would help organizations respond better to intense competition and to rapidly changing products, technology, and human resources.

Conclusion

Our review of the design factors advocated and used by selected sociotechnical systems scholars reveals both similarities and discrepancies. Most of the similarities relate to an almost-exclusive focus on design elements involving core production processes. Our most paradoxical—and perhaps most important—finding is that, although the design principles of the organization as an open system and compatibility with organizational context were frequently employed, principles involving strategic planning were not. Today's environment presents a unique challenge to the design of organizations. The goal of achieving a social and technical system characterized by joint optimization, established by STS founders (Emery, 1959; Rice, 1958; Trist, 1951) and further articulated by others who developed this approach (Cherns, 1978; Cummings & Srivastva, 1977; Davis & Taylor, 1979; Herbst, 1974; Pasmore & Sherwood, 1978; Pava, 1983; Shani & Pasmore, 1985; Susman, 1975; Taylor, 1975; Thorsrud et al., 1976; Walton, 1982), stops short of including the design of an organization capable of effectively performing within a highly turbulent environment.

The most common applications of STS have focused on manufacturing systems, and therefore have led to the notion that the technical system is the best starting point for joint optimization (Elliott, Shani, & Hanna, 1985). A broader-based framework that includes strategic planning is needed. Within the fast-paced "high tech" environment, one can more easily see how strategic changes can force those involved with the technical system to make major choices and can cause a dynamic interaction between the strategic, technical, and social subsystems. Ideally, this can lead to a high-performing organization.

NOTE

The author's names are listed in random order; each contributed equally to the preparation of this chapter. The chapter was developed from a paper presented at the 27th annual meeting of the Western Academy of Management, Reno, Nevada, March 1986.

REFERENCES

Albrecht, K. (1983). *Organization development: A total systems approach to positive change in any business organization.* Englewood Cliffs, NJ: Prentice-Hall.

Andrews, K. R. (1971). *The concept of corporate strategy.* Homewood, IL: Irwin.

Bartlett, B., & Villagomez, E. T. (1981). *Application of sociotechnical systems in the U.S. Army.* Working paper, U.S. Army Organizational Effectiveness Center and School, Fort Ord, CA.

Bushe, G. R. (1984). *Developmental trends of parallel structure interventions.* Paper presented at the 45th National Academy of Management Conference, Boston.

Bushe, G. R., & Shani, A. B. (1988). A review of the literature on the use of parallel learning structure interventions in bureaucratic organizations. In F. Hoy (Ed.), *Best papers proceedings* (pp. 288-262). Academy of Management Conference, Anaheim, CA.

Chandler, A. D. (1967). *Strategy and structure: Chapters in the history of American enterprise.* Cambridge, MA: MIT Press.

Cherns, A. B. (1978). The principles of sociotechnical design. In A. Pasmore & J. J. Sherwood (Eds.), *Sociotechnical systems: A sourcebook.* La Jolla, CA: University Associates.

Cummings, T. G. (1978). Sociotechnical experimentation: A review of sixteen studies. In W. A. Pasmore & J. J. Sherwood (Eds.), *Sociotechnical systems: A sourcebook.* La Jolla, CA: University Associates.

Cummings, T. G. (1985). Designing work for productivity and quality of work life. In D. D. Warrick (Ed.), *Contemporary organization development: Current thinking and applications* (pp. 69-76). Chicago: Scott, Foresman.

Cummings, T. G., & Srivastva, S. (1977). *Management of work: A sociotechnical systems approach.* Kent, OH: Kent State University Press.

Davis, L. E. (1978). The design of work and quality of working life. In W. A. Pasmore & J. J. Sherwood (Eds.), *Sociotechnical systems: A sourcebook*. La Jolla, CA: University Associates.

Davis, L. E. (1983). Workers and technology: The necessary joint basis for organizational effectiveness. *National Productivity Review, 3*(1), 7-14.

Davis, L. E., & Taylor, J. C. (Eds.). (1979). *Design of jobs*. San Diego: Goodyear.

Elden, M. (1979). Three generations of work-democracy experiments in Norway: Beyond classical sociotechnical systems analysis. In L. Cooper & E. Mumford (Eds.), *Quality of working life in Western Europe*. London: Associated Business Press.

Elliott, O. (1984). *Beyond sociotechnical/open system design*. Paper presented at the 45th National Academy of Management Conference, Boston.

Elliott, O., Shani, A. B., & Hanna, D. (1985). *Strategic thinking and sociotechnical system design: A high tech merger*. Paper presented at the 26th annual conference of the Western Academy of Management, San Diego.

Emery, F. (1959). *Characteristics of sociotechnical systems*. London: Tavistock.

Emery, M. D., & Emery, F. E. (1978). Searching for new directions. In J. Sutherland (Ed.), *A management handbook for public administrators*. New York: Van Nostrand Reinhold.

Golomb, N. (1981). *A sociotechnical strategy for improving the effectiveness and the Q.W.L. of three Kibbutz plants and one governmental institute*. Working paper, the Ruppin Institute Kibbutz Management Center, Israel.

Hackman, J. R. (1982). Sociotechnical systems theory: A commentary. In A. H. Van de Ven & W. F. Joyce (Eds.), *Perspectives on organization design and behavior* (pp. 75-88). New York: Wiley.

Hanna, D. (1988). *Designing organizations for high performance*. Reading, MA: Addison-Wesley.

Herbst, P. G. (1974). *Sociotechnical design: Strategies in multidisciplinary research*. London: Tavistock.

Kolodny, H., & Dresner, B. (1986, Winter). Linking arrangements and new work designs. *Organizational Dynamics*, pp. 33-51.

Macy, B. A. (1982). The Bolivar quality of work life program: Success or failure? In R. Zager & M. P. Roson (Eds.), *The innovative organization* (pp. 184-221). New York: Pergamon Press.

Margulies, N., & Coflesh, L. (1985). An organizational development approach to the planning and implementation of new technology. In D. D. Warrick (Ed.), *Contemporary organization development: Current thinking and applications* (pp. 231-253). Chicago: Scott, Foresman.

Miles, R. H. (1980). *Macro organizational behavior*. San Diego : Goodyear.

Pasmore, W. A. (1988). *Designing effective organizations: The sociotechnical systems perspective*. New York: Wiley.

Pasmore, W. A., Francis, C., Haldeman, J., & Shani, A. B. (1982). Sociotechnical systems: A North American reflection on empirical studies of the seventies. *Human Relations, 35*(12), 1179-1204.

Pasmore, W. A., & Sherwood, J. J. (Eds.). (1978). *Sociotechnical systems: A sourcebook*. La Jolla, CA: University Associates.

Pava, C. H. (1983). *Managing new office technology*. New York: Free Press.

Pava, C. H. (1986). Redesigning sociotechnical systems designs: Concepts and methods for the 1990s. *Journal of Applied Behavioral Science, 22*(3), 201-221.

Peters, T. J., & Waterman, R. H., Jr. (1982). *In search of excellence: Lessons from America's best run companies*. New York: Harper & Row.

Rice, A. K. (1958). *Productivity and social organization: The Ahmedabad experiment*. London: Tavistock Institute.

Rubenstein, D., & Woodman, R. N. (1984). Spiderman and the Burma Raiders: Collateral organization theory in action. *Journal of Applied Behavioral Science, 20*(1), 1-21.

Schendel, D. E., & Hofer, C. W. (1979). *Strategic management: A new view of business policy and planning*. Boston: Little, Brown.

Shani, A. B. (1985). *The durability of sociotechnical systems in small business organizations: Some research findings.* Technical report, Bureau of Business and Economic Research.

Shani, A. B., & Elliott, O. (1988). Applying sociotechnical systems design to the strategic apex: An illustration. *Organization Development Journal, 6*(2), 53-66.

Shani, A. B., & Pasmore, W. A. (1983). Durability of sociotechnical systems and quality of life work efforts: Beyond the boundaries of the initial process. In *Proceedings of the Organization Development Network Annual Conference.* Los Angeles: Organization Development Network.

Shani, A. B., & Pasmore, W. A. (1985). Toward a new model of the action research process. In D. D. Warrick (Ed.), *Contemporary organization development: Current thinking and applications* (pp. 438-449). Chicago: Illinois.

Shani, A. B., & Stebbins, M. W. (1987). Organization design: Emerging trends. *Consultation, 6*(3), 187-193.

Smircich, L., & Stubbant, C. (1985). Strategic management in an enacted world. *Academy of Management Review, 10*(4), 724-736.

Susman, G. (1975). Technological prerequisites for delegation of decision making to work groups. In L. Davis & A. Cherns (Eds.), *The quality of working life* (Vol. 1). New York: Free Press.

Taylor, J. C. (1975). The human side of work: The sociotechnical approach to work system design. *Personnel Review, 4*(3), 3-10.

Taylor, J. C. (1986). Long-term sociotechnical systems change in a computer operations department. *Journal of Applied Behavioral Science, 22*(3), 303-314.

Thorsrud, E., Bjorg, S., & Bjorn, G. (1976). Sociotechnical approach to industrial democracy in Norway. In R. Dubin (Ed.), *Handbook of work organization and society.* New York: Rand McNally.

Trist, E. L. (1951). *Some observations on the machine face as a sociotechnical system* (Tavistock Document Series). London: Tavistock Institute.

Trist, E. L. (1982). The sociotechnical perspective. In A. H. Van de Ven & W. F. Joyce (Eds.), *Perspectives on organization design and behavior* (pp. 19-75). New York: Wiley.

Van de Ven, A. H. (1979). Review of organization-environment interfaces. *Administrative Science Quarterly, 24,* 323-326.

Venkatraman, N., & Camillus, J. C. (1984). Exploring the concept of fit in strategic management. *Academy of Management Review, 9*(3), 513-525.

Walton, R. E. (1982). The Topeka work system: Optimistic visions, pessimistic hypotheses, and reality. In R. Zager & M. P. Rosow (Eds.), *The innovative organization* (pp. 260-290). New York: Pergamon Press.

Zand, D. E. (1981). *Information, organization and power.* New York: McGraw-Hill.

Theory, Method, and Process: Key Dynamics in Designing High-Performing Organizations from an Open Sociotechnical Systems Perspective

Bernard J. Mohr

High-performing systems: Characteristics and requisite conditions

Any organizational system is an intricate web of roles, management practices, structures, processes, tasks, technology, and people. How these elements interact with one another determines how successfully an organization can produce a service or product within the constraints of cost, quality, timeliness, safety, and customer requirements. Organizations that continually succeed within these constraints can be considered **high-performing systems.**[1]

One can measure or evaluate a high-performing system (HPS) from an individual level, a "people" level, a system level, or organizational level. Organizations seeking to become high-performing systems must design their work systems to ensure that the following three conditions are met.

1. People must be able to do what is expected of them. This means guaranteeing the availability of appropriate skills, resources, technology, and opportunities within the work system.

2. People must want to do these tasks. This implies a level of individual commitment that can only result from appropriate management practices, reward systems, company norms and culture, and work designed to be intrinsically fulfilling.

---

3. **People must be allowed to do these tasks.** This requires management of responsibility and discretion, the elimination of unnecessary boundaries, and increased access to information needed for operations.

Every work system devises its own way of modifying roles, tasks, processes, and technology to create these conditions. What matters is that they exist, through whatever process. The conscious creation of these conditions—a process called organization design—is how the infrastructure for an HPS is developed.

In addition to knowing about these "people conditions," one should also learn the system- or organization-level description of an HPS. According to this description, high-performing systems have the following characteristics.

1. **An HPS largely achieves both its human and business/service goals.** Contrary to some widespread ideas, an HPS is not a "perfect" system that achieves 100% of what it strives for. Rather, an HPS performs in the "top range" most of the time. It may not meet every deadline, constraint, or individual need, but observers of high-performing systems describe them as consistently ranking in the "top ten" of their fields.

2. **An HPS can adapt to changing requirements with minimal disruption to goal achievement and minimal cost (economic or otherwise) to the organization's members.** The pace and quantity of changes confronting organizations today are greater than ever before. They must address new demands from employees, customers, competitors, and regulatory agencies. The hallmark of an HPS is its having the flexibility to modify its operations in response to these demands—through ways other than going out of business. An HPS can adapt to change without incurring the economic, psychological, and emotional trauma often associated with major organizational transitions.

3. **An HPS is characterized by an alignment of the organization's culture, vision, and structure.** OD consultants often find organizations that have worked hard to create their own visions. This refers to a widely shared image of an organization's preferred future. A vision becomes the driving force for deciding what kinds of norms, values, and beliefs are to be inculcated. In modifying these cultural elements, organizations frequently find that the structure of work and authority are major factors influencing their cultures. Only when an organization's vision, culture, and structure are "in sync" can this organization exhibit some of the characteristics of a high-performing system.

For example, an organization in the forest products industry developed a vision of operating as a series of small entrepreneurial businesses (within the structure of the larger plant). To attain this vision, management found the need to make major structural changes affecting supervision, and to support this with changes in the incentive system so that business results would be valued more than individual performance. These changes enabled the organization to align its vision, culture, and structure.

4. An HPS achieves its energy for operation from a high level of individual commitment, which is generated internally within individuals rather than imposed on them externally through mechanisms of control and punishment. The underlying premise is that although all organizations create various amounts of human energy, an HPS both requires and generates more of this. Human energy is needed for productivity, and high-performing systems consume unusually high levels in seeking to be constantly responsive and effective in attaining their goals despite changing environments and pressures to reduce costs (something faced by all organizations, from government to the automobile industry). An HPS can consume so much energy only by ensuring that equivalent or larger amounts are constantly generated.

To evaluate the performance of an HPS, the following measurement criteria can be used.

1. The ratio of resources consumed to the value of what is produced. This is a basic criterion for evaluating all organizations. Unless the perceived value of an organization's ''output''—whether this is a social service, a physical product, information, or, as in the case of symphony orchestra, a pleasurable experience—exceeds the perceived value of the ''input,'' the organization not only cannot be called a high-performing system, but it will soon cease to exist at all.

When examining this criterion, one must not limit one's definitions of input and output to traditional monetary ones. Rather, one should refer to a ''give/get'' ratio. This is the ratio of expected return on ''gives'' (EROG) to actual return on ''gives'' (AROG), based on perceptions of stakeholders who provide the resources enabling the organization to operate. When the ''gives'' include such resources as labor, energy, commitment, electoral mandates, political support, information, physical materials, and money, the ''gets'' (i.e., return for one's investment) include enhanced power and status in addition to valued products and services, job satisfaction, and money.

2. The timeliness and quality of the system's output. No matter how excellent a symphony orchestra is, unless it produces its ''product'' at the times its customers want to ''consume'' it, it cannot be considered an HPS. Similarly, a company may offer a highly popular toy, but if it cannot make this available in stores until the week after Christmas, the company cannot be considered an HPS. With respect to quality, the American automobile industry offers classic examples of organizations able to meet deadlines, but having more difficulty ensuring sufficient product quality to maintain their historical shares of the market. Although these companies have put forth major efforts to improve this, they continue to suffer from a perceived ''quality gap'' in the minds of a significant number of potential customers.

3. The appropriateness of the output for the primary receiving system. The primary receiving system consists of those individuals or groups an organization is primarily in the business of serving. A hospital's primary receiving system is its patients; an accounting firm's primary receiving system is its clients. The output of an HPS is typically considered desirable and relevant for its primary receiving system. Examples of organizations meeting this criterion include accounting firms that deliver advice on taxes when asked and bookkeeping services upon request. An accounting firm that fails to provide its clients with necessary financial planning advice, however—or provides advice its clients' consider useless—would not be considered a high-performing system.

4. The degree to which the internal individual commitment—rather than control—of organization members is the primary source of energy for operations. As discussed above in the section on system-level characteristics, the issue is the balance between control versus internal commitment (Walton, 1985) as strategies for generating human energy in an organization. All organizations require some degree of internal control as a mechanism of coordination and general management. High-performing systems tend to rely more on members' commitment to the work place as a way of achieving necessary behaviors rather than on such controlling tactics as use of time cards, close supervision, piece-rate compensation, and the like.

These four major criteria, along with the descriptions of system-level and "people" characteristics, form the framework for understanding high-performing systems and for evaluating the extent to which a system can be considered high performing. The following section discusses how to create (i.e., design) such a system, whether one is modifying an existing organization or starting a new one.

Organization design, open sociotechnical systems, and high-performing systems

This chapter previously referred to the organizational system as an intricate web of roles, management practices, structures, processes, tasks, technology, and people. Organization design is an umbrella term for the **conscious creation** of an HPS through the **systematic and systemic modification** of some or all of the above elements making up the "intricate web."

A systematic approach is one based on a thoughtful consideration of change and the politics involved with this, and on a comprehensive diagnosis of what exists (this differs from an approach that simply adopts the latest management fad, such as management by walking around, quality circles, or the like). A systemic approach is one based on the recognition of the interconnections of these elements and the tendency of organizations to resist change unless a "critical mass" of the elements are modified to support the change. For example, attempts to modify people's work responsibilities to make them more entrepreneurial are unrealistic unless simultaneous changes are made in incentives, decision making, and information dissemination, and opportunities are provided to develop required skills.

The rest of this section examines in more detail some of the major organizational elements typically analyzed and modified during an organizational design—or redesign—process. Individual skills invariably need development, for new work roles require behaviors different from those learned over the years in the organization. The types of skills needing development are skills related to team and interpersonal relations and technical skills.

In the case of the redesign of a major railway organization, the number of work role classifications was reduced from 16 to 8. Because of this, employees needed extensive retraining in technical skills. For example, persons who had worked as porters needed to learn how to be waiters, make coffee, and the like. Moreover, the redesigned organization called for work teams to meet at the start of a trip so that members could assign tasks, determine food requirements, and so forth, creating the need to develop skills in problem solving and team decision making.

Organizational redesign affects the availability and allocation of physical and financial resources within the work system. Because the processes for distributing scarce resources can be designed in many ways—each having a dramatically different impact on system performance—the organizational design process requires careful assessment of alternatives. One frequently used option is to assign responsibility for supplies procurement to the work group actually responsible for using those supplies. This movement toward semi-autonomous work teams has systemic implications for the traditional staff functions of purchasing and finance. The organizational design process must also note how the roles associated with these functions will need to be modified.

Technology design is another part of the overall design process that can aid in achieving the desired level of total system performance. Technology can be designed so as to either minimize or maximize the operator's control, or to provide little or much data. For example, when Ford Motor Company sought to improve product quality, it gave each assembly-line operator access to a button that, if pressed, would shut down the line. This modification gave the operators more control over the technology, an important variable of the overall quality improvement program. Of course, such modifications make sense only if operators have timely access to data enabling them to take action appropriately. Technology can often be designed so that additional ''readouts'' of information become available to operators.

Modifying management practices is an essential component of organization design. Such practices as determining how decisions are made and the level of involvement of various parties in this process, employing formal goal setting versus an activity orientation, devising incentives to encourage various behaviors, and deciding whether to connect rewards with achievement of results rather than seniority have strong influences on the total system's performance.

As noted previously, the alignment between an organization's culture, vision, and structure is important. All three elements can be changed through the organization design process. In corporate culture, the design process explores and determines the existing norms and values that shape and guide daily activities. The design process identifies organization rites and rituals, the ways culture becomes communicated through management practices, the changes necessary, and how such changes may be implemented. Design mechanisms such as philosophy and mission statements—and statements about what constitutes good management practices—can communicate and guide the design process as it addresses job design and help the remainder of the organization become aware of the new culture.

Perhaps the most visible aspect of an organization's culture is the way it chooses to design individual jobs or work roles. The design process involves making choices about what jobs include or exclude, the extent to which jobs are interconnected, the levels of autonomy associated with various jobs, and the challenges and development opportunities they offer. Choices made involving these elements have some of the strongest impacts on the organization's culture and the concomitant energy levels within it, as the daily work required by people's jobs is the setting in which the design process's best intentions either fly or falter.

Along with designing individual jobs, the design process must also consider and choose from among alternatives for connecting and aggregating jobs. This involves answering such questions as the following.

- Should people work individually, or as teams?
- How many teams should a unit have? What is the best basis for determining unit boundaries and thus avoiding overfragmentation of the work system?
- How will communication occur within the teams and among teams and units? Who will have the authority to make what kinds of decisions?
- What types of information are required by individuals? By teams? By units? By divisions? How can this be made available so that the necessary data for self-correction is timely and accessible?

All of these decisions must be made as part of the organization design process—but only after extensively assessing how the work system currently performs. Indeed, such an assessment—consisting of the technical system analysis and social system analysis—is part of the design process. It must occur, however, before one chooses options in the areas discussed previously.

Both the analysis and subsequent design process seek to consciously and systematically create a high-performing system having the organizational characteristics described previously and leading to a situation in which

- persons **are able** to do what is expected of them,
- persons **want** to do these tasks, and
- persons **are allowed** to do these tasks.

Open sociotechnical systems

Open sociotechnical systems is an approach to designing organizations based on a theory and procedure (Pava, 1983) different from those associated with traditional design approaches. According to the perspective of open sociotechnical systems, an organizations is

- influenced by and needs to respond continually to its external environments as it converts input (i.e., raw materials or information) into output (i.e., products or services),
- through a work system composed of a social system **interacting** with a technical system to convert or transform input into output,
- with the technical system consisting of any combination of techniques, machines, instructions, or tools used to produce desired output, and
- with the social system consisting of the work-related interactions among persons managing the technical systems (i.e., the transformation of input into output).

Sociotechnical theory holds that a high-performing system results from finding, through comprehensive analysis (i.e., designing), the "best match" or most mutually enhancing "fit" between the technical and social systems of an organization.

This theory of designing to achieve "joint optimization"—the best fit—substantially differs from traditional designs such as scientific management, which seeks maximum automation and job simplification. Sociotechnical theory assumes that social systems can adapt to the needs of technical systems rather easily. The drawback of the traditional approach is evident in Calvin Pava's description of the General Motors plant at Lordstown:

> [I]n 1972 . . . labour strife dramatically underscored the need for a fundamental transformation in how work is organized. At the time, Lordstown housed America's most technologically advanced automotive assembly line. In accord with the Taylorist principles of efficiency, automation was maximized and worker roles greatly simplified. Workers went on strike to protest the low quality of their jobs in this supposedly optimal system. Over-optimization of technology by itself and subpar development of the plant's social system led to a deterioration in the overall performance of the facility. The Lordstown episode marked a watershed in American management of human resources. It signified

the need to obtain superior performance in ways that depart from traditional reliance upon simple work and purely technological optimization. (1983, p. 128)

The open sociotechnical systems approach to organization design not only provides a theoretical perspective, but also a specific set of participation procedures for analysis and design activities. These activities are carried out in five phases (Cotter, 1983):

- initial planning,
- technical systems analysis,
- social systems analysis,
- development of alternatives,
- implementation planning.

Technical systems analysis involves identifying the sequence of the self-contained steps or operations for converting input into desired output. It emphasizes identifying any variances or problems occurring within each operation, how they are currently dealt with, and the consequences for operations ''downstream'' if variances are not adequately dealt with at the source.

Social systems analysis involves describing the existing interactions of employees, not only with respect to who controls what variances, and how this is done, but also with respect to coordination among groups and individuals, particularly in solving unexpected problems arising from unpredicted events in the organization's external environment. Social system analysis also examines existing organizational processes for recruitment, incentives, performance evaluation, training, career management, and the like and how these influence employees' commitment and the organization's capacity for self-renewal and development over time.

The technical and social system analyses provide information necessary for considering alternative organization designs. Developing and evaluating design alternatives involves assessing the extent to which possible new jobs and arrangements for connecting them do the following:

- allow for variances to be controlled as much as possible at their source, thereby minimizing or reducing costly work flow problems;
- provide meaningful work as defined by the employees themselves;
- create situations in which persons are able to, want to, and are allowed to do the tasks necessary for both the short- and long-term success of the organization.

Processes and structures for open sociotechnical systems design

Both the theory and procedures of the open sociotechnical systems approach to organization design are of little use when implemented through a traditional process of unilaterally developing—by a staff or external consultant—analyses and recommendations. Alternatively, the open sociotechnical systems approach prescribes a heavily participative process, one in which the structures for participation are created and agreed to during the first step of the design activity sequence (the initial planning phase), which

> . . . includes the formation of an approval body and a design team. The approval body is composed of senior managers who have a stake in the final outcome, and whose responsibility it is to guide and approve proposals from the team formed to design the new organization. The design team is charged with the task of envisioning the ideal future state, analyzing the current work system, and recommending a new organization design to the approval body. (Ranney & Carder, 1974, p. 171)

Problems with traditional approaches to organization design

By more closely exploring the dynamics of traditional approaches to organization design, we can also move closer to understanding the role of the methodology, procedures, and theoretical perspective of the open sociotechnical system's approach to the successful design of high-performing systems.

Managers and employers who have personally been involved in traditional design approaches frequently describe their experiences with them by using statements such as the following.

- "It's what we do every five years—move from centralization to decentralization, or vice versa, often without any lasting impact on the way we really do things around here."
- "That's what those people in the head office do to us when they have nothing else to keep them busy."
- "My job is to get the work done in this plant, not to spend my time worrying about academic theories."

Traditional organizational design processes frequently evoke such unflattering images in part because managers and workers alike consider them as

- something done by one group (usually senior management or staff) to another group (usually middle managers and their subordinates),
- relatively unconnected to the operational problems of the production process, partly because they do not include any analysis of the technical or social systems,
- political maneuvers by incoming managers that will have little impact on work done on a daily basis,
- something line managers are not responsible for (''Let the personnel office do it''),
- belonging to a small set of previously used—and discarded—design ''solutions'' (''It's either functional or product or matrix, so why get excited?''),
- focusing on only authority and reporting relationships (i.e., changing the boxes on an organization chart) rather than representing the more comprehensive approach of open sociotechnical systems design.

Indeed, much of the popular management literature is consistent with these characterizations. For example, the literature suggests only three or four basic organizational configurations (product, functional, matrix, or geographical), and finds the task of the staff expert (or senior management) to be to determine which of these configurations is best for the particular organization.

Experience suggests that the likelihood of successfully designing a high-performing system by using such traditional approaches is low, because such approaches

- are not based on a detailed operational analysis of actual, current work practices,
- have not meaningfully involved those persons closest to the operational process (i.e., workers and line managers),
- focus on solving only today's—or even yesterday's—problems rather than creating an organization capable of flexibly responding to tomorrow's challenges,
- do not have the necessary commitment and support of those at lower levels, which are required for successful implementation,
- are based on the false assumption that modifying only authority/reporting relationships will be sufficient for obtaining intended results,
- use analytic perspectives that make the ''designers'' prisoners of their own histories, cultures, and traditions, and
- stem from a constraint orientation emphasizing all that **cannot** be changed, rather than from an inventive/creative orientation central to effective organizational change.

Successfully implementing the open sociotechnical system approach to designing high-performing systems

The following factors must be present to achieve a successful outcome using an open sociotechnical systems approach:

- the proper analytic perspective, methodology, and procedures for focusing on the right questions (i.e., an open sociotechnical systems perspective),
- a design approach characterized by innovation, invention, and experimentation,
- analysis and design activities that involve not only technical/staff personnel and senior management, but also those who will do the actual work, and
- recognition by both the participants and those providing resources that the organization design process is a social activity with some human, nonlinear aspects and that it needs widespread, ongoing organizational support.

The fourth factor cited above emphasizes the need to consider organization design an activity that—as much as any other key activity—must be managed so that it receives appropriate resources and widespread support, and achieves congruence between the process used and end results.[2]

Table 1 presents other implications for action associated with nine key dimensions moving from a traditional approach to an open sociotechnical systems approach when designing high-performing systems (Mohr, 1984).

Conclusions

Traditional design approaches for creating high-performing systems are severely limited by inadequate theoretical frameworks, methodology, and procedures for analysis and design, and by their failure to focus on the political processes and organizational structures used for implementing open sociotechnical systems theory, methods, and procedures.

Experience suggests that successful movement along the ten dimensions discussed in Table 1 can help eliminate many of the problems associated with traditional approaches. Moreover, organizations using open sociotechnical systems approach to design will begin to effectively use organization design, one of management's most powerful interventions for improvement. To reap the benefits available, however, management must fully understand the essential **creative, human, and political nature** of the actual design activities, the need for detailed operational analysis, and the need for participative structures for conducting analysis and design.

Table 1
Implications for Action Associated with Moving from a Traditional Approach to an Open Sociotechnical Systems Approach when Designing High-Performing Systems

Dimension	Movement required
1. Participation	Movement **from** restricting analysis and design to technical specialists and senior managers **toward** also including operational employees, middle managers, and key organization stakeholders (e.g., union officials, personnel specialists, other staff organization members)
2. Data base	Movement **from** overdependence on individual perceptions and theories as to strengths and weaknesses **toward** a collection of detailed data on the behavioral and factual aspects of the current operational processes, which consider actual responses to operational problems (i.e., technical system factors) and specific activities of the social system intended to support goal achievement, adaptation to the environment, integration of efforts, and long-term system development
3. Area of inquiry	Movement **from** singular, exclusive foci (e.g., those limiting analysis to either structure or equipment, or to either procedures or human relations) **toward** a multiple, inclusive scope of inquiry that includes technology, individual differences, the organization, the environment, and management practices and styles
4. Causality	Movement **from** viewing organizational elements as having simple cause-and-effect relationships (e.g., higher pay leads to increased motivation) **toward** a systemic understanding of multiple causes and effects, not all of which are fully predicted (although one may anticipate their existence)
5. Time orientation	Movement **from** emphasizing solutions for today's—or yesterday's—problems **toward** emphasizing the creation of an organizational setting capable of continual, effective progress toward clearly defined goals
6. Design goals	Movement **from** an either/or orientation (e.g., one calling for choosing between economic or human goals, or between short-term responses or long-term development) **toward** an orientation with multiple goals (e.g., productivity and QWL, or short-term results and long-term flexibility)
7. Customization	Movement **from** a tendency to limit one's choice of design solutions to the three or four structures dominating the literature **toward** creating a setting uniquely tailored to the organization's own current and future needs
8. Maximization	Movement **from** designing either the best possible technical system or the best possible social system toward designing the sociotechnical system with the best fit
9. Finality	Movement **from** expecting the organization design to be completed "once and for all" **toward** setting a goal of developing the appropriate skills, experience, and flexibility within the organization so that future design activity can be a part of its regular operations, not a separate activity.

NOTES

1. I am indebted to Peter Vaill, whose work on high-performing systems provides the origins for the notions I present on this concept.

2. These concepts, often referred to as the set of knowledge and skills related to the "management of organizational change," are discussed in more detail by Beckhard and Harris (1977).

REFERENCES

Beckhard, R., & Harris, R. (1979). *Organizational transitions: Managing complex change.* Reading, MA: Addison-Wesley.

Cotter, J. (1983). *Designing organizations that work: An open socio-technical systems perspective.* Unpublished working paper.

Mohr, B. (1985). *Art, analysis, and participation: Key dynamics in designing organizations from the open socio-technical systems perspective.* Unpublished working paper.

Pava, C. (1983). Designing managerial and professional work for high performance: A sociotechnical approach. *National Productivity Review, 2,* 126-135.

Ranney, J., & Carder, C. (1984). Socio-technical design methods in office settings: Two cases. *Office Technology and People, 2,* 169-184.

Walton, R. E. (1985, March/April). From control to commitment in the workplace. *Harvard Business Review,* pp. 77-84.

Management Development and Adult Learning

Robert A. Luke, Jr.

Relationships between individuals—particularly managers—and organizations represent a major area of inquiry for many behavioral scientists interested in understanding and facilitating improvements in the quality and effectiveness of individual and organizational functioning. Recently, I became interested in the possibility that adult learning could provide an informative perspective on the manager's role in mediating relationships between individuals and organizations. This chapter describes some behavioral and developmental parallels in the behavioral science and adult learning literature. It also includes implications for management development programs.

Behavioral science and the manager's role

One can characterize the applied behavioral scientists who conducted major research into the relationships between individuals and organizations according to three terms: sages, empiricists, and experimenters. The **sages** were notable for their philosophical observations, such as those of Claude Saint-Simon, Charles Fourier, and Emile Durkheim, and addressed the issue of individual-organization relationships from a position of advocacy. Although they disagreed as to the form or structure organizations should take—some proposed that individual needs should serve as the guiding force for designing organizations, whereas others argued that societal needs should do so—the sages' writings indicate the following assumptions about the relationship individuals should have with organizations.

- Individuals must be controlled, because if they are left unchecked they will destroy and oppress themselves and others.

- Individuals must choose between their needs for self-direction and society's need for collective action.
- A society managed by individuals should be replaced by a society managed by principles discerned by intellectuals.

The **empiricists** were grounded in increasingly sophisticated research methodology (e.g., anthropological participant observation, experimental design, and various forms of survey techniques and instruments), as characterized by the work of Fritz J. Roethlisberger, Kurt Lewin, Ronald Lippitt, and Ralph K. White. These researchers identified and described various types of relationships between individuals and organizations, and, contrary to what the sages concluded, found that the needs of each are not necessarily mutually exclusive. The empiricists' writings suggest the following.

- The conscious manipulation of a manager's use of authority can change a group's behavior, cohesion, morale, and productivity.
- Individuals can use intelligence and reason to affect the pattern of relationships among individuals in task or problem-solving groups.
- Human behavior in groups and organizations is greatly influenced by the social and physical environment, and not determined solely by dynamics endemic to human nature.

The **experimenters** worked in the context of social laboratories—often referred to as cultural islands—to establish supportive, relatively risk-free environments. Under these relatively controlled conditions, they could study and experiment with the interplay among individual and organizational needs. Such "cultural island" programs, often known as sensitivity training groups, provided the first sustained demonstrations that, within a group context, individuals could effectively understand and alter both their individual behavior and the group structures governing their behavior (Bradford, Benne, & Gibb, 1964). Many of the behavioral scientists first involved in sensitivity training were instrumental in bridging the gap between cultural islands and the more complex arenas of business, industry, education, volunteer agencies, and government, both in the U.S. and abroad, as the field of organization development flourished. Experimenters such as Douglas McGregor, Robert Blake and Jane Mouton, Rensis Likert, and Chris Argyris have contributed such classic models of individual-organization relationships as Theories X and Y, the Managerial Grid, Systems 1, 2, 3, 4, and Interpersonal Competence.

By the 1970s, applied behavioral scientists had completed the transition from detached observer to active participant in the process of integrating the needs of individuals and organizations. Some of their more visible results included typologies of managerial styles—including the collaborative, confrontational, accommodating, situational, transactional, consultative, and developmental modes—and nontraditional organizational forms such as the matrix, flat, and "adhocracy" structures, which offered alternatives to the ominous spectacle of the bureaucracy. Many management development programs emerged from the applied behavioral scientists' findings.

It occurred to me (Luke, 1975) that although behavioral models may well provide useful guidance and points of reference for managers, managers might also benefit from the behavioral scientists' methodology of research, discovery, and experimentation. A potential trap of management development programs based on typologies is that they may imply that one or several models are superior to others. Such an implication ignores the unique environmental, historical, and personnel dynamics a particular manager faces. I have suggested that managers consider adopting a learning posture toward the demands of management and become leaders in establishing a learning process and climate within their organizations. To me, learning acts as a promising prism through which managers can view the interplay of individual and organizational needs, something I have since discovered that many managers already recognize. Following my recent exposure to the literature on effective management and adult learning, I came to speculate that management development could be profitably informed by the concepts of adult learning.

Adult learning and management development

My intuition tells me that effective managers are effective learners as they go about making numerous decisions each day in a changing, competitive, world. Research supports this hunch. Hall (1976) found that high-achieving managers could be distinguished by their active pursuit of information and a willingness to share it. Mintzberg (1975) found that a key component of a manager's job is processing information. According to Skinner and Sasser (1977), a characteristic of successful managers is their acquisition of in-depth information with sufficient detail to provide both the necessary data and confidence to make decisions. Andrew Carnegie attributed his success to hiring people who knew more than he did. Such efforts to seek advice and help, Skinner and Sasser found (1977), is another characteristic of effective managers. McClelland and Burnham (1975) determined that effective managers demonstrate greater maturity in that they are less egotistical and more willing to seek advice from experts. Similarly, in describing how Presidents Franklin D. Roosevelt, Truman, and Eisenhower sought information, Mintzberg (1975, p. 57) relates:

> To help himself he must reach out as widely as he can for every scrap of fact, opinion, and gossip bearing on his interests and relationship as President. He becomes his own director of his own central intelligence. Roberts (1985) has shown that a positive relationship exists between one's readiness for self-directed learning and one's level of management, performance ratings, creativity, and problem-solving ability.

In the course of management development programs, managers are challenged to learn, acquire, and perhaps modify their skills, knowledge, and attitudes. Those designing these programs, however, often give limited consideration to the processes of learning beyond attempts to create a social and physical culture conducive to inquiry, risk taking, experimentation, self-disclosure, and feedback. Supportive environments can be mixed blessing, both for the participants and program staff. They facilitate participative learning, but the culture in which this occurs often differs significantly from the participants' work cultures. These differences frequently contribute to the well-known dilemmas of transferability, accountability, and meaningful evaluation. Recent findings about adults' learning styles and preferences offer some ideas for obviating some of these dilemmas and providing assistance, such as creating end-of-program action plans, support groups, and participant reunions. These ideas focus on using existing adult learning methodology to develop individual management development experiences.

Adult learning preferences

Knowles (1975, 1980) has developed a system for planning self-directed learning, one based on the following set of assumptions he found helpful for working with adults in university and workshop settings.

- Adults have a need to be self-directed in establishing and implementing their learning objectives, which tend to be **practical, short term, and intended to enhance competence.**
- Adults desire to integrate their past experiences with new learning and to revise and adapt their learning processes to suit changing needs and conditions.

Knowles popularized the term "andragogy"—defined as the art and science of helping adults learn—to denote his system of self-directed learning. Research on adult learning (Tough, 1982) supports this system. Tough found that adults overwhelmingly prefer to plan their own learning projects, because they wish to control the pace and substance of their learning and to retain the option of changing and revising strategies. He notes that adults' preference for self-directed learning is apparent in their ranking of locations for obtaining learning: (1) their homes, (2) their job sites, (3) outdoors, (4) in discussion groups, (5), classrooms, (6) libraries, and (7) public events.

Some implications for management development

Research findings for adult learning can provide a base of concepts and confidence from which we can identify a wide variety of management development strategies capitalizing on adults' learning preferences. What is necessary is a systematic approach for providing managers with relevant learning experiences enabling them to perform at consistently higher levels. Such learning experiences can be considered both in terms of content and process.

Ideally, I believe that the content of management development programs should be proposed by corporate leaders with the experience and vision to articulate which managerial skills, knowledge, and attitudes are most productive for their organizations. Often this information is not readily accessible in written form, and must be determined by reviewing the history, folklore, myths, and stories of an organization. A workshop with a title such as "What We Expect of Our Managers" might provide a potent program for corporate leaders and help obtain support and commitment for management development efforts. Those responsible for management development can act as consultants and facilitators for these workshops, and introduce ideas and concepts they consider appropriate. Clearly, the action research approach incorporates this concept.

With respect to process, I feel that an emphasis on adult learning should lead to heightened consideration of alternative formats other than group encounters in hotels, cultural islands, and other "off-site" settings. Appropriate processes could be selected with the multiple objectives of developing job skills, providing on-the-job feedback about using new skills, and minimizing cost. These objectives lead me to think that processes could be devised that provide a maximum amount of individualized learning on important organizational matters, yet also pay attention to important social and reinforcement goals served by group learning activities.

Specific process ideas that have occurred to me are probably familiar to the reader. These include self-study packets and instruments, videotapes and audiotapes, personal computer disks, on-the-job training, field trips, coaching, "mentoring," learning contracts (also known as individual development plans), "at-the-elbow" consulting, and formalized support groups. Ideally, whatever management activities are used will directly focus on a manager's performance appraisals—both those given and received. In the final analysis, choosing a particular learning activity matters less than paying attention to organizational expectations for managers and ensuring that the learning activities give managers optimum opportunities for involvement, flexibility, and control of the learning pace.

Summary

I have seen managers become enamored of typologies, only to find that their attempts to emulate them encounter significant resistance based on disparities between the environments of the learning experience and the job site. This led me to consider the importance of learning as a developmental strategy available to managers caught in the dilemma of choosing from among many behavioral models those most appropriate for their own circumstances. More recently, I have become intrigued by the potential for self-directed learning to act as a guiding force for designing and delivering management development programs.

The advantages of self-directed learning include an increased probability that the learning will be applied and personalized. The locus of control is vested in, or at least shared by, the manager. Moreover, self-directed management development places the educator in a facilitator/consultant role, and enables the manager to take a more active, self-responsible stance (whether this is an advantage or disadvantage depends on the educator's "training" preference and the manager's formal learning experiences). A major disadvantage of self-directed learning is that it often involves increased costs, including those of time, travel, and materials. Administrative work may be considerably increased as management development becomes increasingly personalized. Apart from its other attributes, group work can be comparatively efficient in terms of logistics and administration.

I have always considered management development one of the preeminent challenges and opportunities available to behavioral scientists. After all, managers have much of the leadership responsibilities for society, and therefore have provided—and will continue to provide—one avenue for the behavioral sciences to make societal contributions. I thus believe that concepts of adult learning are worthy of consideration by those addressing the management development process.

REFERENCES

Bradford, L. P., Benne, K. D., & Gibb, J. R. (Eds.). (1964). *T-Group theory and the laboratory method.* New York: John Wiley and Sons.

Hall, J. (1976). To achieve or not: The manager's choice. *California Management Review, 18*(4), 26-41.

Knowles, M. (1975). *Self-directed learning: A guide for learners and teachers.* Chicago: Association Press.

Knowles, M. (1980). *The modern practice of adult education: From pedagogy to andragogy.* Chicago: Follett.

Luke, R. A., Jr. (1975, May-June). Matching the individual and the organization. *Harvard Business Review,* pp. 18-22.

McClelland, D., & Burnham, D. H. (1977, November-December). Power is the great motivator. *Harvard Business Review,* pp. 121-135.

Mintzberg, H. (1975, July-August). The manager's job: Folklore and fact. *Harvard Business Review,* pp. 48-61.

Roberts, D. G. (1985). *A study of the use of the self-directed learning readiness scale in making selected organizational decisions.* Unpublished doctoral dissertation, The George Washington University, Washington, DC.

Skinner, W., & Sasser, W. E. (1977, November-December). Managers with impact: Versatile and inconsistent. *Harvard Business Review,* pp. 55-68.

Tough, A. (1982). *The adult's learning projects.* Austin, TX: Learning Concepts.

Shadow Consulting: An Emerging Role

Mikki Ritvo
Ronald Lippitt

The concept of shadow consulting did not exist when most of us received our professional training or orientation in organization development consulting. During the past several years, however, in conversations with our colleagues we have noted many examples of what we call shadow consulting and an increasing recognition of the important, unique aspects of this role. This chapter presents a working definition of shadow consulting, a description and clarification of some of the dimensions of the shadow consultant-client relationship, and a discussion of the key issues.

Shadow consulting: A working definition

A shadow consultant works exclusively with one client—whether this is an individual or a small team—and has no connection to the rest of the system. This is done, for example, to facilitate effective performance, to support the problems associated with the "loneliness at the top" leaders feel, or to help someone manage stress caused by the complexity and rate of change. The contract between the client and consultant usually is made with the knowledge and support of other significant persons associated with the client.

As you read this definition, reflect on your own experiences that can be called shadow consulting. We invite you to assess the definition we provide and to suggest any revisions or additions.

The following examples represent a small sample of the types of shadow consultant-client relationships existing today.

- The chief executive officer of a high-tech firm requests regular monthly telephone conferences to the consultant. A week before these conferences, he sends memoranda or drafts covering what he wants to discuss. The consultation usually focuses on decisions, strategies for action, and issues related to key staff members' resistance to change.
- A former student/trainee of the consultant now holds a responsible position as director of training. She makes a one-time-only call to the consultant to get some reactions to a tentative design for an off-site, two-day staff planning meeting. She expects—and gets—from the consultant several alternatives for consideration.
- The head of a department of a hospital meets periodically with the consultant in 7:30 am breakfast meetings to get advice with staff leadership, conflict resolution, and the development of quality assurance procedures.
- A university vice president holds a series of breakfast and telephone meetings with the consultant to discuss his relationships with the president and his colleagues, and images of the future concerning various ideas for programs.
- Young professionals participate in monthly "consultation-in-the-round" sessions in which the consultant, working with one person at a time, generates as many ideas as possible and asks for suggestions from others.
- One of three brothers owning an international manufacturing company asks the consultant to help him with strains resulting from sibling relationships and with change interaction patterns.
- The administrator of a large hospital wants to learn about theories, innovative practices, and coping with resistance to change. The consultant first acts as a teacher, but then comes to review change strategies.
- The CEO of an architectural firm asks the consultant to give him ideas for team building with his interdisciplinary staff. He asks the consultant to change roles and work directly with the staff.
- A statewide educational administration network asks the consultant to interact with it monthly through a computer linkage, responding to questions and encouraging ideas for issues and images of the future.
- A personnel director had supported hiring practices that neglected affirmative action mandates. The consultant helps clarify the malpractice that occurred and develop appropriate action plans and commitments.

How the client benefits from shadow consulting

Perhaps the most important benefit for the client is the ready availability of the shadow consultant, usually by telephone, at the moment consulting is needed. Contracts confirm the availability of the consultant at any time of the day or week.

Another benefit is that the shadow consultant is free to produce as many ideas for action as possible, because the consultant has no responsibility for advocating any single suggestion or solution. This usually results in a rich menu of ideas for the client to consider.

The shadow consultant also provides the client with an opportunity for rehearsal, for trying out plans and ideas in a not-for-keeps situation.

By internalizing the shadow consultant's ideas as part of her or his own thoughts, the client also benefits from having the shadow consultant available psychologically as a source of support and a guiding alter ego.

Finally, many clients have also said that the shadow consultant provides an antidote to loneliness and stress. The consultant thus serves as a mental health resource.

How the shadow consultant gains satisfaction

The shadow consultant takes part in a significant relationship with the client, one in which both learn a great deal and trust is of central importance. Working with a client whom one can challenge to think, feel, and act beyond that person's perceived limits is satisfying. Empowering a client means indirectly affecting the larger system.

Being able to influence action without having responsibility for implementing ideas is quite different from conventional OD consulting situations. It enables the shadow consultant to be more creative and experimental in generating ideas, as the client is responsible for "reality testing," decision making, and risk taking.

Of major appeal to the shadow consultant is the freedom to choose when and where to work with the client. The setting is not limited to the office or work site. Because the shadow consultant-client relationship is close and trusting, much of the consulting successfully occurs over the telephone or, more recently, the computer. By reducing or eliminating travel, both the consultant and client have more time available.

Although the client may represent only a small part of the system, increasing her or his effectiveness may attract the attention of other parts of the system, thereby leading to new in-house consulting contracts of a "nonshadow" nature.

We have also noted the following other sources of satisfaction for the shadow consultant:

- experiencing the client's growth, as demonstrated by movement from a narrow vision of issues to a more systemic one,
- the opportunity to give and receive ongoing, direct feedback,
- having a close, collaborative relationship with flexibility in how, when, and where to conduct it,
- the opportunity to test a range of intervention strategies, and
- enabling the client to acquire skills related to diagnosis, problem solving, and performance, and thus make the consultant less necessary.

Role variations and work patterns

The small number of illustrations we provide indicate a wide variety of shadow consulting relationships and roles.

A key difference is whether the relationship is conducted mostly or entirely at a distance—by using telephones or computers, for example—or through face-to-face interactions. Often the work pattern consists of periodic meetings, with telephone conferences held in between to meet the client's pressing needs. The telephone calls often occur just before or after an important event, such as a major presentation, a staff retreat, or a new policy decision.

One of the consultant's more satisfying roles is that of a "brainstorm" resource—that is, a means of generating visions of "preferred futures," current societal trends with implications for strategy planning, ideas for alternative ways of implementing goals, and advice for getting all necessary persons involved.

Another important role is that of coach and director of rehearsals and simulations. Legitimizing and initiating a rehearsal in anticipation of an important event is an often-neglected quality assurance procedure. Successful endeavors often depend on one's "working the bugs out" through such drills, but most leaders lack the proper perspective or feel too uncomfortable to perform this useful precursor to success.

Many times the "lonesome leader" needs an opportunity to share doubts and feelings of inadequacy and risk. Acting as a supporter and champion of the client's taking risks is another crucial role of the shadow consultant.

In connecting the organization and its environment, the shadow consultant can often provide a link to external resources and widen perspectives. Leaders often focus their energy on the pressing internal requirements of "running the business," and thus must be made aware of the importance and challenges of looking inward. A shadow consultant often occupies the best position to provide such a link and make "external affairs" a priority.

The specific roles played by the shadow consultant should be familiar to those aware of other consulting relationships: counselor, confronter, advisor, clarifier, teacher, coach, rehearser, reality tester, strategist, supporter, friend, giver of feedback, mentor, diagnostician, referral agent, "futurist." In scanning our own experiences, we have doubtless forgotten other roles.

Traps, temptations, and ethical issues

One pitfall inherent to shadow consulting is potential client dependency. In a close, continuing relationship, the person with greater expertise can become comfortable directing, advising, and controlling the other. Moreover, the client may feel so grateful for the personal growth and achievements gained that he or she may resist autonomy and fear the loss of the relationship with the consultant.

The shadow consultant must actively use her or his participant observer skills to avoid serving the client's needs and interests to the detriment of the larger system. The intensity of the relationship may result in the shadow consultant's easily becoming part of the client's social circle. This does not constitute an ethical issue per se, but too much of this sort of exposure and contact with a client may adversely affect the consultant's objectivity.

The following list cites several other temptations the shadow consultant may face:

- misusing one's influence over a vulnerable client,
- becoming a positional advocate (i.e., telling a client what to do),
- using only data supplied by the client, particularly if one has not stimulated the client to perform appropriate checkup, scanning, and data collecting procedures,
- assuming the status of a senior adviser,
- acting as a therapist, Rasputin (e.g., the power behind the throne), or Pygmalion.

The extent to which the client makes the shadow consultant contract known to others must be reviewed. Too much secrecy can have awkward consequences, an issue that must be understood and addressed.

Special requirements and opportunities

An important requirement of the shadow consultant, and opportunity for the client, is the consultant's availability when needed. The two persons must interact when need arises, rather than through scheduled meetings, training events, or off-site staff gatherings.

Shadow consulting gives the consultant the satisfying opportunity to produce as many ideas as possible, without being required to focus on their being accepted or acted upon. The client has the opportunity—indeed, the responsibility—to choose which ones seem appropriate to the client's situation and style.

The shadow consultant is required to remain barely visible—often invisible—to the other groups and important members of the client's system. The consultant derives ego satisfaction from having a creative relationship with a single client, rather than from directly influencing the key persons and groups in a system.

We have found that one of the more demanding requirements of the shadow consultants is achieving a balance between being involved with the client and her or his needs and retaining some detachment from the operating situation. To do this, one must not only "put oneself in the client's shoes," but also remain an objective observer of the client's behavior and situation. Such detachment can be one of the client's largest sources of help.

Feedback from our clients has indicated the importance of the mental health aspects of the shadow consultant-client relationship. This is particularly important with respect to attention to feelings of loneliness and discouragement, support for taking risks, and encouragement of actively seeking to confront and solve complex problems.

An invitation to explore, experiment, clarify, and share

As we reflect on our current OD activities, the opportunities and challenges of the shadow consultant-client relationship become increasingly clear and important. Having the freedom to stimulate innovation and creativity—rather than the responsibility for acting as a responsible change agent—can be fun. And providing mental health support for "lonesome leaders" is rewarding and increasingly important work, particularly now that CEOs must address ever-complex environments and heavier work loads in response to rapid change.

We recommend that readers explore the shadow consulting role as a significant complement to the more traditional parts of the OD repertoire—and encourage you to share your experiences.

Microcomputer Support for Organization Development

Tom Armor

Microcomputers are playing an increasingly larger role in professional and personal life. Their image, however, has often been that of either the enormous number-crunching mainframe machines or of extravagant, expensive typewriters. Indeed, most of us lack a good understanding of the real potential of this technology. Organization development (OD) practitioners are among those least likely to consider microcomputers an important tool for their professions. This is unfortunate, for this technology can make great contributions to the practice of OD.

Many years ago, Fritz Steele wrote an interesting article comparing the methods of fictitious British detectives with those of OD consultants. Among the analogies he devised, one related the inductive processes required to pursue criminals to those used to make organizational diagnoses:

> The British detective often uses intuition as a mode of operation. He generates hypotheses from within which he then attempts to test either by gathering new data or by sifting through the old data again. He often does not know for a considerable length of time why he is looking at a particular corner of the data pile, but his intuition keeps him there until the connections are made.
>
> I think that this process is also a very important one for consultants. I find that sometimes I almost stop trying to control **where** I focus and let natural awareness lead me in whatever direction it will. In a sense, I try to stop **staring** (looking hard without really seeing) at the data and allow the figure and ground relationships to shift around and take on new meanings or new potencies for me. I do not believe that a consultant can do this without some intuition—some way to generate contextual notions so that he can understand what is he sees as he lets his eye and mind roam over the situation. (Steele, 1969, pp. 191-192)

Compare Steele's comments to a recent news item describing how police in England use technology to support their traditional detective work. This report refers to a computer program called Major Incidents Computer Applications (MICA), which was developed after the Yorkshire Ripper case to help police solve crimes.

> The great advantage of MICA is that it can cross-reference all [previously entered] indexes simultaneously. Police officers can interrogate the computer to see whether, for example, a red Cortina has ever been associated with a woman wearing a brown coat. In the Nominal Document Index, different statements many thousands of words long can be studied by entering key words. The program will then highlight those sentences where these words appear . . . . MICA also compares two or more major incidents. It can, for example, compare the sequence of events in one with another. So everything that happened on Thursday morning in two seemingly separate incidents can be listed in the order that they occurred. This could give officers working on the two cases a better idea of the events leading up to or following an incident. As one officer said, "The hope is to generate new lines of enquiries." (Connor, 1984, p. 6)

Similar to the ways in which they aid modern detectives, computers can help organization development practitioners by supporting both organizational diagnosis and intervention.

Data base management

Data base management (DBM) is a useful paradigm for conceptually and operationally using microcomputers in direct support of OD. I propose that much of the behavioral data generated and used for OD diagnoses, intervention, and evaluation can be collected, stored, retrieved, and manipulated—in the best sense of the word—with the help of microcomputers.

Briefly, DBM refers to the collection and storage of data (of any kind) in the smallest, most discrete pieces having inherent meaning or value. These data are cross referenced to one another in one or more ways, allowing them to be retrieved according to many different criteria. They can be counted, sorted, searched, combined, and otherwise manipulated to yield great amounts and varieties of information about the underlying source of the original data. A familiar example is that of accounting data from a business being used to provide a great deal of financial information about a company (e.g., current ratios of debt to equity, book value, cash on hand, sales volume per employee, accounts payable, and the like).

For technical reasons, this ability has not been widely available for "free form," text-oriented material until recently. Most of the initial work with DBM required numerical data and proscribed text-oriented material. Now, large mainframe computers allow one to use sophisticated DBM methods with this material. The example given above of the English police illustrates this potential. Although somewhat limited when compared to mainframes, the new microcomputer programs support some useful DBM applications for text-oriented material.

Why and how to use microcomputers for OD

Establishing a data base model. Much of the literature on organization development emphasizes the "data orientation" necessary for effectively dealing with human—especially individual—behavioral phenomena. This approach underscores the nonjudgmental nature of the process, reduces defensiveness, allows data to be accessible and shared in the best tradition of the scientific method, and seeks to encourage the client to "own" the data—and thus take responsibility for change.

We have not, however, been good at clearly distinguishing among "data" and the information derived from it through analysis. This is often a difficult distinction to make in our profession, for much analysis is inductive and intuitive. The so-called data often take the form of loosely written notes, undocumented conversations, and observations. These data are seldom saved after the analysis is made. For example, consider the interview process typically undertaken for a team building effort. The consultant's interview notes are not treated as "data" in the DBM sense, because they are usually quite unstructured, and no method has been devised for saving them in a meaningful form.

Now technology has made it feasible to record text-oriented data, such as interview notes, in a microcomputer data base for later use or analysis. This takes us a step closer to differentiating the data from the derived information. These principles have long been practiced with numerical data used with OD work (e.g., that generated by surveys), but have not been practical for text-oriented material because of the difficulty of organizing, filing, and retrieving such material in a useful way.

Although these programs require more consistency and discipline for the analytical process, they do not unduly restrict intuition and inductive reasoning. Certainly, some learning is required to use these programs, and in the early phases some confusion and frustration may occur. I propose, however, that a more flexible and clear approach to analysis will result.

A computer-supported approach to OD data collection and analysis makes it practical to establish a data base for one or more OD efforts. The following are the benefits of doing so.

• Programmatic OD efforts in large organizations can make better use of multiple staff resources. This enables several consultants to share their interview and observation findings in more meaningful ways.

• The same data can be used to test the usefulness of various diagnostic models. One can thus develop new or modified models from data originally collected under a different rubric or for different purposes.

• Those conducting OD efforts will be able to aggregate or separate data from several departments and use it to diagnose both department-specific and organization-wide situations. One can use multiple criteria in conducting these analyses (e.g., gender, position, specialty, job characteristics, and more).

• OD practitioners can more easily establish "client ownership" of the data and the credibility of the analysis because of the more explicit methods this approach requires. These programs also establish a well-documented "path" through the collection and analysis process that can be shared and reviewed as needed.

• The mere act of recording data into an electronic storage medium makes its long-term availability more realistic. This in turn permits later analysis of the data by others, of the correlation of long-term performance indicators, and of the cost effectiveness of the OD effort itself.

Some practical aspects. Most OD consultants use a variety of "simple" activities to generate important information for understanding or resolving issues facing an organization or group. Such matters as role negotiation, needs assessment, goal clarification, objective setting, leadership style, and others come to mind as important topics for OD.

These activities often involve structured approaches for generating data, reorganizing it so as to produce useful information, providing a context for reviewing that information, and taking action to change behavior as indicated. For example, consider the "nominal group" exercise. In this exercise, issues are first identified by groups formed for this purpose. Then, different groups are formed to address the previously generated data, which is "stored" on newsprint and "recalled" in a new aggregation, in which several sheets of newsprint from the initial groups are presented to the new "solution" groups.

Many of the steps in this activity can be taken using a computer to record the material as it is generated by both sets of groups. The reorganized "issue" lists can be created with a few keystrokes (as opposed to shuffling and recopying sheets of newsprint) and distributed immediately to the solution groups. Perhaps most important, the process—and resulting list of action steps—is documented in an immediately usable form. One can even produce and distribute a "report" before the participants leave the meetings! The flexibility of this approach even enables practitioners to conduct the process with the groups separated by time and place.

The following are examples of how practitioners can use this new technology to directly support OD activities.

1. Consultants can "cross-categorize" interview notes involving different issues, different persons, and so forth as they are entered into a text-oriented data base system. They can identify new relationships or issues searching for various combinations of important terms. They can generate specialized feedback reports by retrieving information according to specific key terms, names, or issues.

2. Consultants can take advantage of new methods of data collection and analysis. For example, they can ask people to "write a paragraph or two describing how you feel your department deals with conflict." The computer can then analyze these collective descriptions for counting the frequency with which certain words appear, the number of negative or positive words used, the use of first-, second-, and third-person pronouns, the juxtaposition of important terms, and more.

3. "Organization mirroring" exercises can be designed to collect input from individuals before departmental and interdepartmental meetings, enabling consultants to collate various aggregations of these data for discussion at the meetings. This saves time without compromising the need for group discussion. Multigroup "mirroring" designs become more practical because of the consultants' ability to selectively generate the most useful feedback reports for different purposes at different stages in the intervention.

4. Exercises in role expectations and negotiation can be adapted to a computer format, thus enabling members of groups or departments to identify individually any areas of common agreement or disagreement as to their expectations for one another. Individuals can respond to computer-organized questions about the roles and expectations of other members' of their groups or departments. The consultants can then sort the resulting data by "target" names, pairs, functions, or any other means considered most useful. This could then provided the basis for discussions and negotiations.

5. Many instruments using pencil and paper to measure "traits" (e.g., the FIRO-B or the Myers-Briggs Type Indicator) result in multiple scores or measurements that have greater meaning when compared to those of the persons with whom an individual has functional relationships. A microcomputer program can quickly and flexibly compare scores for group members, whereas a manual means of comparison would be limited by the number of combinations under consideration.

6. Meeting agenda can be developed through an iterative process for seeking agenda items from individuals, collating them, returning them to all who

will attend the meeting so that they may review them and set priorities, putting them into sequence for attention, relating issues, and the like. This information can provide the basis for constructing tentative agenda by a computer evaluation of the ratings of initial agenda items. One may do this across time and distance by communicating through computers, which requires only a few moments of each person's time.

This list of microcomputer applications to OD illustrates both the possibilities now available and ways of conducting familiar activities with more flexibility and ease. In addition, data generated during these activities can be documented and preserved in an electronic form during the activities themselves. This creates a data base useful for additional OD work, either in meeting the initial agenda or conducting a programmatic approach.

Examples

A planned meeting. A regional group of professionals wanted to revitalize their loose organization and identify some future directions for the group. The group's current viability resulted largely from its informality and diversity of activities. It sought a "revitalization" effort so as to preserve this informality yet define more salient structures and activities.

To accomplish this, different members of the group hosted a series of small dinner parties throughout several weeks. The group attempted to ensure that all interested members were invited to one of these parties. Each party was both a social event and a vehicle for collecting preliminary information about members' wishes for the future of the organization. The means of generating this information varied from party to party, but each host or hostess generated a short "report." Some of the reports were actually created on newsprint during the parties, and a few others consisted of short notes the host or hostess took to record the discussion of the issues.

Those who attended the parties—a total of about 100 persons—received a subsequent invitation to a weekend retreat to synthesize the data and develop plans and methods for the revitalization effort. Only 23 were able to attend the retreat, a number consistent with the group's previous experience. For the retreat, the group decided to use a microcomputer "text data base" approach for organizing the information generated at the dinner parties.

These data were entered into the data base in the form of short items (one or two sentences long), each tagged with as many as 10 key terms for later retrieval. This work was done by three of the group members who had, between themselves, attended most of the dinner parties so as to provide continuity. The data entry resulted in 72 items and 88 key terms.

A list of all the items (and their key terms) was prepared and distributed to everyone attending the retreat. At the appropriate time, the retreat participants were asked to read the list to get an impression of the issues identified by those attending the parties. They had access to a computer for generating selected lists based on key terms, which was useful for subgroups working on specific issues (e.g., topics for quarterly meetings, governance of the group, and functional structure). In addition, a subgroup was chartered to meet after the retreat to design a general meeting according to a list of items relevant to that task.

Organizational mirroring. This example of a typical organizational mirroring intervention was enhanced by and conducted with the support of a microcomputer used by the consultant. The intervention took place in a large organization with some experience and familiarity with OD methods. Thus, when two departments that experienced difficulty working with each other asked for help from the internal OD staff, they were prepared to undergo an exercise such as this.

The consultant suspected that even though the two departments initiating the request—which I call Departments A and B—considered the problem theirs, any lasting solution might involve third department, Department C. The design initially focused only on Departments A and B, however, and each department met at different times with the consultant to address the following questions.

1. What things does the other department do best?
2. What things does the other department do least well?
3. What do you need from the other department to make your work go more smoothly?
4. What do you predict the other group will say about you?

After each meeting, the consultant entered the responses to these questions into a text data base, using the following key terms: FRA ("from Department A"), FRB ("from Department B"), TWA ("toward Department A"), TWB ("toward Department B"), and Q1, Q2, Q3, and Q4 to signify a response to questions number 1, 2, 3, and 4, respectively.

At that time, the consultant selected the key terms while thinking that if the third department or other questions became involved later, the data could be regenerated in a useful way. For example, if Department C underwent the same process, then a list of everything said about Department A could be recalled without necessarily indicating who made the comments. The permutations and combinations possible for the design grow quickly when the number of groups involved increases to more than two or three.

In this example, lists were made and printed in several ways and in several formats (e.g., FRA + TWB + Q4 could be listed beside FRB + TWA + [Q1 or Q2], in Boolean terms). These lists were made and used during the second meeting each group had alone with the consultant. Although the consultant could have generated the lists during the meetings themselves, this was not done because the objective for the meetings was to develop the agenda for a joint meeting of the two groups. The groups exchanged their agenda prior to the joint meeting, and their reconciliation provided a starting point for the meeting.

The meeting was considered a success. All present felt that its productivity was enhanced by the use of the lists during the second meeting of each group. A potential elaboration of the design to include the third department was discussed, but no action taken.

Issues

Interpersonal processes and microcomputer methods. The appropriate integration of microcomputer methods and the underlying processes of laboratory training and OD is crucial and should be mutually supportive. I am **not** suggesting that computerized information analysis and interchange replace direct, face-to-face meetings. Such meetings, however, can be made more productive by early use of computers to collect and organize the information base for the meeting.

Obviously, one should be certain that a clear context exists for discussing and resolving the information one seeks to collect and make available to an individual or group. This might require careful control of the timing and means of distributing feedback, perhaps delaying this even when the technology permits a much faster dissemination schedule.

We can expect to see a cultural drift toward more acceptance of computers in this role. Fears about computers' making decisions requiring human judgment have lessened as people have gained a wider understanding of the potential and limitations of this technology. The distinction between data related to human behavior (e.g., scores from paper-and-pencil instruments, written descriptions of important interactions) and the behavior itself (e.g., exercising leadership in a real situation, yelling at one's spouse) will become clearer as computers give us more flexibility in collecting and understanding the "data about" so as to make real behavior more effective.

Participation in data analysis. One of the more powerful aspects of computer technology is its ability to analyze data interactively. The computer's speed and flexibility allow one to do this in "real time" and without any special training or expertise. This means that a consultant and client group can collaboratively review information stored in a data base to test new and emergent relationships or issues.

One of the important issues related to feedback is ensuring clients' ownership of the data. If a consultant's interview notes are entered into a text data base and an edited version is prepared to protect people's anonymity, clients can then review the data and retrieve information in the ways most meaningful to them.

For longer-term efforts, especially those in which client groups have access to computer network systems, consultants can develop iterative methods. Organizational diagnosis and the design of interventions based on this can function together as a process, rather than as separate steps. As this develops, so will the data base, which will provide opportunities for retrospective research on successful and unsuccessful activities.

Conclusions

This chapter proposes that recently available microcomputer programs allowing one to collect text material and analyze it with data base management techniques holds promise for improving OD efforts. A major benefit is that this enables practitioners to produce documented records of data and information otherwise difficult to retain and gain access to using traditional means. In operation, these microcomputer programs permit one to collect new organizational diagnosis data and analyze them, and offer the possibility of innovative intervention designs not heretofore practical.

To date, the OD profession has responded to the needs of people and organizations challenged by the rapid changes technology has induced. We can now use aspects of this changing technology to directly support our own practice. A synthesis of OD methodology and current trends in the modern work place will improve both.

REFERENCES

Steele, F. I. (1969). Consultants and detectives. *Journal of Applied Behavioral Science, 5*(2), 191-202.

Connor, S. (1984, February 9). Clues to four murders analyzed by computer. *New Scientist, 101,* 6.

Marketing and Selling Professional OD Services

Allan Drexler
Weld Coxe

A friend of ours who teaches organization development at a university says that the question his students ask him most frequently is, "How do I get clients?" In response, he usually just mumbles something not terribly helpful.

Our friend is not the only one who has difficulty with this issue. Many programs avoid the topic of building an OD practice. The majority of OD consultants—both internal and external—receive no training in marketing their services or building a base of clients. To market and sell OD services intelligently and professionally, one needs to understand principles of marketing. This chapter seeks to help you as an OD consultant get clients by developing answers to the following basic questions.

- What is marketing, and how does it apply to the unique role of an external or internal OD consultant?
- What is required for a marketing program, and how should the program be tailored to an individual's goals and capabilities?
- How should a consultant seek and obtain new business?

The recommendations and procedures outlined in this chapter provide a framework enabling an individual OD practitioner to create a marketing program tailored to that person's unique needs. Obviously, the marketing needs of a one-person firm, 30-person firm, or internal consultant differ widely, but the principles presented in this chapter provide basic guidelines one can adapt to fit any of these scenarios.

What is a marketing program?

Many of us find out about marketing programs the hard way. One consultant we worked with went into business for himself, and had several clients who kept his business going for a few years. Then three contracts ended abruptly, and seemingly overnight he lost 65% of his business revenues. Moreover, he had no idea how he would get any more clients. As do many consultants, he lacked any knowledge of marketing, and did not seek to learn about it until his business was endangered. That is usually too late to start: Without a marketing plan, the consultant was forced to take work he found neither rewarding nor fulfilling, and had to face the stress of possible business failure and its impacts on his personal and professional life.

Marketing need not be overly complex. Basically, it enables you as an OD consultant to do the following:

- pursue the specific type of work that you wish to do,
- create a network of contacts with clients you want to work with,
- work in the areas in which you are most qualified.

No matter what size your consulting firm is, if you want to control the quality or type of work you do, or the location in which you do it, you must have a marketing program. Today clients are more sophisticated in choosing consultants; even in many large organizations, managers do not feel obligated to use the internal consultants. Despite this sophistication, however, most clients still have no formal standards for selecting consultants. Therefore, professional OD consultants are responsible for making their qualifications and interests known to desirable potential clients.

Marketing versus selling

Most persons consider the term ''marketing'' a synonym for ''selling.'' Sales, however, is only one element of marketing. The overall definition of marketing embraces all facets of business. Marketing involves the **analysis, planning, and control** of all that is required for developing a service appropriate for particular clients and building a client base. Selling addresses **how** one gets a client to buy one's service; a marketing plan must address both **what** one sells and **to whom** one is selling it.

With respect to products, **what** is sold and **how** it is sold are distinct aspects. Once a car rolls off an assembly line, the first aspect is complete. Except for various optional features, the customer chooses either to buy or not to buy that particular product. OD consulting differs somewhat from this in that, unlike assembly-line industries, we can more readily redesign our product—our consulting services—to fit each client's needs. The skillful consultant adapts the services offered to meet the particular client's needs, thus performing selling and other marketing functions almost simultaneously. Indeed, a potential client's decision on obtaining a consultant's service may hinge not only on just the type of service offered (i.e., the product), but also on the way the consultant operates and the chemistry between the potential client and consultant (i.e., how the consultant conducts the sale). In selling the service, a consultant must convince the potential client of the value of that consultant's unique approach or skills—after all, no two team-building sessions are alike.

What a marketing plan requires

OD professionals are often involved in strategic planning with line managers. This planning is based on the assumption that a vision must precede movement toward a goal. OD consultants have helped others create long-term plans for their businesses, but frequently do not follow their own advise in this respect.

As often happens with their clients, when OD consultants begin creating a marketing plan, they usually find this is much easier than they had expected. Indeed, sometimes it is even enjoyable!

When making a marketing plan, you must make sure you do the following.

- Define the market: Determine where you want to look for work and what types of clients you want.
- Determine your capabilities and message: Clarify what skills and unique contributions you can offer.
- Create a plan: Determine how you intend to develop and pursue the market for your services.

Defining the market

Some OD consultants concentrate on one specific field or market, such as health care, higher education, or design. Some specify locations in which they will work. Others are not as specific, and will take any type of work they can get. The latter strategy is often risky, particularly during periods in which consulting work is hard to obtain.

The first important step in making a marketing plan is to determine to whom and where you will sell your services. This requires market research. Market research is not difficult, and begins with questions such as the following: What organizations hire OD consultants? Does a market for my work exist in the New England states? What functions or divisions within a particular organization use OD services? How does that organization perceive OD? How can I judge the competition for my services? What are my competitors' strengths and weaknesses?

At the least, the answers to these types of questions should enable you to decide whether or not to invest further effort in pursuing a particular market. Getting answers often simply means finding someone who already has that information, and many times potential clients are the best source. For example, a manufacturing plant's personnel manager should be able to speak knowledgeably about the market for OD services in the manufacturing industry. An executive vice president can generally describe that particular corporation's readiness or desire for OD services.

In virtually every field knowledgeable persons exist who, if asked, would be glad to share their views of the markets in which they work. In our experience, most people have been delighted to have the opportunity to discuss their expertise in their own fields. Almost all those we have approached when conducting market research welcomed our contact with them and freely gave their time and knowledge. Indeed, the problem will probably not be how to find someone who can answer your questions, but rather how to narrow the field of prospective sources of information. You should generally need to interview only three to five "experts" to get useful information on a market.

Determining your capabilities and message

An OD professional's product is that person's capabilities. These capabilities must match the needs of the market being pursued. For example, you may have excellent process skills, but these may not appear essential to a client in need of skill-building training.

Once you have defined the market, you must assess whether you can serve that market in light of the market's demands and the competition. For example, if you decide to target the high-tech training and development market, you must have experience and knowledge in project management, matrix structure, and multifunctional disciplines. Simply knowing how to train or to design team building is insufficient.

If you are interested in a market for which your skills are not yet strong enough or appropriate to deliver a high-quality service, three options exist.

- You may develop the necessary skills by attending seminars or courses, or by working with another consultant who has expertise in this area (internal consultants often do this by hiring external consultants).

- You may consciously decide to attempt to sell your current capabilities, despite their poor fit with the market. Doing this means recognizing that you will have difficulty securing work and a relatively low return for your marketing efforts.

- You may stay out of that market and devote your efforts to targeting markets more suitable to your capabilities.

When evaluating your capabilities, you must also examine how unique they are and what value your distinctiveness has for a client. If clients can do the work proposed themselves, they do not need your services. You must stress to the client what you can do—and the benefits of this—that the client cannot, and perhaps help the client feel comfortable with asking for help. Virtually all of the most successful OD professionals are those most capable of communicating clearly what is distinctive about themselves and their work, thus enabling clients to determine the services they can expect to receive.

Creating a plan

One way of obtaining clients is to write a best-selling book. Peters and Waterman have found this technique effective. Most of us, however, cannot rely on such a strategy. A simpler one is to specialize and become associated with a narrow field, enabling clients with an interest in that field to turn to you automatically. Internal consultants can use this strategy by treating the various divisions or departments of their firms as specialized markets.

The best marketing system is one in which a consultant does such good work that that person's clients come back repeatedly with new assignments. Building a reputation, expertise, references, and personal relationships are all valid business development approaches, and most OD consultants derive at least some of their work from them. But such systems depend on clients' seeking the consultant. A new practitioner or an established firm seeking to broaden its client base must adopt systems whereby they seek clients, and thus develop new business.

Developing new business

The process of developing new business involves six separate but closely related steps. Not every project for obtaining clients requires all six steps, but those steps it does take tend to follow the sequence given below.

1. Market selection. Some consider this part of a business development plan, whereas others find it should be performed before one develops such a plan—but in either case market research should be the first step taken.

Market research has two objectives: determining what kind of work you want to do, and how to find clients who will agree to have you do it. In performing research, you should ask the following questions:

- What market should I investigate?
- What area should I study?
- Who are the sources of information I should contact?

2. Prospecting. Sometimes referred to as "bird dogging," this process involves seeking and finding clients, **not** selling one's services and closing the deal. Remember: Most clients are just as anxious to be found as consultants are to find them. Unless such clients are offered alternatives, they may select OD consultants through such means as soliciting references from those who have obtained OD consulting. We have observed that about 50% of our new clients have been referred to us by previous clients, and that these persons frequently did not consider any of our competitors before signing contracts with us. This situation may appear to be fine for those fortunate enough to get constant referrals, but relying exclusively on referrals actually limits one's choices and leaves one unprepared should the "well run dry." Moreover, this is not the best way for a client to select an OD consultant suited to fill that client's needs. The latter factor is the one most often overlooked by OD professionals who criticize the practices of prospecting for and selling OD services.

Many OD consultants resist making prospecting part of their business development plans. Prospecting only occasionally results in a contract; those who perform prospecting with the goal of obtaining a contract will get discouraged. No one enjoys having a door slammed in one's face, and one can understand OD professionals' desiring to avoid such rejection. This alone would justify eliminating bird dogging were it merely a sales function. But bird dogging is intelligence gathering, not sales. The expression comes from hunting with bird dogs, whereby the dog seeks information the hunter can use. When a dog points to a target, it only provides directions—it does not get the bird for the hunter. Similarly, when you go prospecting, you should have a dual objective: to introduce yourself and to gather information that may ultimately lead to your obtaining clients.

Imagine that you are an OD consultant talking to the president of a hospital, or an internal OD consultant talking to your firm's senior vice president of marketing. If this represents your first contact with that person, you must of course introduce yourself and describe the services you provide. Should you try to sell your services during this initial meeting, you will be making a pitch to someone whose needs you do not know. Without this knowledge, you may end up doing something as silly as trying to sell snow to Eskimos. If, however, you use the opportunity to perform prospecting, you are in effect asking for information from a potential client whom you are treating as an authority in her or his field of expertise. This should make both of you feel good about this contact. If you are lucky, this may eventually lead to a sale— but that is not the objective of this stage.

Sometimes during prospecting, those being interviewed offer then and there to establish a contract for the consultant's services. When this happens during this step, one friend of ours replies, "I appreciate what you are asking for, but I came prepared only to gather information. I would love to make an appointment to discuss this further at a later date when I can be fully prepared to do so.'' By making another appointment, this consultant keeps the objectives of prospecting and selling separate.

3. Strategy research. Imagine that you have received a call from a desirable prospective client who is seeking professional OD services. We find this one of the most exciting moments in the process of selling. The potential clients will ask many questions, and how you answer them may determine whether or not this person continues to consider obtaining your services. You must, therefore, know a good deal about this person, the possible project, and the organization before answering these questions, or else you cannot give appropriate answers. This is why we emphasize interviewing prospective clients before they interview you. An OD consultant can more easily respond to the question ''Do you do strategic planning?'' when that consultant knows that this is being asked by someone from a 200-person, family-owned firm that held a retreat the previous year—and has learned what ''didn't work.''

Do not try to do a ''hard sell'' during this step. Instead, learn what you need so that you can more effectively sell your services later. Remember, as an OD professional you can market and design your service as you sell it; this is a strength. The more information you have, the more you can shape your services to fit the potential client's needs. To sell your services effectively, you must know the following:

- Who is the prospective client? A working knowledge of the organization and its members is valuable. This will help you talk to the prospective client in the language of the organization and to know more about the person you are dealing with.

- What is the project? The potential client has some sort of program in mind, and a wise OD consultant will try to learn all that can be learned about it before beginning to sell one's own services.

- How does the organization select consultants? Most OD consultants do not treat this information as important, but they should realize that the prospective client is in charge of all the rules that influence the consultant's selling strategy. One should determine how many consultants are being considered, the selection criteria—and how important the price is—and who will make the final decision on the selection. To be successful in selling, one must know these rules before planning a sales campaign.

- What are the timetables for the project and for the selection of a consultant? Knowing this may provide one with opportunities for performing follow-up work and making personal contact.

No reasonable prospective client should hesitate to answer these questions. These answers will reveal much about the services the prospective client seeks, and should enable that person to see what sort of professional OD consultant one is.

Strategy research thus leads one to ask: Do I want the job? Do I have any chance of getting it? If I pursue it, what strategy is best for winning? Most OD consultants do not ask the first two questions, but simply decide to "just go for it." This is unfortunate, as taking everything that is offered does not enhance one's personal image. If you think you have no chance of getting a job, or that it is not suited to your services, politely withdraw yourself from consideration. This will gain respect for your professional judgment. If, however, the answers to these questions indicate a desirable opportunity for you, plan your strategy according to the following model.

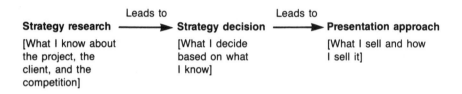

Figure 1. Strategy model

Finding or developing markets, building a list of potential clients, prospecting, and devising a strategy are all activities that should come before selling begins. Do not start direct sales efforts until you have developed a strategy for a specific target that incorporates the final two elements of the business development process.

4. Courting. Getting prospective clients to know you requires that you establish a professional relationship with them so that they will feel comfortable with the idea of working with you. The "chemistry" between a client and consultant has a large impact on the selling of the consultant's services. The basic rule is to build rapport with the potential client and increase that person's confidence in you. Be known, be credible, be helpful.

5. Proposals and presentations. In our field, some potential clients ask consultants to begin negotiations with a written proposal, others ask to start with a face-to-face meeting, and many require both. If you have done good strategy research, submitting a proposal will merely require you to demonstrate in writing your understanding of the clients' objectives, give a clear definition of your approach, and set your price.

Interviews and face-to-face meetings are held to determine if any "sparks" result from the contact between the prospective client and consultant. In this setting, facts matter less than personal interaction. Your goal should be to convince the prospective client that working with you will be enlightening and rewarding. Note that this will probably be your only opportunity to show the prospective client who you are and what kind of experience can result from your services. Take risks, go for broke—if you "play it safe" you will not likely be offered the job.

6. Closing the sale. This final step calls for closing the sale with follow-up activities. You may find it appropriate to encourage the client to contact the references supplied. Writing a letter of thanks for the interview that contains a summary of the highlights will allow you to restate your strengths and provides a final opportunity to demonstrate your genuine interest in the assignment. A client once told one of us, "We chose you because you cared about us. The other two consultants cared only about getting the job."

After the decision

When the decision following a proposal is communicated through a telephone call, this probably signals that you have been selected to provide your services. When this is communicated through a letter, it probably means your proposal has been declined. Whether you "win" or "lose," try to find out why that particular decision was made. This information can be vital for your business development process. If you do not get the job, do **not** begin by asking, "What did I do wrong?" Instead, ask, "Can you tell me what primary factors influenced the final decision?" The most valuable information will be what the prospective client required for a contract to be awarded, and what any "winning" consultant did, said, or proposed. Asking this even when you have obtained an assignment helps you reinforce or revise your business development plan.

Conclusion

Many professional OD consultants lack an organized approach to marketing and merely respond to requests for their services. Although they may be skilled at contacting potential clients and responding with proposals, they are only reacting to the market and are subject to its whims. If the market dries up or tough competitors enter it, they have little control over their fate. This chapter provides suggestions as to how you can take a more active stance in determining the work you will do, how you will obtain it, and how you can build the foundation for your future work.

Section VI.
A Look Ahead

OD in the Future: The Challenge of Integrating Human Systems and Technology

Joseph Potts

The term "high tech/high touch" was coined by John Naisbitt (1982) in his book *Megatrends*. It refers to a megatrend that has already started to affect the business community. Some organization development (OD) practitioners have recognized this trend, and a few have even been on the leading edge of it, but most have avoided consulting in this area. The reasons for this resistance are somewhat fuzzy, but seem related to a fear of technology by those more oriented toward people and relationships, and the lack of a theoretical basis for understanding the complex interaction between technology and the social system. Although little theory exists related to this issue, a theoretical base could be developed as part of the process for doing this work. Fortunately, most of the immediate problems encountered in situations involving technology are actually "people problems," and the short-term solutions to these require skills OD practitioners already possess.

The influence of technology on work systems

Technology, especially in the form of microcomputers, is now exploding into our lives at an unprecedented rate. As recently as a decade ago, computers were large machines enclosed in air-conditioned rooms that required swarms of persons to maintain them and occasionally program them to do new tasks. In most cases, the management information system (MIS) specialist was the person who told the organization's management what they should ask of the computer and how long it would take to provide the information. When the computer

---

completed its tasks, management often did not use the information generated because it did not really perceive a need for it. In short, managers did not usually use the type of information that MIS specialists considered important.

Now one can find microcomputers in nearly every office complex, and in many organizations they sit on the desks of all managers and secretaries. Moreover, they are used daily to manage business in the ways individuals find most useful. These machines have profoundly influenced the way work is done in offices. Their impact will grow as more organizations find more ways of improving productivity and decreasing costs by using this technology.

Microcomputers allow organizations to see for the first time that information management is the central activity supporting their operations. Whether the main product of an organization is information or something more tangible, the key to remaining competitive and to producing a high-quality product is managing information and converting it into knowledge.

Microcomputers have resulted in some rather subtle but profound changes in the social system we commonly label "the office." Two of the most significant of these involve handling information.

The importance of information for managing organizations has become much clearer since the advent of the microcomputer, because it makes information readily available to any layer in an organization. The sheer volume of information available has forced organizations into taking a position supported by OD professionals for years: that **people are the most important resource for organizational success.** People convert information into something more usable—knowledge. That is, information must be converted and condensed so that it has a proper context, and this task requires people. Thus, computers are indirectly causing organizations to treat people better—not worse, as was predicted in the early days of automation.

Middle management has traditionally served as the main information channel between top management and the work force. That is, managers have been required to filter information from both directions and to be the key actors in organizational problem-solving and decision-making processes. As the function of computers has changed, so have those of top management and workers. Now **people at all levels in a firm can have access to information through a computer terminal.** Top management can gain access to data bases without the intervention of middle managers, and decisions can be communicated to all personnel without relying on a management chain. This means that those at all three levels must redefine their roles and expectations for one another.

Both of these changes support the values and skills of OD practitioners. This trend is favorable to the practice of OD and the humanization of the work force. Rather than resisting and fearing technological change, those of us on the "touch" (i.e., social science) side should feel encouraged by this trend.

We must recognize that information management and microcomputers are **not** a fantasy, but already exist. For example, Naisbitt (1982) reports that 85% of the employees of Exxon—a manufacturing-oriented organization—hold jobs that essentially involve handling information or using knowledge. We could safely assume that most large organizations are in a similar situation. This is crucial information for the OD practitioner. Imagine what an organization would be like if it were designed to manage information as if it were its key product. The organization's structure and procedures would surely differ from those of organizations designed to produce tangible items. Managers must come to recognize that **people** are as important as technology—indeed, more so—and practitioners must grapple with ways of designing organizations for which the product is information.

The impact of current technology on OD

Which technology is important for the practice of OD, both now and in the near future? Three applications of existing technology to existing organizational problems have resulted in new solutions.

Microcomputers as support for OD. The use of microcomputers to support OD is a relatively recent phenomenon. In 1985, Tom Armor conducted a workshop with the OD Network on microcomputer support for OD and laboratory training, and even before this one of my colleagues and I were using some of these ideas in managing a series of complex projects involving both OD efforts and technical decision making. In general, practitioners can use microcomputers to support OD efforts because computer software is available that allows users to manipulate **ideas** as well as numbers. This class of programs is called idea processing. The programs permit the user to enter data in chunks that make sense to that person, and then to assemble or break down the data in ways the user finds useful.

Idea processing allows several persons involved in collecting data to enter the data into their own portable computers in chunks that each considers reasonable. The only constraint is that they must use common notations for the demographic data for each person interviewed so that the data can be sorted later. Moreover, multiple diagnostic models can be used to understand the data. The computerized data base enables the client to become completely involved in the diagnosis, and may even aid the development of the diagnostic model. This approach is appealing because it enables one to use the computer to sort the data for any group to uncover desired characteristics, which can help one find common themes or differences among groups or across levels.

Idea processing software also allows one to perform a "content analysis" of the information in the data base, and thus to search for themes, hostile or friendly descriptions of other departments or individuals, the frequency with which certain issues are mentioned (e.g., race and gender, policies and procedures), and the like.

Consultants often use instruments such as the FIRO-B, the Myers-Briggs Type Indicator, and the Strength Deployment Inventory to help their clients understand one another and develop better working relationships. Unfortunately, comparisons among members are usually difficult to obtain for groups of eight persons or more. Using a computerized data base allows one to perform comparisons across relatively large groups, because the computer can store the data and quickly report the comparisons one seeks. Instead of being recorded on pieces of paper scattered throughout several files, information stored in a computer is found in one location. This permits the practitioner to review successes and failures based on recorded information, not just recollections. This alone does not correct poor work, but allows consultants to determine if they overlooked important data that had been gathered and/or if they used the wrong diagnostic model. Just as we tell our clients, we should try to learn from our own experience!

Microcomputers as mechanisms for management development.
Applications of microcomputers that serve as management development tools are being developed at a rapid pace. These tools tend to be designed for individual use, and are "expert" systems based on psychological theories of how individuals behave in a work environment. These software packages use the concept of interactive programmed learning, and are capable of "branching." They instruct the user to answer a series of questions, and use the responses to provide a diagnosis and opportunities to experiment with new approaches to various situations through simulations, case studies, or working with colleagues "off line." The programs keep track of each person using the system, and provide suggestions about their areas of concentration.

These tools have been designed to tap into the enormous market for training. Most of the software packages are designed for use independently of external consulting assistance, and sometimes in place of internal training staff. My experience leads me to believe that these programs fail to achieve their potential when they are used alone. When, however, clients use them between face-to-face meetings or workshops as a means of building skills and expanding awareness, the programs can be important supplements for training/consulting efforts—especially when the software addresses the same information and issues addressed in the larger training design.

Many such systems are being sold. I briefly discuss two of these below. Both are run on IBM-compatible personal computers, and neither requires computer expertise beyond finding the "on/off" switch and loading the program diskettes. Once they they are brought up, they guide the user with clear directions through each step. Thus, the systems are truly "user friendly."

Thoughtware (produced by Thoughtware, Inc. of 2699 South Bayshore Drive, Coconut Grove, Florida 33133) is a program for teaching managers about managing, motivating others, appraising performance, interaction, and conducting successful meetings. It is based on a series of surveys for which the user or the user's subordinates provide answers. The results of these surveys are often compared to those of a national sample. Thoughtware uses the findings to develop an action plan for applying what is learned.

Acumen (produced by Human Factors-Advanced Technology Group of 4340 Redwood Highway, Suite 26, San Rafael, California 94903) is a program designed to help managers identify productive and counterproductive thinking styles and behaviors, develop the best ways of handling management responsibilities, manage conflict, plan, control, and provide leadership. The program's major focus is on learning about oneself, but it also pays significant attention to assessing others and improving work relationships. Acumen uses the Life Styles Inventory as the basis for its survey questions.

Both programs take a serious approach to applying psychological theory to self-development. Both focus on the personal side of management and help managers recognize their own styles and how these affect others. They also encourage managers to try new behaviors, and thus can be considered self-directed learning devices. They give consultants opportunities to make their presence felt even after the face-to-face contact is over, and to feel assured that the clients are being exposed to accurate information and acquiring this in an interactive way that is consistent with the adult learning paradigm.

Microcomputers as mechanisms for understanding groups. Microcomputers are now being used to support people's understanding of the group process by allowing complex computations to be performed quickly and flexibly. The most important work of this type is that of the Symlog Consulting Group (producers of the software entitled Symlog; they are located at 18550 Polvera Drive, San Diego, California 92128). This group worked with Freed Bales to computerize his approach to understanding group process. Bales worked on developing a model of group behavior for more than 40 years, back to the time of the first T Groups conducted in Bethel, Maine. His highly complex research tool is now a practical tool for the OD practitioner, with this progress resulting mainly from the advent of the personal computer.

Bales's underlying theory suggests that one must consider three dimensions if one is to understand group process: dominance/submission, friendliness/unfriendliness, and acceptance/rejection of tasks by established authority. The microcomputer can compile the necessary information in seconds and, even more important, can provide many different perspectives on the data. What formerly took researchers weeks to do can now be done with several keystrokes on an IBM-compatible personal computer. The system has been modified so that one can answer 26 questions about oneself and each member of one's group.

The forms used for gathering data can be read directly by the computer, which can make the results for the entire group available within minutes.

What I find most impressive about Symlog is its capability of allowing managers to determine and understand clearly the **dynamics** of their groups. Symlog takes some of the "magic" out of consultants' interventions, allowing clients to see in a graphic format—that is, a field diagram—"snapshots" of their interactions. The visual display presents dimensions intuitively meaningful to most managers, so that clients can respond more quickly upon learning which key issues should be addressed, with an understanding of the process issues likely to arise. Symlog also enables a group to comprehend that **group dynamics** as well as interpersonal dynamics are important to its functioning.

In all of the examples I mention, technology permits practitioners to do things they already know how to do—but in a more effective way, and/or at a level of greater depth, quality, and complexity, than they could do previously because of the extent of data manipulation required. None of the actual interventions presented above are new. The microcomputer simply makes them easier to perform, thus allowing practitioners to deliver their services more effectively.

Organization development has proven successful in office automation applications. In 1983, Ava Albert Schnidman and Susan L. Colantuono presented an NTL workshop entitled "Introducing Automated Technologies— What's Gone Wrong, What To Do about It." During this workshop, they described 15 of 18 efforts to put computers into offices (office automation) that could be termed business failures because the systems did not fulfill the purposes for which they had been designed. The reasons for this were "people problems." That is, all of the systems met the technical requirements set for them, but no one had adequately considered the needs of the workers using them. The fundamental premise of OD is that people are much more likely to support the implementation of decisions when they have been involved in making them. Organizations investing $250,000 to $10 million in office automation, however, often fail to involve their workers in its installation. This occurs for the distressingly obvious reason that people still tend to view computers as tools to be installed solely by technical experts. Office automation systems are generally developed by persons with software expertise, who unfortunately tend to prepare them with other programmers in mind, not those who will use the information they generate.

OD consultants working in this arena have been selling the idea that office automation represents a major change in the work environment, that they change work flow and even the actual tasks people perform. Because of this, the consultants emphasize that attempts to initiate such change without involving those who will be affected by it have resulted in failure.

Successful office automation projects rely on multidisciplinary teams, which should reflect a balance of persons with different technical expertise, a sponsor, those having process consulting expertise, and the workers to be affected by the change as well as management. Moreover, those involved in successful projects recognize that automation does not reach its full potential after just one attempt at implementing it. Whenever an organization expects this to involve an iterative process, with the project team getting closer and closer to an optimum solution as it works with various stakeholders, it prevents the level of frustration from getting high enough to terminate the project prematurely.

The governing principle is that any change outside the organization's experience (office automation requires a knowledge of what computers can really do and how they can both enrich the people working with them and increase organizational effectiveness) requires the organization to implement the change in series of small adjustments that are more easily understood and integrated. In effect, the strategies that have proven successful for office automation involve the users' saying what they think they want, the technical experts providing this, and the users' responding by saying that they now understand what they had asked for and want something different. As this has occurred, OD consultants have supported the development of the social aspects of this "sociotechnical" human/computer system and played key roles in managing the processes of the project teams.

Organizations that have accomplished office automation have undergone important shifts in the ways in which people relate to their work and to their coworkers and supervisors. Task relationships change when computers cause job reorganization. Instead of relating by direct physical contact with others or a product, following automation people accomplish tasks through the medium of information, with physical contact limited to the keyboard of a computer terminal. Feedback about the task often comes through a terminal—or not at all. This makes work more abstract and symbolic, and people may easily come to feel out of control. Even when computer systems do provide appropriate feedback, many individuals dislike being judged by an inanimate object. The OD practitioner's role is to work with the organization members and the system on these issues.

People in automated offices must adjust to shifts in human interaction. Information previously obtained in conversations with other persons often becomes available via computer terminals. Face-to-face encounters, which most people find satisfying, become less necessary. Similarly, computers can possibly affect relationships between individuals and their supervisors—another source of satisfaction and productivity—by allowing for remote monitoring of employees and the measurement of productive according to more "objective" criteria.

The overall effectiveness of the system depends on balancing the efficiency computers make possible with the satisfaction provided by relationships at work. Other than trial and error, however, at this time we lack any theoretical basis for determining how to best achieve this balance. In effect, workers have some grounds for resisting the change office automation is likely to achieve, as they know intuitively that this will alter their interactions. Until the advent of the high-tech environment, we did not need to know the specific value of relationships in the work place and how they affect task performance.

The impact of future technology
on organization development

Where will technology lead us in the years to come? What other events will occur that we OD practitioners must address as we develop our own skills and awareness?

Until now, we have viewed computers as tools to help us do our tasks more effectively. Paul Kellman (1984) differentiates brain work (e.g., tasks such as calculating, sorting, and comparing) from mind work (e.g., considering, conceptualizing, and creating). Although such functions are related, they are also distinct. When we are free from having to bother with the detailed requirements of brain work, we can concentrate on work of a more theoretical nature. Thus, tools that help us in this regard include idea processors that provide structures to help us think and create new concepts. Programs are being created to keep track of details important for task completion, yet also allow users to extract general principles from their work and develop new, creative solutions to old, nagging problems.

Alvin Toffler (1980) states that computers are teaching us different ways of thinking about problems, and that they will allow us to explore alternative future scenarios by simulating possibilities. This will ease us into the future. Perhaps personal counseling programs will lead users through series of questions, use the responses to select appropriate theoretical bases, and suggest alternatives for consideration. They may even allow us to examine problems based on our own unique histories.

I note above that the impact of microcomputers on the overall social system is congruent with the values expressed by most OD practitioners—which support the empowerment of people. Programs that allow users to work more independently and that reduce the influence of centralized work organizations will proliferate. These include educational programs that can teach children faster and more efficiently than the existing educational system can. In such cases, microcomputers can allow children to learn through an "adult education" mode of experiential learning.

Software and communication links are being developed that will allow both managers and employees to work from their homes or other locations away from the organization, at least part of the time. This will cause practitioners to confront the need to assist organizations in managing changes in their existing authority structures and informal cultures. Consultants may also be able to work from home—at least part of the time—as they interact with client systems.

Telecommunication is cheaper and, in some cases, more effective for the organization, for it reduces the expense and time of commuting, overhead, and office space requirements. Moreover, some employees feel better about work when they can do it from home. Some problems will likely arise, however, particularly with respect to isolation and alienation, removal from the information flow, distractions involving people's homes and personal lives, and trusting employees who cannot be observed while working.

Expert systems based on the concepts of artificial intelligence have begun to emerge, with most applied to data base management. These allow users to ask microcomputers questions in "plain English," which are then restructured into a language the computer can understand. When applied to a multitude of programs, such systems allow users to manage complex projects even when they are not "computer literate." They also decrease the need to remember all the various relationships among different parts of data bases, as computers with expert systems can look for appropriate relationships when given relevant principles.

Networks: How we get there from here

"Networking" is an area for which social systems theory is almost totally nonexistent. This is unfortunate, for I consider it the area in which the highest payoffs can be obtained from understanding its social systems component. Networking per se is an old concept that most of us use in an informal manner. Sociologists have studied networks as work structures and described some of their fundamental characteristics. Virginia Hine (1984) points out that networks are characterized by their decentralized nature and common values, adding that they may be humans' oldest social invention.

With microcomputers, the scale of possible of interconnections becomes so large that what networks have already done for families and neighborhoods they may now do for organizations, special interest groups (including OD practitioners), and whole societies (see Grayson, 1984). OD practitioners may find them important because by their very nature networks result in a more egalitarian approach to management. Networking does not necessarily preclude positional power, but it certainly enhances power based on knowledge.

Computer networks will become a major part of the structures of existing hierarchical organizations, and will have to be integrated into these structures. This means that organizations and networks will have to be modified to accommodate the formalization of a previously informal process, for networks will become part of a larger organizational context rather than free-standing entities.

Computer networking—also known as computer conferencing—allows individual users to sit at terminals in their homes, offices, or away from home (particularly if they have portable computers) and interact with as many as

200-300 persons, without regard to space or time. One initiates this process by dialing the phone number of a central computer and connecting one's personal computer to it through a telephone modem. The messages of other users are stored in the central computer, and when each user "logs on"—or connects with the network—the central computer tells that person which messages have been left since he or she last logged on. Users can have "conversations" with one another by responding to messages transmitted by the network. The system has the capacity to make all messages available to all users, or to allow some to be communicated privately to specific users. Equally important, all conversations are captured permanently by the central computer, allowing users to "go back" as far as they wish in any conversation and track all responses following a given message.

Computer networks can expand the level of connection among people far beyond anything in our previous experience. Networks promote egalitarian decision making and power based on knowledge. Despite this, our understanding of the social systems underlying computer networks is virtually nil. This lack is certain to cause problems, for computer networks will have to be integrated into organizations with already existing cultures and structures that, in most cases, are not democratic, egalitarian, or horizontal in nature.

Computer networks will never completely replace face-to-face meetings or telephone conversations. They do, however, supplement them by offering the following advantages:

- they reduce the need for travel,
- they reduce the incidence of "telephone tag" whereby callers repeatedly fail to connect with each other,
- they produce permanent written records of what is communicated,
- they allow for "asynchronous" communication, meaning that people do not have to communicate simultaneously, but can leave messages of any length for one another and respond to these in "conversations" whenever this is convenient,
- they enable communications to occur independent of location, requiring only that telephone lines and computer terminals be available,
- they enable many more persons to take part in the communication than is possible with face-to-face meetings or telephone conference calls,
- they allow for more varied communication linkages, with the only constraint being the availability of telephone lines and computer terminals,
- they enable news and information to be disseminated quickly,
- they allow individuals belonging to a network to develop a sense of community independent of geographic location,

- they do not require people to be computer literate or fast typists to engage in the networks, and
- they enable greater knowledge to be generated and more appropriate decisions to be made.

The last advantage listed is especially important. Organizations and the people within them are bombarded with data and information. Much of this stems from the increasing complexity of the environment and our acknowledgment that we must pay attention to the environment if we are to succeed. Moreover, computers themselves have increased the ease with which we can collect and manipulate data. Unfortunately, data is usually summarized into chunks of information represented in graphs, charts, and reports. What is often missing is any dialogue that makes sense of the information—that makes knowledge. Knowledge is what gives organizations the ability to perform high-quality problem solving, make good decision, and be effective. Computer networks enable dialogues to occur among those having relevant points of view and transform information into a knowledge base.

George Bugliarello (1984) calls this aspect of computer networking "hyperintelligence." He states that the presence of millions of computers that are interconnected can be considered the most recent step in our ability to sense, reason, and remember. The interaction of more experts and nonexperts in a coherent manner will allow problem solving to occur in ways not previously possible because of our inability to gather a truly large number of "high-powered" persons together in one place.

In addition to the previously mentioned lack of knowledge about networks in organizations, several smaller problems—or micro issues—are associated with computer networks.

One problem is that identifying differences of opinion and making positions clear is relatively easy with computer networks, but resolving conflicts through this mode of communication is nearly impossible. Because the users cannot see or hear one another, they cannot rely on facial expressions, tone of voice, or other such indicators to sense others' feelings as they make or respond to statements. Thus, arguments that might otherwise be resolved in minutes with the help of a little body language can get rather intense.

Decision making can be difficult if a computer network is set up in accordance with common values rather than an existing decision-making structure. Even if such a structure is in place, time boundaries for decision deadlines can be troublesome to deal with.

Another problems arises when some users do not actively participate in a computer conference. During face-to-face meetings, such persons can be easily identified and brought into a conversation, and the reason for their nonparticipation easily determined. The problem is more complex and difficult to resolve for computer networking.

Some networks may get rather large, causing users to grow frustrated over their inability to develop a good "mental map" of the various facets of an electronic meeting. During a well-run face-to-face meeting, one issue is dealt with at a time, making the mental map rather simple. During a good computer conference, 10 or more matters may be addressed at the same time by various users.

Another issue concerns the record of network communication. Sometimes people are willing to make various statements out loud, but unwilling to put them in writing. Such concerns are that much greater when they are not sure who will eventually see their statements.

The power dynamic of granting access to a computer conference and declaring some conversations "off limits" to certain users is often not spoken about. As is the case with all interactions, setting "in/out" boundaries is important. The boundaries are clearer in this communications medium than in most, making the issue particularly salient.

Rewards for participation in computer networks are unclear, as is their distribution. The norms for "on-line" behavior and the process for establishing them are also unclear.

Finally, the varied meaning of typing in some organizations can cause problems. In some cases this poses a major block to the participation of high-level organization members, who could derive the greatest benefits from participating in computer networks.

Networks in action

Despite all the problems associated with computer networks, numerous systems have been established, and many have proven successful. The following are some examples.

Bill Paul and Susanna Opper developed a system enabling OD practitioners in the Exxon Corporation to work with another through computer networking. When this system—called Exnet—was initiated, external OD practitioners were invited to join the network and serve as resources for the internal OD personnel. Later, several Exxon line managers joined the system and began using it to discuss common problems and act as resources for one another.

The Electronic Networking Association was formed in the spring of 1985 during an informal meeting of persons interested in computer networking. This group decided to hold a conference entitled "Using the Medium," which they planned almost entirely through computer networking during a six-month period. The conference drew nearly 200 persons and was a financial success. Many of those attending met for the first time at the conference, and all the participants agreed that this was their first experience with "knowing" others well before actually meeting them.

NTL Institute now uses a computer conference system to conduct its governance between meetings of the Board of Directors. All Board members and the chairs of key committees, as well as administrative liaisons, belong to a computer network.

Western Behavioral Sciences Institute set up an educational effort for top-level executives that uses computer conferences. A series of lectures is available by computer, and executives interact with the instructor by using computer terminals. In addition to the computer linkages, the executives involved in the effort meet face to face four times during a two-year period.

In all of these cases, the organizations had to overcome problems. These problems arose almost entirely from a lack of understanding of the social systems involved, either at the macro or micro level. The groups responded by accepting the idea that the technology would not work perfectly at the beginning of its implementation, and took an ''action research'' approach to correcting difficulties.

Conclusions

Microcomputers offer OD practitioners unique opportunities to do their existing work more effectively. They also provide opportunities for doing new kinds of work as organizations come to understand that computer systems change organizations, and that experts in managing change are necessary if large investments in office automation are to be made effectively. Microcomputers are changing the nature of organizations, and thus changing the type of work OD practitioners do.

Technical advances are occurring at an increasingly fast pace. The major problems with their implementation involve the social system. As experts in the social system aspects of the change process, OD practitioners must develop a theory base that will allow people to gain the maximum value from computer technology. If we can gather sufficient momentum from the ''social system side,'' we can harness the potential of the ''technical side''—and address social system issues by creating new programs to enhance human interaction.

REFERENCES

Bugliarello, G. (1984, December). Hyperintelligence. *The Futurist,* pp. 6-11.

Grayson, C. J. (1984, June). Networking by computer. *The Futurist,* pp. 14-17.

Hine, V. (1984, June). Networks in a global society. *The Futurist,* pp. 11-13.

Kellman, P. (1984, June). The cognitive revolution—An evolutionary human advance. *LIST,* pp. 66-75.

Naisbitt, J. (1982). *Megatrends.* New York: Warner.

Toffler, A. (1980). *The third wave.* New York: Bantam.

Seven Process Frontiers for Organization Development

Peter B. Vaill

The basic thesis of this chapter is that organization development is in danger of becoming defunct as both a profession and an organizational function. The following is a new definition of OD designed to replace the dozens that have been offered up until now.

> Organization development is an organizational process for understanding and improving any and all substantive processes an organization may develop for performing any tasks and pursuing any objectives.

A "process for improving processes"—that is what OD has basically sought to be for approximately 25 years. This definition helps us understand why explaining OD is so difficult: Without keeping substantive organizational processes in mind (e.g., planning, group meetings, superior-subordinate communications), one will find it nearly impossible to state just what OD can contribute. An individual must know quite a bit about such substantive processes—and about the various ways in which they can become distorted and blocked—before that person can imagine the existence of some professional specializing in helping others determine how such processes are supposed to work, why they are not, and what can be done to remedy this.

The definition also helps explain why OD has always been a collection of loosely related concepts, theories, research findings, and techniques (with some accused of being "gimmicks"). When responding to the full range of processes found in the modern organization, OD is limited to only one theory or doctrine at its peril. Therefore, those involved with OD have been and continue to be unable to explicitly describe what it is about.

The definition clarifies another of OD's most frustrating features: its failure to take a stand and declare how things ought to be. OD specialists **have** written eloquently and movingly about what organizations should do, but when addressing particular organizational projects such consultants are usually hesitant about making judgments and prescriptions. Unfortunately, this has given terms such as "facilitator" and "process consultant" connotations of indecisiveness, "wishy-washiness," and even lack of moral courage. The definition presented above, however, clearly indicates that OD focuses on the substantive process and what is needed for this to work better. The OD practitioner usually does not want to take responsibility for prescribing ways of improving the process, for this tends to require technical expertise that the consultant lacks. The underlying assumption of OD is that almost any organizational process will work if those involved with it want to make it work—the **problem** lies in the ways in which people work with one another in dealing with the process.

These are not merely abstract questions and criticisms directed at a profession claiming to offer a process for improving process. They can provide the basis for tough, even destructive charges launched by persons who consider themselves competent enough to conduct their organizations' processes without needing outside "facilitation." OD specialists have endured much sarcasm, been the subject of many jokes, come to doubt themselves and their own motives, and been tempted to give in and play the same power games everyone else plays: the games that disrupt the organization's rational processes for performing the work it is in business to perform.

Faced with this pressure to justify itself—to "pay its own way"—OD has come to offer extraordinary assistance with a few organizational processes. Sadly, however, the field has drifted away from its goal of serving as a process for improving process. The remainder of this chapter discusses some of the processes for which OD has been useful, identifies some of the ways OD has departed from its historic areas of competence, and reviews briefly seven organizational processes that greatly need the kind of assistance OD can provide.

Organization development successes

Any declaration of OD's primary achievements is guaranteed to invite controversy, but I am willing to risk this and offer the following nominations.

In general, OD has demonstrated a great ability to improve organizational processes involving **power sharing** and **lateral communication,** especially that occurring "around the table" in a team or committee meeting.

Power sharing. This term applies to all efforts to help managers encourage the participation of others, become more accepting of feedback and disagreement, and seek the opinions of those down the organizational hierarchy. It also refers to the attempts of OD specialists to encourage managers to change their attitudes about their subordinates, and to encourage lower-level personnel to view those higher up differently. This interest and skill in addressing the process of power sharing probably stems from the enormous influence of Douglas McGregor's work, and from research done in the 1940s, 1950s, and 1960s that produced findings favoring democratic rather than authoritarian leadership.

I consider it significant that OD's work on power **sharing** has not been matched by an equal degree of interest or skill in addressing the processes associated with the concentration of power in the offices of supervisors, managers, and leaders. Those in OD tend to call such processes "politics" or "power games," and seldom offer much help in dealing with them. In today's turbulent organization, quite often legitimate situations arise in which establishing and clarifying power is as important as sharing power. Although this issue is not considered one of the seven "frontiers" discussed below, it can be rather significant.

The other major type of expertise OD specialists have developed is that of helping persons talk to one another when they have relatively equal status and must work together to achieve some task or goal. This applies to meetings of committees such as task forces, project groups, and interagency study groups, and also to the millions of group meetings arising on a more-or-less ad hoc basis (e.g., in voluntary organizations, family decision-making situations, and cases in which persons are assembled for a particular reason). OD can help people work well together under these conditions, providing the essence of what has traditionally been called "process consultation." The key skill is that of determining the **way** a group works, not just the content of its task or what is being said. Despite the purported increase in people's awareness of "group process issues," in the heat of the moment such understanding often deserts a person precisely when one needs it most. Therefore, we will always need process consultants—as long as people continue to have feelings that sometimes lead them to say and do things differently than they would during calmer moments.

Just as OD's work with power sharing has been influenced by McGregor, its work in facilitating lateral relationships probably is rooted in the experience of the T Group and individual psychotherapy. For those involved in T Groups and therapy, the **meaning** of what one says—not just its manifest content—is what one primarily seeks to understand. OD has proved itself good at helping people come to see one another's intentions, based on specialists' long experience with groups whose sole purpose is to help persons understand themselves and one another.

In addition to facilitating power sharing and lateral communication, OD has developed expertise in helping with a few other organizational processes. These include career planning and development, stress management, and communication across the deep gulfs of gender, race, and ethnic differences. Particular OD specialists also have many other different types of expertise, such as helping organizations undergo reductions or mergers in honest, healthy ways, and helping companies conduct executive searches. I wish to emphasize, however, that only a few organizational processes are understood and addressed by nearly all OD specialists, even though some consultants have become adept at helping organizations with other processes not considered to be at the core of OD.

Wrong directions OD has taken

The seven frontiers mentioned in this chapter's title refer to ways in which mainstream OD can expand and address modern organizations. Before I describe these, however, I discuss what I think the profession has done wrong during the past ten years.

In brief, I believe OD has lost its focus on process. This is the "dark side" of its response to pressure and criticism from "hard-nosed" managers oriented toward the "bottom line." Although OD has demonstrated its ability to help with a few kinds of organizational processes, because OD specialists have not understood the definition of OD I present at the beginning of the chapter, they have drifted toward the substantive and sought to become experts on "leading-edge" issues of human resource management and development. I am not saying that we do not need such experts. Indeed, line managers seem to be realizing that all their plans for the future depend on having the right persons—who are selected, trained, and rewarded in the right ways (although this can never be done with the precision of, say, engineering)—in the right places at the right times, and on having systems to provide assistance to employees having difficulty coping with organizational life.

Such expertise, however, has not been the traditional goal of OD, and does not match the definition given at the beginning of this chapter. It will never eliminate the need for a process for understanding and improving any and all substantive organizational processes. The more organizations try to do, the more flexible they try to be, the more carefully they allocate their resources, the wider the variety of people they try to employ—in general, the more they try to remain internally coherent and externally adaptive to their turbulent environments—the more they will need a profession meeting the definition of OD this chapter provides.

So many OD professionals have come to specialize in one or two particular types of substantive processes, creating the risk that the general process skills they employ in doing this work will not be noticed. Process skills are terribly ethereal; we can just barely describe them even when conducting team development or helping superiors share power with their subordinates. When process skills are used in more unusual circumstances, such as when one facilitates the installation of a computer-based management information system, what the consultant actually does to help the process go forward is nearly certain to be invisible to line management, the rest of the profession, and—even newcomers to OD. Such "invisible" exercise of process skills is becoming more and more common in OD. Specialists are exercising process skills in increasingly disparate settings, making it harder and harder to sustain the generic view of OD that this chapter's definition declares.

The definition is also becoming more difficult to maintain through the practice of consultants who, when trying to tell colleagues and people outside the profession just what they do, discuss only the substance of their contributions to organizations. That is, they speak of the theories they teach their clients, the instruments they use for collecting data, the ways they arrange data in tables and graphs, the workshop "designs" they employ, and—as if this were not enough—their plans for transferring their consulting expertise into sets of things they can leave with a client, do for a client, or **sell** to a client. Explaining what a process consultant does is hard; it is easier to say, "Read this book," "Go through this exercise," "Watch this videotape" than to say, "I will charge you money for sitting with you and helping you think about how you have been doing, what you want to do next, and how you might do this."

Of course, the clients themselves, who are under pressure to show what the OD consultant can "deliver," do not like the latter statement either. They want to show the vice president for human resources the terrific workbook the OD consultant will disseminate throughout the company.

Process skills are as important now as they ever have been, but when OD specialists "talk shop" these days, they show an increasing interest in copyright, marketing strategies, and the prospects for putting a questionnaire into a computer, and speak less frequently about the process itself of working with particular clients and how they feel about this.

OD today

My feelings about the current situation of OD alternate between sadness and amusement. I feel sad when I realize that we will have to invent process skills all over again, for we cannot get along without them. Terrible things happen in organizations when substantive processes are out of control and inaccessible to intervention (remember the Internal Revenue Service's computer system debacle? Or Exxon's $2 billion loss from office systems?). I feel amused when I realize that all the systems, instruments, and behavioral objectives OD consultants are selling today will **themselves** require much old-fashioned process facilitation if they are ever to accomplish in organizations what the specialists promise they will. I wonder how many OD consulting groups have yet recognized how much they need an OD consultant to help themselves connect all this technology to their client organizations.

I argue that the core of OD is not the content of organizational operations, which I call substantive process. Neither is it the proliferation of ideas,
techniques, and paraphernalia that supposedly represent what OD can "do"
for its clients. The main thing OD can do for organizations that nothing else
can is help them design, implement, evaluate, and improve the substantive
processes they need to operate, fulfill their missions, and be the types of organizations they want to be. OD's expertise lies in developing processes to help with
processes.

This means that OD must respond to the ways in which operational
processes evolve. Because most OD professionals do not clearly recognize that
OD is in the business of developing processes to help with processes, OD has
become increasingly unaware of the problems confronting organizations, much
less able to offer interventions to help address them. In saying that OD is
"unaware" of these problems, I do not mean to ignore those individual professionals working on the problems on their own, for I recognize and applaud
their efforts. What I wish to call attention to is a general absence of awareness
within the profession of just what is happening and is at stake. Indeed, many
of the "leading-edge" OD specialists themselves wonder whether anyone else
in the field cares about the needs of modern organizations. The remainder of
this chapter discusses briefly seven areas in which new operational processes
acutely need assistance from OD.

1. Top management development

Everything managers do in organizations involves "organizational behavior."
From its very beginning, OD has sought to address organizational behavior.
Yet OD has not had much influence on the processes affecting how top managers
are chosen, what they do, or how they work together. Its impact on the top
level of organizational operations has been minimal partly because OD
specialists generally do not understand top managers' needs, partly because
these specialists are in awe of those with power and authority, and partly because
the top managers' own roles and self-concepts keep them from asking for help.

This situation has begun to change. More and more published works
describe what top managers are like and what they do, with some of these
accounts written by top managers themselves. *Fortune* 500 companies now
recognize the need to consciously aid the development of men and women
qualified to assume positions of broad responsibility and leadership. Those
persons assuming these positions are increasingly aware of their own needs for
continued development, and under the right conditions are more easily
approached than were their counterparts of the previous generation.

This means that OD's opportunities to help such persons become more
effective are improving. Many have spoken glibly of the "loneliness of com-

mand," but for too long those in OD have not drawn the obvious conclusion: Loneliness is an acutely felt emotion, indicating unmet needs that can produce enormous amounts of personal stress and distort the leadership and decision-making processes. Rather than treating the situation as a cliche, those in OD should recognize it as an opportunity—indeed, a responsibility.

2. Determining what business we are in

For about 25 years, the classic question asked in MBA courses and executive strategic planning seminars has been, "What business are you in?" OD professionals are relatively unaware that changes in technology, economic reality, global competition, and consumer tastes have forced more and more organizations to answer this question, whether they are for-profit corporations, not-for-profit associations, government agencies, educational systems, health care structures, or firms in any other sector. Each firm is finding that its basic reason for existing and the basic terms of its success are changing **beyond** those contained by traditional mission statements.

Pain, confusion, and acrimony sweep through those organizations struggling to redefine themselves, both for now and for the future. No **personal** anarchy need be present; indeed, each person may feel assured of understanding the firm's new needs. Collectively, however, the effect may be anarchical, as one version of the company's mission vies with another. Each day, newspapers report how some faction in a large organization has "won out" in a struggle for redefinition. Those in OD should at least ask, "**Must** this articulation of new missions result from a power-based political process? Should we assume that a Darwinian process is the only one available for determining basic directions? Is the process of deciding which business one is in inevitably one of playing games?"

We know two things: that power politics need not provide the only means for resolving differences among people, and that large organizations are not immune to making large mistakes resulting in large social and economic costs. At least OD has never acquiesced to claims that realpolitik is the only valid option. The ways OD specialists intervene and can be of help, however, have largely remained unexplored.

3. Digesting new technology

The classic situation of manufacturing has called for several kinds of engineering skills in order to produce a product and meet certain requirements of quantity, quality, and cost. These include product development engineering, manufacturing engineering, industrial engineering, and—more recently—

quality and value engineering. Systems engineering seeks to integrate these various disciplines.

OD has never demonstrated much interest in the ways organizations seek to adopt and absorb new technology associated with these and other types of engineering. Indeed, many in OD consider engineers the "bad guys," and many "rational" designs have included unrealistic, even inhumane assumptions and requirements for the persons involved in engineering.

This situation has changed markedly in the past decade, for two main reasons. One is the increasing willingness of those with technical skills to consider the implications of technology for human beings. Until recently the term "human factors" was generally restricted to only the physiological aspects of the human body, but lately human psychological and interpersonal dimensions have also come under consideration when devising technical systems. The rapid rise of the field of ergonomics provides evidence of this. OD specialists may be surprised to discover that some of the technical personnel they had labeled as "cold and inhumane" now know more about the "whole employee" than do many in OD.

The other reason is the sheer spread of new technology and its extension into all facets of organizational life, which means that former approaches and structures of systems engineering may be inadequate for the rapid rate of change. Systems engineers need as much help in dealing with one another as in dealing with system users, which is readily apparent in both the hardware and software engineering areas of computer systems. The power and promise of new technology is not fully realized—or even comprehended—by organizations. Thousands of computer specialists know how to work with others of equal sophistication in their own fields, but are less capable in communicating and functioning with those of different kinds and degrees of expertise. They need **a lot** of help with this.

I do not feel I am exaggerating when I say that we need an entire new subprofession of persons with OD process skills who can facilitate communication among those representing various elements of the computer industry. This is particularly essential for addressing the industry's impact on the user lacking technical skills, who today alternates between feeling mystified and furious about the effects of this technology.

4. Integrating new ideas about human resources

Previously in this chapter I note that line managers have finally come to realize that **the** factor determining whether or not an organization can survive and develop is the state of its human resources. One must also note, however, that much of the human resource expertise OD professionals make available is the esoteric sort of "new technology" described above. When line management asks for a new reward system, a series of workshops on gender awareness, or a study of workers' attitudes within an organization, it may not realize that this makes a great deal of professional expertise available, which will continue to increase.

Someone with an OD mentality might ask, "Do we really want to take the common sense understanding of the employee away from the line manager? Do we really want to contribute to a situation in which the human resources staff alone has behavioral science knowledge?" Such a person may seek to use various interventions to fight the dehumanization of the work force by recasting employees into the abstract categories of modern human resource management. Examples include "high potential" programs, "competency-based" management development, "organizational behavior modification," and "pay-for-performance" programs.

Because no one seems to be paying much attention to such substantive processes of human resource management, OD specialists risk helping management become as cut off from employees as ever. Managers' own Theory X assumptions and suspicions used to cause this before. Now, if human resources continues developing as it has, managers will be cut off because the work force will become unrecognizable to them.

5. Sophisticated diagnostic processes

Nearly everyone in OD complains about the highly analytical, impersonal style MBA students develop in America's business schools today. Even if the extremely technical approaches employed recently were dropped, however, I still feel that management would remain a far more analytical, quasi-scientific enterprise than it was when OD first began. Cognitive styles in organizational life seem to have changed permanently toward a greater reliance on rational thinking, especially for identifying and solving problems.

When an employee today tells the boss, "We've got a problem," the evidence is rarely rumor, hunches, or intuition, but usually data, particularly quantitative data. An analytical model may well be in the background, and if the data is computer generated, a consciously constructed model will almost certainly be present. In everyday life, people also operate from models, frames, and other abstractions, but the processes for developing these differ greatly from those used to develop, test, refine, and use highly analytical models. OD's process skills were developed to help persons with different "models" of situations communicate better with one another, increase mutual understanding, and thus improve their effectiveness at work. OD offers little knowledge about the process skills appropriate for competing definitions of "reality" arising from consciously developed analytical models purportedly free from distortions caused by human quirks and idiosyncracies.

This problem has manifested itself throughout the organizational world. With such competing models, process skills must be used to help managers determine what this all means. OD has already addressed dozens of organizational subjects; I am personally familiar with "strategic planning" and "excellence." The process skills needed must combine traditional OD help with the interpersonal dimension and help with basic thinking process that have become increasingly important. Process skills in the future will require much more ability related to logic, data, determining what science is and is not—and can and cannot do—and how interpersonal communication relates this to other psychological factors. In brief, we are moving rapidly toward using new language systems and forms of consciousness for which traditional process skills are simply inadequate.

6. Permanent white water strategies

Many years ago, Kurt Lewin created a simple but vivid model of the change process—called "unfreezing-moving-refreezing"— which OD has presented in various guises since that time. Even the most contemporary thinkers addressing such topics as transitions and organizational transformation still seem to assume that companies will "settle down" after changes are enacted. Lewin's model is analogous to a wild river of white water connecting two stable, tranquil lakes.

I think I detect a growing awareness that firms may be in a "permanent white water" situation. Today, one of the key strategic objectives of most organizations is flexibility. Of course, we have described the environment as "turbulent" for years. General Electric CEO John Welch uses the term "light and agile" to describe what he wants for his company. Despite all the criticisms of the "fast track's" superficiality, it nevertheless signals people's desire to keep moving and not get entangled in intractable problems. People are now planning for second and third careers, rather than scrambling to create them after being jolted out of previous ones.

Adjusting to the existential fluidity and uncertainty now characterizing our culture requires high-order process skills. OD has not been indifferent to this, but most of its efforts in this area have concentrated on the personal level, with the goal of helping individuals cope with stress and transition. The need for this at the institutional level is acute, but OD professionals are doing little at this level and do not seem to understand the issues. Imagine the process skills that could help an organization having the size and traditions of General Electric become more light and agile. To do this with something other than a "meat ax approach," some thoughtful facilitation must occur.

The permanent white water problem is obviously influenced strongly by the other issues I raise in this chapter. I treat this as a separate matter, however, because a failure to address it directly may lead one to view the other six issues in terms of unfreezing, moving, and refreezing.

7. The manager as a moral agent

Mainstream management textbooks do not describe managers and leaders as moral agents—that is, as individuals whose actions and inactivity have a major impact on their organizations. Neither are they usually considered amoral persons, of course. Rather, people generally assume that the overriding moral issue has been settled: The organization's primary moral standard is the pursuit of its mission within the boundaries of the law. This is a form of instrumental morality, whereby the more effectively and efficiently one pursues the firm's objectives, the more moral one's behavior. This concept can be traced back through John Dewey to William James and the Pragmatists. Chester Barnard was among the first to articulate it thoroughly as an ethical standard for managers.

Not surprisingly, OD has only addressed the morals and ethics whenever OD professionals consider client-managers to be behaving unethically—by OD's standards. OD's morals and ethics were set **against** management's whenever a confrontation was felt necessary. This has also been the strategy adopted by those in various technical and staff positions within organizations, and by external stakeholders. Just as OD professionals have done, whenever these other groups think that management has acted wrongly according to their own standards of right and wrong, they have spoken out. The resulting cacophony of pronouncements on morality has made managers feel they occupy an impossible situation, one requiring them to be "all things to all people." Such aphorisms as "You can't please everybody" and "You can't win, you can't break even, you can't even get out of the game" have great appeal to practicing managers.

This means that each of us really does view the manager as a moral agent, as do managers themselves. They want to feel that they are "doing the right thing" by their own standards, and this may be one explanation for why the mythical "bottom line" has become so important to them in the past 10-15 years: Perhaps managers cling to it so desperately because it is not just some accounting device, but actually a moral standard.

All the evaluation of managers across various groups of stakeholders results in conflict, misunderstanding, and resentment more than in mutual respect and commitment. Various members and constituencies of organizations need help in dealing with values, morals, and standards. They need the process skills provided by OD consultants, provided that the highest value of these consultants themselves is helping others with respect to values. OD has not taken on this task with much energy, but must do better so that organizations and their managers can avoid paralysis.

Conclusion

This chapter names and discusses seven broad aspects of organizational life that, I argue, have great need of the type of process facilitation organization development has traditionally practiced. From my criticism of OD, I have shown how the profession has neglected to apply process skills to these issues.

I wish to emphasize that the skills unique to OD are those used to help other organizational processes go more smoothly and effectively—something that many in OD do not understand. Indeed, as organizations and life itself have grown more disconnected and problematic, the process skills addressing substantive processes are needed now more than ever. Who else besides the OD professional has the competence and will to deliver them?

Biographical Sketches
of the Contributors

Tom Armor is an organization development consultant living in Los Angeles. His interest and work in sociotechnical systems have led him to adapt computer applications to both organization development and training. He also has extensive experience applying OD and training techniques to Third World development projects.

Gene Boccialetti, Ph.D. is an associate professor in the Department of Organizational Behavior at the Whittemore School of Business and Economics at the University of New Hampshire. His primary consulting and research activity involves authority relations in organizations, particularly how these affect team operations, organizational effectiveness, and career development. Dr. Boccialetti is a member of NTL Institute and the Academy of Management, and is on the editorial board of the journal *Group and Organization Studies.*

L. David Brown, Ph.D. is professor of organizational behavior at the Boston University School of Management and president of the Institute for Development Research, a nonprofit center providing assistance to agencies promoting social and economic development. A member of NTL Institute, Dr. Brown works as a consultant and action researcher with development organizations in the U.S. and developing countries.

Lee Butler, Ph.D. is director of planning and institutional research at the University of Maryland at Baltimore. As a trainer, consultant, and manager, he has specialized in change processes and personal growth and development. Dr. Butler is a member of NTL Institute, and has worked with various public and private organizations for the past 20 years.

Robert Chasnoff, Ed.D. had a long, prestigious career in training and consultation, was a member of NTL Institute, and wrote numerous articles and books on cooperative learning. A particularly noteworthy and influential intervention of his involved the entire South Brunswick, New Jersey, school system. Dr. Chasnoff was also a professor at Kean College, served as director of the Laboratory for Applied Science, and was the director of NTL Institute's National Health Service Corps in the 1970s. He died on October 18, 1985.

Jane G. Covey is executive director of the Institute for Development Research in Boston. This institute provides strategic management and organization development consultation, action research, and educational services to social development organizations in the U.S. and developing countries.

Weld Coxe, founder of the Coxe Group, is the author of *Managing Architectural and Engineering Practice* and of *Marketing Architectural and Engineering Services.* He has conducted professional workshops for AIA, ACEC, ASLA, ASCP, and ASID, and lectured at numerous universities. Mr. Coxe is a certified member of the Institute of Management Consultants and a charter member of the Professional Services Management Association and the Society for Marketing Professional Services. In 1976 he was elected an honorary member of the American Institute of Architects.

Allan B. Drexler, Ph.D. is president of Drexler & Associates, Inc. of Annapolis, Maryland, and since 1971 has consulted to businesses seeking organizational and strategic change. He has developed organization-wide programs for General Mills, ARA Food Services, the U.S. Naval Academy, and the International Monetary Fund, among others. His current work has been on team performance and effectiveness at all levels in the organization. Dr. Drexler is a member of NTL Institute and a lecturer in the American University/NTL Institute master's degree program in human resources development.

Ord Elliott is an organization development consultant living in Woodside, California. He specializes in the reorganization and strategic development of both large and "start-up" enterprises.

Katharine Esty, Ph.D. is executive vice president of Ibis Consulting Group, an affiliate of Goodmeasure, located in Cambridge, Massachusetts. A member of NTL Institute, she specializes in the implementation of change in large organizations, and is currently focusing on affirmative action, women in management, and work/family issues.

Daryl Funches is president of Daryl Funches Associates, Inc., a consulting firm in Washington, D. C. offering services in managing strategic change, team building, conflict resolution, coaching/counseling, and managing issues of diversity. She works with various for-profit and nonprofit organizations, and is particularly interested in creating and managing change at the individual, group, and large system levels. Ms. Funches is a member of NTL Institute and a consultant, trainer, manager, teacher, and writer in the field of organization development.

Jack Gant, Ph.D. is a retired dean of the College of Education at Florida State University and presently president of Gant Associates, Inc. He is a trainer and consultant specializing in team building, institution building, and management training in education and health care systems. A member of NTL

Institute, Dr. Gant has worked with various organizations in the U.S. and to a limited extent in Indonesia, Africa, and the Caribbean.

Jean Thomas Griffin, Ed.D. is a professor in social psychology at the University of Massachusetts/Boston and an adjunct professor of the Union Graduate School of Ohio. She provides consulting in issues of diversity and organization development. Dr. Griffin is a member of NTL Institute.

Philip G. Hanson, Ph.D. recently retired from the VA Medical Center (VAMC) where he was chief of the Psychology Service. He currently is a consultant to the VAMC and an associate professor of psychology at the Baylor College of Medicine and the University of Houston. An NTL member, Dr. Hanson has been associated with NTL since 1964, and has published approximately 70 articles and three books.

Carl L. Jennings is an organization and management development consultant with research interests in multicultural diversity in organizations. He is managing director of Jennings and Jennings, and a senior associate of Nichols and Associates. Mr. Jennings is a member of the OD Network and of NTL Institute.

Jimmy E. Jones is an Islamic chaplain working in the Connecticut Penal System and an associate professor of human services at Springfield College. A member of NTL Institute, he consults to both nonprofit and business organizations in the areas of cross-cultural relations and human resources development.

Ronald Lippitt, Ph.D. was professor emeritus of the University of Michigan and a cofounder of NTL Institute (with Kurt Lewin, Leland Bradford, and Ken Benne) in 1947. He held a doctorate in social psychology—having studied under Lewin—and a child development diploma from his work with Jean Piaget. He was codeveloper of the concept of group dynamics with Lewin in 1940, and wrote the basic book entitled *Dynamics of Planned Change* in 1957. Dr. Lippitt most recently worked with communities, school and health systems, industries, and colleges on long-range planning, team building, and participative management. He died on October 28, 1986.

Bernard Lubin, Ph.D. is a professor in and former chair of the Department of Psychology at the University of Missouri at Kansas City. A member of NTL Institute, he provides consultation on organization, management, and executive development to a variety of organizations.

Robert A. Luke, Jr. is a principal scientist with Applied Science Associates, Inc. in Landover, Maryland, a firm specializing in improving individual and organizational performance through training and education. A member of NTL Institute, he works in management training and group problem-solving processes.

Henry Malcolm is a senior organization development specialist for the Westinghouse Institute for Resource Development in Columbia, Maryland. He specializes in long-term OD change efforts, cultural change, participative systems, and developing teams for improving organizational effectiveness. A member of NTL Institute, Mr. Malcolm is a founding member of Certified Consultants International, and teaches training design and facilitation for the American University/NTL Institute master's degree program in human resource development.

Catharine J. Martin, Ph.D. is a trainer, consultant, and educator. She is codeveloper of the Martin Operating Styles Inventory, a line of products for assessing personality style and improving relationships. As vice-president of Organization Improvement Systems, Dr. Martin conducts organization development projects in companies across the U.S., in Costa Rica, and in Jamaica.

Haywood H. Martin, Ph.D. is president and founder of Organization Improvement Systems, a firm specializing in training and organization development. He is a member of NTL Institute and the National Speakers Association, and codeveloper of the Martin Operating Styles Inventory, a line of products for assessing personality style and improving relationships.

C. James Maselko is a partner in the Plainfield, New Jersey, office of the consulting firm of Block-Petrella-Weisbord. He has consulted to various organizations. As a principal of BPW Designed Learning, Inc., Mr. Maselko currently focuses on developing conflict resolution models and the transfer of skills in organizations.

Bernard J. Mohr is president of Synapse Group, Inc. (located in Portland, Maine, Ottawa, New York City, and San Francisco), a firm specializing in helping organizations use participative processes in the transition toward greater flexibility, productivity, and quality of life. As a consultant his practice focuses on work redesign, team building, and the planning and implementation of major changes in organizational culture. As a trainer he conducts programs on sociotechnical systems, managing change in complex organizations, interpersonal development, and organization development. Mr. Mohr is a member of NTL Institute.

Peter Muniz is the president of Peter Muniz, Inc. He provides consultation and training services in both English and Spanish to organizations in the private and public sectors in the U.S. and abroad. Mr. Muniz earned an MBA degree from the City University of New York, and spent one year in Panama training Panamanian trainers and consultants. He has published several books and articles on a wide range of training and consulting topics, and is on the editorial advisory board of *Supervisory Management.*

Thomas H. Patten, Jr., Ph.D. is a professor of management and human resources at the California State Polytechnic University in Pomona. He has facilitated and written extensively about organization development through team building, and has worked internationally in employee compensation systems and performance appraisal. A member of NTL Institute, Dr. Patten has an extensive consulting practice.

Joseph Potts, Ph.D. is president of his own consulting and training firm, which focuses on developing democratic leadership. His work addresses leadership development, team building, conflict management, and managing diversity. A member and former executive director of NTL Institute (1983-1987), Dr. Potts is an adjunct faculty member of American University.

Miriam "Mikki" Ritvo is president of Ritvo and Associates, a firm specializing in organization development, executive and management training, consultation to family-owned businesses, and the change process, with clients in both the public and private sectors. She is a member of NTL Institute, consults to a wide variety of organization, and is a co-trainer of the Exeter Conference, and has been a college professor and dean, special deputy commissioner of education, and director of management development in Massachusetts. Ms. Ritvo has been a director of many corporations, and is currently a member of the boards of seven companies.

Russell R. Rogers, Ph.D. is a professor of human resources development at Azusa Pacific University (Azusa, California) and an HRD consultant with InterAct Associates (Chicago and Pasadena, California). In his work as professor, author, and consultant/trainer, he specializes in organizing for accountable performance, applied change processes, and methods of organizational forgiveness. Dr. Rogers's clients have represented a diverse array of organizational types, both in higher education and business.

Abraham B. Shani, Ph.D. is a professor in the School of Business at California Polytechnic State University in San Luis Obispo. He is a member of International Certified Consultants. Dr. Shani has worked as an action researcher with diverse organizations and industries in the U.S., Europe, Israel, and Canada, and has published articles on sociotechnical systems design, parallel organizations, and action research methodology. His current interests include creative organization designs fostering innovation and improving product quality, productivity, and the quality of work life.

Walter Sikes, Ph.D. is president of the Center for Creative Change in Yellow Springs, Ohio. He works with various organizations on a wide range of managerial issues. A member of NTL Institute, Dr. Sikes is a clinical professor in the School of Professional Psychology at Wright State University and an adjunct professor at Antioch College. He is a principal of the Coxe

Group, which is based in Philadelphia and specializes in management consultation to architectural and engineering firms.

Claire Sokoloff, Ph.D. is an associate of Synectics, Inc., of Cambridge, Massachusetts, an international management consulting firm specializing in innovation and creative problem solving. She works with companies on various management issues, including mergers and acquisitions, strategic visions, management development, and new product development.

Oron South, Ph.D. is a consultant, researcher, and sometimes college professor specializing in consulting on capacity building at the top of public organizations. His current interests include managing complexity and strategic education. Dr. South lives in Montgomery, Alabama.

Peter B. Vaill, DBA, is a professor of human systems in the School of Government and Business Administration at the George Washington University. A well-known thinker and consultant, he was editor of the American Management Association's journal *Organizational Dynamics* from 1985 to 1988, and is a member of NTL Institute. Dr. Vaill's most recent book is *Managing as a Performing Art: New Ideas for a World of Chaotic Change.*

Marvin R. Weisbord is a partner in the Ardmore, Pennsylvania, office of the consulting firm Block-Petrella-Weisbord, which specializes in work place improvement. A member of NTL Institute and a consultant since 1969, he is the author of the book *Productive Workplaces: Organizing and Managing for Dignity, Meaning, and Community.*

Leroy Wells, Jr., Ph.D. is an associate professor in the School of Business at Howard University. He was awarded a doctorate in organizational behavior from Yale University. His research interests are the unconscious aspects of organizational life, intergroup relations, and organizational diagnosis and change. Dr. Wells has consulted to organizations in the U.S. and Australia, including Telecom and Exxon, and is a member of NTL Institute.